At Liberty

At Liberty

Joseph E. Illick

The University of Tennessee Press KNOXVILLE

The Story of a Community and a Generation

The Bethlehem, Pennsylvania, High School Class of 1952

Frontispiece: Liberty High School from the *Cauldron*.

The paper in this book meets the minimum requirements
of the American National Standard for Permanence
of Paper for Printed Library Materials.
∞
The binding materials have been chosen
for strength and durability.

Library of Congress Cataloging in Publication Data

Illick, Joseph E.
    At liberty : the story of a community and a generation :
the Bethlehem, Pennsylvania, high school class of 1952 /
Joseph E. Illick. — 1st ed.
    p.   cm.
Bibliography: p.
Includes index.
ISBN 0-87049-610-7 (cloth: alk. paper)
    1. Bethlehem (Pa.) — Biography.   2. High school graduates —
Pennsylvania — Bethlehem — Biography.   3. Bethlehem (Pa.)
— Social conditions.   4. Oral biography.   5. Sociology —
Pennsylvania — Bethlehem — Biographical methods.
I. Title.   II. Title: Class of '52.
F159.B5145   1989
974.8'22 — dc19   89-5433   CIP

*For Flex, Kit, and Tom
who followed me to Liberty;*

*And in Memory of Phil Phillippi,
Tom Ryther, Nancy Vaitekunes,
Jim Ramberger, and especially,
my dear cousin and closest friend,
John Walzer.*

Contents

Illustrations

Tables

Acknowledgments

My deepest debt is to those many members of the Bethlehem High School Class of 1952 who cooperated with me in gathering the materials for this book by filling out long questionnaires, submitting to taped conversations, and showing continued interest in a project that seemed to take forever. Frank and Eileen Bunsa Donchez were especially helpful in locating classmates.

The late Tom Ryther helped me design a questionnaire. After the second mailing my sisters-in-law and niece—Jan, Gini, and Gwen Illick—boldly prodded recalcitrant class members for information by telephone. San Francisco State University and the American Philosophical Society awarded me grants that helped cover travel expenses incurred as I visited classmates. Henry Glassie raised my sensitivity to the responsibilities an interviewer should assume.

Thomas P. Vadasz generously lent me his University of Virginia doctoral dissertation, "The History of an Industrial Community: Bethlehem, Pennsylvania, 1741–1920" (1975), and took the time to discuss it. At Lehigh University, David Amidon, Roger Simon, and Ross Yates shared their viewpoints on Bethlehem, as well as relevant papers and interviews taped with local residents.

My uncle, the late Dale H. Gramley, former editor of the Bethlehem *Globe-Times*, was a source of both information and inspiration for this book. The late Sam Fishburn and my father-in-law, George Anthony, told enough stories about Bethlehem Steel over the years that I couldn't avoid gaining a perspective not available in official publications.

Local figures whose insights contributed to the narrative of this book include Paul Marcincin, then Mayor of Bethlehem; Joseph Mangan, councilman and parks commissioner; Vivian Ross, city planner; John Betts, long-time head of the Bethlehem Boys Club;

Liberty High School teachers Mary Crow, Ted Martz, and Joseph McIntyre; Bob Thompson, editor, social worker, and school board president. I turned to Margaret Szabo, Anna Herz, and M. Mark Stolarik for clarification of ethnic issues and to Mike Topping, Mike Schweder, and Ed Davies for information on city planning, politics, and leadership.

At San Francisco State University my colleague Bob Cherny instructed me on the mysteries of the computer. Cindy Schmidt helped me prepare key punch sheets. Laura Merlo and Tony Pfeffer, students in a history seminar, analyzed data I gathered on child rearing from the Class of 1952. Regan Harrington and Suzanne Searby typed the manuscript.

Finally I can acknowledge but not thank fully enough the friends, fellow historians, and family members who read my manuscript at various stages and gave me helpful criticism and/or support: John Bodnar, Kathy Bozora, Peter Carroll, Gayle Fitzpatrick, Ray Hiner, Joseph E. Illick, Jr., Toni Illick, Bill Issel, Katherine Ramage, Suzanne Searby, Joyce Seltzer, Barbara Stabile, and John Walzer. Bob Dalva and Jeremy Larner expressed their confidence by taking seriously the idea of making a film based on this book.

At every step of the publishing process, the staff at the University of Tennessee Press was courteous and helpful, always lightening my tasks. I am especially appreciative of Lee Campbell Sioles' excellent editorial judgment and Dariel Mayer's discerning design skills.

Introduction

At Liberty contains the stories of Americans who began their lives during the worst years of the Great Depression, came to maturity at the high point of postwar prosperity, and are now witnessing the industrial decline of the place where they grew up, the steel-producing town of Bethlehem, Pennsylvania.

I began this book, quite unawares, in my classroom around 1970. Seven years earlier I had begun teaching at San Francisco State College, a large and lively institution with a diverse student body and a reputation for innovation. It was a totally new experience for me, a young historian who had been educated in two sedate Ivy League universities and had thus far held a couple of one-year jobs at small, conservative liberal arts colleges. I was excited by and drawn into civil rights and peace activities. But when, in the later 1960s, these liberal causes took a radical turn, I lost my bearings. I welcomed the sabbatical leave that lifted me out of a student-faculty strike at State and into a safe haven in Philadelphia, where I began research on a book about colonial Pennsylvania.

When I returned to San Francisco the strike had been broken, the faculty was demoralized, and the students seemed listless. I searched for a stimulant that would bring my classroom to life and found it in family history. Everyone must care about his or her forebears, I reasoned, and if I could nurture among students an interest in their ancestors, it might be broadened to include a concern for the whole American past.

Three things came of this project. First, students began writing family histories, and they enjoyed it! Second, I quickly realized that these personal essays would only be relevant to what was called "American history" if I reinterpreted that term. My students had no family ties to the politicians, military heroes, and business leaders who appeared in textbooks; their predecessors were immigrants and farmers, slaves and wage workers and housewives, anonymous but real Americans. The only way to locate these people who had left no written records was to abandon the traditional tools of historical inquiry and turn to the techniques used by anthropologists, demographers, sociologists, and psychologists.

Third, as I read my students' themes I reflected on my own family history, and when I began psychotherapy these reflections were intensified. Therapy, in turn, demonstrated to me how much was hidden below the surface of our minds, lodged in the unconscious. Around this time I chanced upon several books—*Akenfield, Working, The Boys of Summer*—based upon personal testimony. Then, purely by coincidence, I discovered that I had a major high school reunion coming up.

I was immediately curious about the men and women whom I had known as classmates almost a quarter century earlier, people whom I studied with, competed against, and dated. Had they experienced life as I did, and if so (or if not), how did their adulthood reflect their earlier years? I knew I wouldn't discover the answers to these questions at a reunion. But I saw no reason why I could not gather the family histories of my classmates (using questionnaires similar to the forms I gave my students), interview some of them (psychotherapy made me confident I would ask the appropriate questions), and write a broad social history of my generation that would appeal not only to scholars but to anyone interested in contemporary America.

My enthusiasm was shared by Tom Ryther, a sociologist and close friend who helped me refine the questionnaire before I mailed it to the 480 (of 554) members of the Liberty High School Class of 1952 whom I could locate; over 200 answered (see Appendix A). In the summer and autumn of 1976 I taped conversations with some 50 of them (see Appendix B). And, by way of a self-interview, I began writing an autobiography.

I did return to my twenty-fifth high school reunion. But, for reasons that had nothing to do with the wealth of material I had gathered, I stopped working. I returned to psychotherapy, I taught abroad for a year, I became an art student, Tom Ryther died. Finally, I realized that I wanted to finish this book. I taped follow-up interviews with classmates, mainly in 1983, and I began writing, confident that I had underway a book that would be a bridge from my ivory tower to the workaday world.

Academic studies abound on such subjects as family, ethnicity, education, work, marriage, and child-rearing, and I asked about these matters on the questionnaire I sent out. The same issues naturally arose again in conversations with my classmates, who candidly stated their positions. For the organization of this book, however, I decided not to present a piece of a person's perspective in a topical chapter, for to have done so would have destroyed the context in which the relevant remarks occurred. Better to leave the conversations — and the persons — whole. Consequently, a person consigned to the chapter on Family can be expected also to deliver opinions on work and/or other topics.

Although I believe the thrust of this book to be strongly egalitarian, insofar as it attempts to provide popular history for scholars while demystifying scholarship for the people, I have chosen to call it "at liberty," suggesting that my real concern is not group equality but personal freedom. Of course the title derives in part from the name of the high school, but it also expresses my feeling about the importance to us all of understanding the past. The technological sophistication that fosters rapid change does not render the past irrelevant; on the contrary, what has gone before remains with us in our personal ideologies. We are left to balance the values of our childhoods, the gifts of our parents and grandparents, with the bewildering activities of the contemporary world. Only through an understanding of the past and present can we set ourselves at liberty, that is, free to act in a manner consistent with both peace of mind and social reality.

I | *Community: Bethlehem, Pennsylvania*

An unsettling calm has descended on Bethlehem, Pennsylvania, a tranquility that disquiets those of us who knew the city at another time. When I worked with twenty-four thousand other men in the plant of the Steel Company during the 1950s, I sometimes punched in on the "graveyard shift"—a term simply signifying that fewer furnaces were in operation than during the day. Today I drive across the New Street Bridge in broad daylight, look down the banks of the Lehigh, and see the mills in repose—no smoke, no noise, no activity—hardly different from Nisky Hill Cemetery across the river. The community has returned to the peaceful state its founders envisioned over two centuries ago.

It was then that the Moravians, a group of religious enthusiasts from Germany, purchased from the proprietors of the Pennsylvania colony a piece of land located where Monocacy Creek flows into the Lehigh River. The region was already occupied by Algonkian-speaking Indians known to other aborigines by two names: the "grandfathers," a term of distinction among a people who venerated age; and the "Wabanaki," meaning "inhabitants of the place where the sun rises." European immigrants at first called them the "Lenapi," or "native men." But the Indians willingly took on the name of "Delaware"—after the major river in the area, itself christened by the foreigners in honor of Lord De la Warr—because they believed that harmony and brotherhood could exist between them and the European newcomers.

This belief was shared by William Penn, who planted Pennsylvania in 1682, and by the Moravians, who gathered at the banks of the Lehigh on Christmas Day, 1741, naming the settlement Bethlehem after the birthplace of the Prince of Peace. They referred to themselves as the *Unitas Fratrum,* or "united brotherhood;" like the

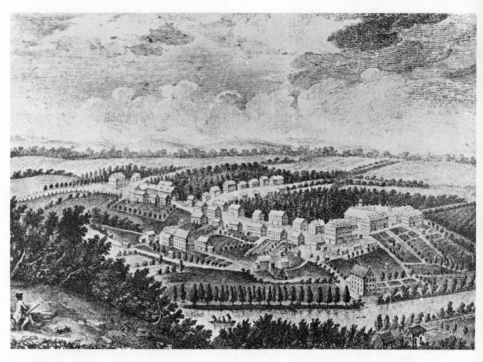

Bethlehem, Pennsylvania, modeled on Herrnhut, Saxony, stood as testimony to the Moravians' cultural conservatism. (Published by permission of The Moravian Archives, Bethlehem, Pennsylvania.)

aborigines, they were spiritual people. One of the founders, reflecting on the moment of their settlement, recalled: "Because of the day and in memory of the Birth of our dear Savior, we went into the stable in the tenth hour and sang with feeling, so that our hearts melted:

> Not Jerusalem
> Rather Bethlehem
> Gives us that which
> Maketh life rich.

The Moravians were so called after the region in eastern Europe where John Hus had begun a movement in the early fifteenth century to reform the Church of Rome. Later they had migrated from Moravia to Saxony, settling in Herrnhut, a village that became the model for Bethlehem. In the wilderness of Pennsylvania, stone buildings were erected in the German architectural style, and a European town plan was copied: a central green was laid out, abutted at its south end by an avenue (now Main Street) which was intersected by three east-west thoroughfares (now Church, Market and Broad streets).

The new settlement in no way resembled the Indian lodgings that went before it. The aborigines had built longhouses by driving posts into the ground, tying horizontal poles to them, and covering the structure with long sheets of bark. The longhouses were scattered in random fashion as if in defiance of the canons of European geometry.

The contrast between the two cultures was striking; the consequences of this contrast proved fatal to the Indians. For however well-intentioned the Moravian missionaries were in bringing their brand of Christianity to the Delawares, native acceptance of the new religion would revolutionize the aboriginal way of life. The respect in which missionaries held Indian culture, seen in the accounts of David Zeisberger and John Heckewelder, did not alter this fact. Where the native religion was inclusive and could have assimilated the European god into the pantheon of tribal deities and even have absorbed some Christian rituals into existing practices, the immigrants' religion was exclusive and could not bear "heathen" additives. The Delawares were not offered the alternatives of compromise and coexistence; they were expected to convert to Christianity.

Delaware domestic relations also differed markedly from the Moravian way of life. The Delaware longhouse, thirty to a hundred feet long and twenty to twenty-five feet wide, housed several families of one lineage—usually husband and wife, their unmarried children and married daughters, as well as their daughters' husbands and children. In contrast, the Moravian residences, built close to the church and the chapel on the central green, housed infants, boys, girls, single men, single women, married men, married women, widowers, and widows in separate units. These so-called choirs, segregated by age, gender, and marital status, served as surrogate families in which members slept, ate, and worked. Like the Indians, however, Bethlehem's residents regarded property as irrelevant to their communal lives; their occupations and even their marriage partners were determined by the church.

The Moravians were unusual in early America, but they were by no means the only sectarians outside the religious mainstream. Pennsylvania attracted many such groups due to its policy of religious toleration. What did distinguish the Moravians, beyond their in-

Preindustrial enterprise was fostered in Bethlehem, making it the commercial center for nearby Moravian communities. (Published by permission of The Moravian Archives, Bethlehem, Pennsylvania.)

terest in and sympathy toward the Indians, was their unusual economic organization, the so-called General Economy. Moravians rejected the capitalistic tenet of individual property ownership. But the church did not dismiss the benefits of vigorous business activity. Bethlehem was to be a commercial center where Moravian farmers from nearby communities, such as Emmaus and Nazareth, sent their agricultural and animal products. Along Monocacy Creek the Moravians built a grist mill, a slaughter house with adjacent tannery and soap boiling house, flax and carding houses, and a fulling mill and dye shop, not to mention a sawmill, a locksmith, a nailsmith, and a cabinetmaker's shop.

Bethlehem also became a manufacturing center. Soon it reached out beyond the nearby communities to Philadelphia and to the frontier. And, like the Puritans and Quakers before them, the Moravians found that economic life was fraught with spiritual stumbling blocks. The liberal, individualistic ethos of American enterprise soon infected otherworldly, communitarian Bethlehem. Its residents began demanding their own shares in the profits until, in 1761, the church officials agreed to abandon the General Economy and lease the already existing industries to their operators and pay wages to workers in church-owned enterprises. Although Moravian authorities supervised business and retained ownership of the land, the choir system dissolved after the General Economy was abandoned. Families began living in single households. These changes did not anchor the younger generation in the community, however, and the population of Bethlehem decreased from 1,000 in 1750 to 543 at the end of the century. Commercial success and spiritual decline were followed by economic stagnation.

Perhaps such failure, seen as a moral lesson, could have pointed out the road back to piety. Instead, national progress took over. The Lehigh Coal and Navigation Company constructed along the river a canal, which passed through Bethlehem in 1829 on its way from the coal regions to nearby Easton on the Delaware. More than ever before, Bethlehem's economic fate would depend on external forces. Indeed, it was the panic and depression of the late 1830s and early 1840s that created a turning point in the town's history. As the church attempted to save its local businessmen from disaster, it went deeply into debt. In early 1844 the system of leasing enterprises was abandoned, and a year later the Commonwealth of Pennsylvania incorporated the borough of Bethlehem. No longer would the town be the exclusive preserve of Moravians.

Nevertheless, the church remained dominant. As the United States moved into its Industrial Revolution in the middle of the century, the *Unitas Fratrum* resisted new business ventures, clinging to such traditional enterprises as tanneries, flour mills, breweries, barrel factories; allowing the construction of iron and copper foundries; but balking at the building of coal furnaces along the river. The community was more commercial than industrial. Its quaint residential and church buildings encouraged tourism, especially in the summer. The population was growing again, reaching one thousand at mid-century and coming close to seven thousand in 1890. Less than 8 percent of its citizens were foreign-born. Rather, newcomers streamed in from local farms, usually speaking low German (Pennsylvania Dutch) and favoring the Lutheran, Reformed, or evangelical denominations rather than the Moravian church. There were also some German-speaking Catholics, as well as English-speaking Methodists, Baptists, Episcopalians, and Presbyterians.

Gradually, this change in the character of the population altered the town's social institutions. Until 1880 political officials were almost always Moravians, but over the next eighteen years two Lutherans, a Presbyterian, and an Episcopalian served in the office of chief burgess of the town. By the end of the century a score of social and fraternal clubs flourished in Bethlehem, lending it a secular complexity quite unlike the days of simple Moravian purity.

Meanwhile, across the Lehigh River a very different community was taking shape. South Bethlehem did not resist industrial development but was created by it. From 1850 to 1870, the railroad commanded the center of American economic life; South Bethlehem lay at the junction of the Lehigh Valley Railroad (carrying anthracite from Mauch Chunk to New York City) and the North Pennsylvania Railroad (which diverted some of the LVRR coal to Philadelphia). Besides its role as a transfer point, South Bethlehem benefited from developments related to the railroad: real estate speculation, rail and carriage production, and exploitation of zinc, limestone, and iron ore deposits found in nearby regions, especially the Saucon Valley. The Bethlehem Iron Company, formed in 1860, and one of the first in the nation to use the Bessemer process, stood among the biggest steel rail manufacturers by 1885.

Within a few years Bethlehem Iron built the first armor plate plant in the country, which assured it of military customers. Converting from Bessemer to open-hearth furnaces, the Company constructed a plant to turn out heavy forgings and castings. It captured another first with its production of high-speed tool steel. These developments lifted Bethlehem Iron out of regional competition into national and international markets, which meant that politics in Washington, technological changes in Chicago, and financial fluctuations in London would affect the heretofore remote town of South Bethlehem.

Bethlehem Iron Company, reorganized as Bethlehem Steel Company in 1899, soon passed into the hands of Charles M. Schwab, who in 1903 left the presidency of United States Steel to assume command at Bethlehem in addition to being its largest stockholder. An authoritative but jovial presence, sometimes referred to as Champagne Charlie, Schwab was always ready to risk on intuition. He was strikingly different from Frederick W. Taylor, the efficiency expert who awaited him at Bethlehem. Watch in hand and notebook at the ready, Taylor had systematized the labor force and pushed a breakthrough on high-speed tool steel. But the scientific approach failed in management relations.

Schwab was not a technician, but he knew his business; he successfully moved Bethlehem into the production of structural steel. And he knew people, succeeding where Taylor had failed with management by introducing two innovations: a bonus system that rewarded individual accomplishment within the bureaucracy; and a promotion system that was entirely internal, without the threat of importing outsiders to fill top positions. In this way he nurtured fidelity and élan; the loyalty of the "Boys of Bethlehem" was legendary. But their fidelity belonged to Schwab and the Company, not to the community. South Bethlehem just happened to be the seat of a steel empire, a fact with different meanings for its resident citizens and the managerial newcomers who commuted to homes a respectable distance from the plant.

Middle-class managers made up only one group of recently arrived persons in South Bethlehem. Industry created jobs for lower-class laborers; immigrants from nearby farms and faraway countries rushed to fill them. The population more than trebled from 1860 to 1870, and again from 1870 to 1890. Foreigners added up to only a third of the 3,500 residents in 1870, only a quarter of the 10,300 inhabitants twenty years later. But by 1910 foreign-born persons and their American-born children comprised two-thirds of South Bethlehem's 20,000 inhabitants, well above the national proportion (two-fifths) and that of Bethlehem across the river (one-sixth), which now boasted a population of almost 13,000 due to its consolidation with the borough of West Bethlehem in 1904.

The earliest settlers of South Bethlehem were Germans: Moravians who drifted over the Lehigh; Lutheran and Reformed churchgoers from the surrounding countryside and from Germany; and, somewhat later, Roman Catholics from Austria. The Irish came almost simultaneously and soon outnumbered the foreign-born Germans. They entered on the ground floor of politics, elected the first chief burgess, and dominated the borough council for several decades. Slovaks began arriving in the late 1870s, initially by way of the nearby anthracite coal regions, establishing Catholic and Lutheran churches. Among the Hungarians there were also both Protestants

The Bethlehem Iron Company of South Bethlehem, fully visible from the Moravian buildings across the Lehigh River, symbolized the force of modernization. South Mountain, in the background, became the home of Lehigh University. (Published by permission of the Bethlehem Steel Corporation.)

and Catholics, while Ruthenians from eastern Hungary formed a separate Catholic congregation. Solvenian (or Windish) Catholics and Lutherans added to the potpourri, which also now included Poles, Italians, Greeks, Russians, Ukranians, Serbians, Croatians, and Jews.

Churches became the centers of social as well as religious life in South Bethlehem, turning the unfamiliar environment of an industrial city into more recognizable landscape. These giant edifices of stone, so much larger than any of the surrounding houses, gave South Bethlehem the appearance of a peasant village. Although the new residents had strayed far from home, they were not basically adventurous. Rather, they had been uprooted by economic need, and they had come to a place where they knew they could find friends and relatives.

National groups in South Bethlehem were drawn from very restricted areas of their respective home countries. Austrians came from the province of Carniola; Slovaks from the provinces of Saris (Catholic) or Zvolen (Lutheran); Hungarians from the counties of

Vas, Veszprem, Sopron, and Zala; Slovenes from the district of Prekmunje; Poles from Galacia; Italians from a cluster of towns near Naples; Greeks from the island of Khios and two mainland villages close by. The organization of churches and mutual benefit societies (insurance companies) along national lines helped these ethnic clusters maintain their separate identities.

But the fact that all these newcomers together faced hostility from the older Irish and German-speaking immigrants served to break down ethnic separation among them, fostering instead a friendliness among Slovaks, Magyars, Poles, and Slovenes which otherwise might not have existed. South Bethlehem was neither the mythical American melting pot, with natives and immigrants mixed together indistinguishably, nor a congeries of isolated ethnic neighborhoods, with each national group standing starkly apart. The scarcity of real estate on the South Side ruled out ghettoes. The steel works and the railroad occupied most of the level land on the south bank of the Lehigh River, leaving a residential area on the slopes of South Mountain approximately a mile in length and only a quar-

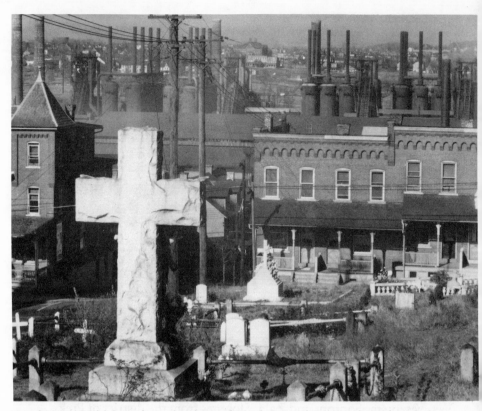

Looking at Bethlehem from the slope of South Mountain: South Side, including Bethlehem Steel Company, in foreground; Moravian buildings in center of background. (Library of Congress Collection. Walker Evans, photographer.)

ter of a mile wide. This limited space made for a chronic housing shortage; people found living quarters where they could, not necessarily where they wanted.

That the location of the mills should determine the placement of the workers' quarters was a familiar feature of the industrial city. In South Bethlehem no power could compete with the Steel Company, which even affected the make-up of the population: for example, a thousand Mexican laborers were imported in the 1920s while black migrants were conspicuous by their absence. Management, guided by the firm hand of President Schwab, set policy which labor was expected to accept and the community to honor.

A test of this maxim came in 1910. Eight hundred machinists, men whose skills classed them among the older residents of South

Bethlehem, went on strike. They were soon joined by hundreds of unskilled workers from the ranks of the newer immigrants. The town police and the local political leaders showed sympathy for the work stoppage, and small businessmen encouraged the Company's employees to unionize. When the strike-breaking Pennsylvania State Police entered the city, the community of workers, small business-men, and politicians stood firmly unified. But Schwab brought eco-nomic and political pressure to bear, including the threat of per-manently shutting down the plant. The borough council wavered and finally supported the Company, the cross-over votes on the council reflecting class and ethnic divisions in South Bethlehem.

Only seven years later the boroughs of South Bethlehem and Beth-lehem merged into the city of Bethlehem, a union Schwab heartily endorsed. The older member of the couple was Anglo-Saxon, Pro-testant, and middle class, the younger a descendent of many nation-alities, predominantly Catholic and working class. In fact, it was a shotgun marriage, pregnant with possibilities for a new political order. The nuptial contract was a new form of city government—the commission plan—depicted at the time as a reform measure be-cause it was nonpartisan, efficient, and economical: "two can live as cheaply as one." Under borough rule councilmen had represented the class and ethnic interests of their wards. The election of com-missioners would be held at-large and without regard to political party. More money would be required for a candidacy, and city-wide prominence rather than neighborhood identification would be the important ingredient of success. The principles of scientific man-agement would supersede grassroots politics; well-known business-men rather than local politicos would run the government.

The merger of the North and South sides into a city followed closely on a very successful campaign to raise funds for a "Hill-to-Hill" bridge, spanning the Lehigh River and thus bringing the two boroughs closer together. Archibald Johnston, a major official of Bethlehem Steel, spearheaded both the bridge and the city consoli-dation efforts, persuasively arguing that municipal unity was synony-mous with patriotism and civilian support of World War I. In 1918 Johnston was chosen mayor in the first city election; the other four commission members were two steel executives, a real estate man who owned a hosiery mill, and a hotel proprietor. Supplementing this official body was an amalgamated chamber of commerce with Schwab on its board of directors.

The emergence of a united and larger Bethlehem under a new form of city government makes 1918 the appropriate year from which to date the modern history of the municipality. Mayor Johnston reigned over a city of fifty thousand in the most urbanized region of the United States; over half the inhabitants of the Middle Atlantic area lived in cities with populations as large as Bethlehem's or larger. By annexing portions of the countryside Johnston expanded the city almost to its current limits, thus allowing for later housing development in the relatively unsettled northeast and northwest sections. Many members of the Liberty High School Class of 1952 took advantage of this option.

From the air Bethlehem looks like the bust of a person wearing the Lehigh River as a string tie: the North Side is the head, with Illick's Mill Road running out of its nose and the old Moravian section, logically enough, at the mouth; the West Side is the right arm, raised as if leading a charge toward Allentown; the South Side is the shoulders and attenuated trunk, with the heart located somewhere near the Steel Corporation plant office. In 1918 half the population resided in five wards on the South Side, but the living conditions did not match the congestion found in such places as the Lower East Side of New York. Families inhabited two-story row houses, not tenements, and the wooded hills of South Mountain were close by.

Slightly over one-fifth of the city's population was foreign-born, while the native sons and daughters of those born overseas constituted yet another fifth. Hungarians were by far the largest recently arrived national group, but enough others were present and distinct in Bethlehem, even a generation later, to prompt the WPA author of a Northampton County guide to proclaim in the 1930s:

> Along Third Street are Greek restaurants, redolent with boiled lamb and syrupy coffee; Italian groceries with windows strung with fiery sausages and Parmigiano and Coceocarollo cheese; Russian tea houses and Roumanian restaurants and Polish pool rooms and Hungarian societies.

Notably absent were Afro-Americans, now streaming steadily out of the rural South into the northern cities but not into Bethlehem, which had an African Methodist Episcopal Church but fewer than four hundred black residents. Another underrepresented urban group were the Jews who, although they played a major role in the retail trade along Third and Fourth streets on the South Side and had

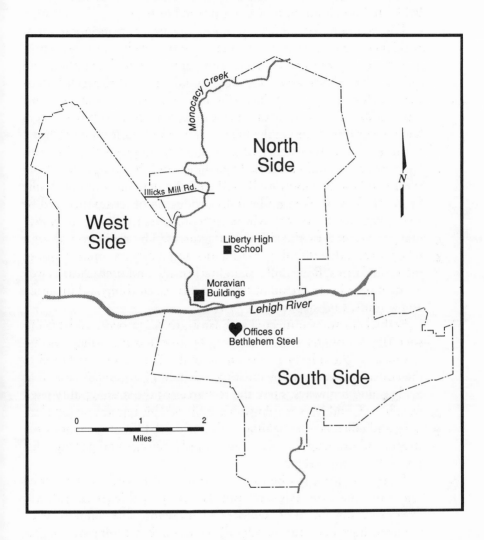

Map of Bethlehem

built a synagogue, numbered only two hundred fifty families when Brith Shalom Community Center opened in 1922.

The economy of the city was less diverse than its population. Bethlehem Steel, of course, dominated; at the height of the war effort in 1918 it employed thirty thousand persons in its local plant and offices. Other companies were functionally related to Steel: foundries, machine shops, electrical equipment plants, chemical concerns, paint mills. Shortly after the turn of the century, South Bethlehem had almost fifty firms employing six thousand people who produced $15 million worth of steel and fabricated metal products. Silk mills had employed hundreds of Bethlehemites until the competition from synthetic fabrics substantially reduced the demand for silk. Some of the slack was taken up by mills producing other textiles and by a small garment industry whose entrepreneurs took over the buildings abandoned by the silk manufacturers. The rapid growth of a labor force aided building contractors and lumber suppliers, not to mention dairies, flour mills, slaughterhouses, and breweries, as well as the more obvious retail outlets—groceries, clothing and furniture emporiums, and department stores.

Bethlehem was connected to Easton, to Allentown, and even to such tiny boroughs as Coopersburg by an extensive trolley system, doomed by the advent of the automobile. But cars contributed to the construction boom by creating a demand for garages as well as bridges and highways. Here the resources of the municipality itself were tested, and Mayor Johnston established his reputation for planning and efficiency by dealing with basic urban matters—not only streets and housing but also water supply, sewage and garbage disposal, parks and recreation.

Johnston, although he established a good record, was removed after only one term. His successor, James M. Yeakle (1922–30), was by comparison a man of mediocre talent, whose sole claim to virtue seems to have been the signing of the city's first zoning ordinance. His tolerance of vice made him notorious, and it has been written that men—not very wise men, perhaps—journeyed from the East (New York and New Jersey) to visit Bethlehem and its red light district.

Yeakle's successor, Robert Peifle (1930–50), was put in office to clean out the whorehouses, the speakeasies, and the police department that tolerated them. Having risen to financial security through the school of hard knocks, Peifle showed compassion for the unfortunate during the Depression, when the steel industry was hard hit.

(In 1929 the Bethlehem plant employed over fourteen thousand persons on a payroll of $25 million; in 1933 less than six thousand persons were at work for $6.5 million.) But local governments were simply not sufficient to the disaster of the 1930s, and Bethlehem was no exception.

The prosperity that followed World War II made it possible for Peifle's successor, Earl Schaffer (1950–62), to tackle those basic issues that Johnston had addressed earlier, but which went almost unnoticed during the Depression and World War II. Most public facilities had failed to keep pace with the growing city; by 1950 Bethlehem had sixty-six thousand inhabitants. Such projects as the Municipal Recreation Area, the Lehigh Valley Industrial Park, the Penn Forest Watershed Storage Dam, and the Redevelopment Authority can be attributed to Schaffer's administration. But Schaffer was denied re-election in 1962 by a renegade in his own Democratic party during the primary.

Bethlehem was and is a Democratic city. The strength of the Party lay on the South Side, organized initially by its first residents, the Germans and, especially, the Irish: the Degnans, Donegans, Quinns, Ganeys, McFaddens, and McCarthys. Joe Mangan, himself a political force in contemporary Bethlehem, recalls that his grandfather, Dinty McCarthy, "always used to say—and I don't mean this as a bigot—that the greatest mistake the Irish made was getting the Hunkies to vote." In a northeastern industrial town, the term "Hunky" refers to any Southern or Eastern European, and the mistake the Irish made was to enfranchise a group that went on to take control of the party from them. Joe Agrest, for example, was an Italian who married a Preletz (Windish) and was close to the Tachovskys, proprietors of the Arcade Hotel on East Third Street where Czechoslovaks lived when they first arrived to work in the mills. Two Agrest protégées, John Bartos and John Peters, were the first Slovak politicians elected to the city council, and they got there by successfully contesting Irish political control.

The most powerful of the Hunkies in the mid-twentieth century was Joe Yosko, whose parents immigrated from Ruthenia to the coal regions of Pennsylvania before coming to Bethlehem. Yosko was working as a law clerk in Northampton County district attorney Russell Mauch's office—a center of power during the time of speakeasies and prostitutes—when he met Pennsylvania State Senator Warren R. Roberts, who drew him into a larger political world. Roberts moved on to the post of auditor general, and Yosko himself was elected state senator in 1947. He had already become, a year earlier, Democratic city chairman. Autocratic and domineering, his 5'7" frame elevated by the senate chair he brought from Harrisburg to his Fourth Street office, Yosko regarded Bethlehem not as the boundary of his ambitions but, rather, as his satrapy.

While Yosko rose to power two more Slovaks, George Ruyak in 1940 and John Soltis in 1949, got themselves elected to city council, political facts that suggested the day of the ethnics was imminent. Yosko knew otherwise. He would not run for mayor, he told his confidants. "I could win the primary hands down. But I'm not that stupid. This town is not ready to elect a Hunky for mayor. My name would kill me." He chose to follow party tradition, backing for mayor a German from the North Side, Earl Schaffer. By recognizing his limits, Yosko kept the party in the city under his control. But his untimely death of a brain tumor in 1958 left the Democrats in disarray and scrambling for power. Yosko's real estate partner, Fred Rooney, jumped into the state senate seat and later went to Congress. Anthony Sacarakis, a Hunky councilman, grabbed the city chairmanship. And Paul Jani, whose origins were truly Hungarian, bucked the party organization and overthrew Shaffer in the 1962 primary, only to be beaten by Republican Anglo-Saxon Gordon Payrow in the general election.

For three terms the Democrats were held at bay, not being able to secure the mayor's office again until 1973 when Gordon Mowrer, another German, whose father's dairy happened to be a household word, was voted in. (In the primary Mowrer had only squeaked by fellow councilman Charles Donchez, who was of Windish and Hungarian parentage and had strong labor support.) It was not until the election in 1981 of Paul Marcincin, who several decades earlier had been only the second Slovak hired in the Bethlehem public school system, that the Hunkies finally found their mayor.

Marcincin himself denies that ethnicity or class were ingredients of his success: "That North Side, West Side, South Side stuff that was prevalent when I was in high school doesn't matter anymore." While no historian would accept this statement at face value, all would agree that there are perspectives other than organized politics, even politics with a broad ethnic dimension, through which to understand the governance of an American city.

Sociologists and political scientists, for example, have often studied community leadership not from the perspective of political parties but by identifying a governing elite which rules. Taking such an approach in Bethlehem has the virtue of allowing us to look at the emergence of several elites, beginning with the Moravian leaders in the eighteenth century.

The organization of community in Bethlehem was close to unique in early America. Moravians were enthusiasts for group experience; their patron and leader, Count Nicholas von Zinzindorf, decreed that "there can be no Christianity without community." The early Moravians' emphasis on religious experience and emotion, and their outright rejection of rationalism, led them to believe that government was unnecessary. Offices, such as elder or teacher, were established, and numerous committees, many of which had to do with the economy, were installed. Theoretically, Zinzindorf was supreme ruler of the community, but since he usually resided in Europe, primary leadership rested in the office of vicar general in Bethlehem. A historian of the early years observes that "power was dispersed to so many different hands at different times that, with the exception of [the vicar general and his assistants], it is almost impossible to single out certain persons as the wielders of community power."

In the decade following Zinzindorf's death in 1760 Bethlehem was controlled by an interim governing body which, in 1771, established a constitution that lasted almost eighty years. It vested authority in a Unity Elder's Conference in Germany. But this body had no more success than Zinzindorf in arresting local autonomy. In 1845 Bethlehem severed its ties to Germany and leadership fell to a burgess and nine councilmen, all of whom were elected by the citizens of the town, not necessarily Moravians.

Nevertheless, the Moravians were clearly dominant. Moravian leaders opposed the industrialization of the town, but by the 1840s they agreed to sell property on the south side of the Lehigh River to the developers of South Bethlehem, who had industrial objectives. Within a few decades, having drawn upon the nearby zinc, limestone, and iron ore resources and the assets of the not-so-distant coal regions, these developers had created mills, a canal, and a railroad. An upper class emerged from the families of men who managed these concerns: the Sayres, Lindermans, Wilburs, Dodsons, Skeers, and Cleavers.

These families intermarried, built homes on Delaware Avenue in the borough of Fountain Hill adjoining South Bethlehem, established an Episcopal church and academy, supported Lehigh University, and lived as a local aristocracy quite apart from the Moravians of the North Side. Nor did they mingle with the first political leaders of the South Side, the Irish who had arrived as laborers even before the borough was incorporated, comprised the largest ethnic group in South Bethlehem until the end of the century, and dominated its politics as well as many of its business establishments. The Irish can be identified as the third elite in the Bethlehem urban area in the late nineteenth century.

When Charles Schwab took over the Bethlehem Steel Corporation and moved from New York to Bethlehem in 1906, he immediately became a giant among the Fountain Hill gentry. Occupying one of the Linderman homes at the top of Delaware Avenue, he could neither be ignored nor absorbed by the social world around him.

In fact, he created a new social elite from the ranks of his executives. Having instituted at Bethlehem Steel the principle of promotion from within, he fostered the emergence of a group of managers who were not members of any local aristocracy. Representative of these men but more successful than any of them was Eugene G. Grace, the son of a sea captain from Goshen, New Jersey, who graduated from Lehigh as an electrical engineer in 1899 and passed up a career in baseball to take a job at Steel. The choice of work over play was significant, even symbolic. Schwab advocated the "drive system" as the means of successful management, and Grace's forward thrust, his capacity for ceaseless work, was a matter of record. It did him no harm, of course, that he got on famously with Schwab, the stern Presbyterian disciple of toil-and-save complementing the jovial Catholic apostle of earn-and-spend. By 1908 Grace was general manager and a member of the board of directors; in 1913 he became president of the Steel Company.

There was not room for Grace and his cohorts, socially or even physically, at the summit of Delaware Avenue, so they built houses on the west side of Bethlehem, on or near Prospect Avenue. Within a few blocks of Grace's estate lived three vice presidents of the corporation, as well as the treasurer, the comptroller, and the general manager. Junior Steel executives, as well as professional people, resided nearby. Consequently, there emerged in the early twentieth century a fourth elite in Bethlehem, its offices on the South Side and its quarters on the West.

However, the unification of Bethlehem in 1918 left the gentry of Fountain Hill, a borough not included in the consolidation, politically isolated. The group retained some force in the community through Lehigh University, where Warren Wilbur chaired the board of trustees, which included Grace and Schwab. But even this small hold on power was largely forfeited when Grace himself took the chair in 1924. He held it for thirty years, since Bethlehem Steel could nurture the university in ways the fading gentry of Fountain Hill could only dream of.

The new Steel elite focused its attention on Lehigh not only because it had alumni ties there but also, probably, because there were limits to the power it could wield in the larger sphere of the city. When Steel's vice president Arch Johnston had been mayor and appointed Schwab and Grace to his planning commission, a company town appeared to be in the making. But the Irish political organization, now transformed and more robust from an infusion of Hunky blood, could elect the city officials it wanted—that is, if their names were Anglo-Saxon (preferably German) and therefore respectable, rather than "foreign" and thus considered to be working class, ignorant, and not electable—at least until recently.

In Bethlehem today the Fountain Hill gentry is all but forgotten, but some status still attaches to being Moravian. Power is largely divided between the dominant industry and a popular political party. No one doubted until very recently the economic clout of Steel. Many people believed, at least until the dramatic decline of the steel industry in the 1980s, that if called upon the Company would help the city meet its payrolls or contribute materials to street repair in return for low property taxes or special rates on city-supplied water. But it is also evident that the Democratic party, which included no Steel Company officials, almost always could and still can elect the candidates of its choice.

In a community where economic might and political power are so divided, there is sometimes room for a third force—a citizens' group, service club, or the like—to act as vehicle of political change. Bethlehem has had some reform movements, the most notable occurring when the city council in 1958 turned down a Junior Chamber of Commerce request that a charter study question be put on the ballot. The Jaycees went into the community with petitions and ultimately brought about a strong-mayor plan of government—and helped in the election of a Republican leader as well. But there have been few such instances of local political reform.

The "third force" in Bethlehem, which has acted not to divide but to draw Steel and city officialdom together, is the federal government. For Bethlehem, like every other American city, is no longer administered at the local level alone. In the 1930s, politics in the United States was transformed under the auspices of the New Deal, when the only humane policy available to the federal government was to undertake what local agencies could no longer do—provide for the jobless, the homeless, the poverty-stricken. Industrial leaders had no mind for his task. Eugene Grace, in 1935 chairman of the board of Bethlehem Steel and one of the highest-paid executives in the land, expressed his opposition to the Social Security Act by observing: "This country was built by our forefathers on the cornerstone of economy and self-denial." The people around Franklin Roosevelt, on the other hand, believed that suffering did not build character but destroyed lives.

The institutionalization of welfare on the federal level not only offended business leaders but undermined local politicians by taking from them the functions of providing jobs, food, and housing for their constituents. In Bethlehem the Roosevelt administration's manifest friendliness to labor was not only an affront to capital but led to the formation of Political Action Committees among the workers, which posed a threat to ward bosses and minions of city hall.

As power relationships shifted with federal involvement in local affairs, the nature and locus of community decision-making changed too, as is evident in the field of city planning. Although Bethlehem, like a number of early American towns, began its urban life with a design, not until 1918 did it have a city planning commission, a local agency whose work—municipal zoning—was sanctioned by a Supreme Court decision eight years later. Under the New Deal, the legislative and executive branches of the federal government initiatied action. Congress passed a Housing Act in 1937 to provide "decent, safe, and sanitary dwellings for families of low income," administered by a national Housing Authority; Bethlehem responded with the creation of its own Housing Authority in 1939.

Then, after World War II, came redevelopment—slum clearance, later labeled urban renewal (or, by its opponents, urban removal)— a concept considered separate from, though of course related to, public housing. Generous funding was available from the federal government when Bethlehem created its Redevelopment Authority in 1953. And Steel was quick to cooperate with local officials, even to lead the way, in drawing upon the national coffers to remodel the city, recognizing that Washington could as easily be a friend as an enemy.

The results were stunning: a new city hall and library, facing one another across a grand plaza on the north bank of the Lehigh River which afforded visitors a panoramic view of the steel works, the South Side, and beyond; a spur route through the West Side, tying the steel plant to U.S. 22, a major highway; redevelopment projects on the North and South sides; and the creation of Historic Bethlehem to preserve the eighteenth-century past in the midst of twentieth-century growth and change. Enthusiasm ran so high that the president of the city's largest bank convinced merchants in the somnolent commercial district of the North Side that their decrepit stores should be replaced by a brand-new shopping mall and a multi-story office building that would house—his bank!

There were some dissenting voices, none of which was more articulate than that of Bob Thompson, a graduate of Liberty High School ('54) and Amherst College, who came home to teach high schoolers and stayed to edit a newspaper. In *Polis*, "An Independent Monthly for Inspired Citizenship," Thompson hammered away for two years in the mid 1960s on community themes—urban renewal, education, youth activities—and related subjects, especially Vietnam. He reported on meetings between city officials and angry residents, he philosophized about the relationship between urban and rural rejuvenation, and he attacked Bethlehem Steel and Lehigh University for joining forces to form a "pincers movement" that would displace the South Side residents whose homes were between the two expanding institutions. If he was heard he was not heeded. He eventually gave up teaching, took up social work at a much lower salary, and served as president of the Bethlehem School Board.

A similar point of view was also voiced at city hall, as can be found by looking back over the Community Redevelopment Reports issued in 1967. And it is clearly articulated by Vivian Ross, formerly senior planner in the city's Bureau of Planning and Development, which was translating federal legislation into a program for Bethlehem's future. Ross's point of view, a preservationist philosophy, is that South Side neighborhoods could have been kept intact and ethnic diversity maintained if urban renewal could have been slowed to a block-by-block pace, if the retail shopping area could have been sustained, and if small-scale manufacturing could have been developed between Third and Fourth streets so that a job base existed to allow people to walk to work. But the best the preservationists could achieve was blocking the highway that would have superseded Third Street. Otherwise, developers demolished residences and neighborhoods disappeared.

Downtown Bethlehem today: Moravian buildings in right foreground; fifteen-story office building in right background; mall parking garage in left background. (Published by permission of the City of Bethlehem.)

The North Side held even more possibilities for success or failure from the preservationist point of view. "You make a town like Bethlehem work," Ross asserts, "by recognizing that it's historic, by building on its assets. It has a historical group of buildings which are magnificent; it has a certain amount of charm in its downtown residential area; it has a certian amount of stability; and it's small scale. When you begin to destroy that you destroy everything it's good for. In trying to preserve it we were being very practical, we thought." In fact, the old Moravian buildings were saved and the industrial works along Monocacy Creek were reconstructed, largely through Steel money and the leadership of the wives of top executives. And Main Street north of the historic section is handsome for a couple of blocks.

But the pedestrian walking east on Broad Street from Main is dramatically confronted with an enormous mall, capped by an eleven-story structure, Bethlehem's downtown skyscraper. This modern mammoth is incongruous with the historic houses, the Main Street shops, and the surrounding residences. Commercially, the project has been a huge failure. The women who played a major role in the preservation and restoration of eighteenth-century Bethlehem have obviously been more successful than the men who speculated on growth and change in downtown North Side. (Perhaps the course of urban redevelopment ultimately can be reduced to gender: men, who are concerned with power, want to erect large structures and look for rises in property values; women, who are typically more sensitive to personal relationships and usually must conduct daily activities like shopping and chauffeuring, see the workings of the city from a human-size perspective.)

Working in favor of the women, of course, was the presence of a rich cultural heritage from the Moravians—Bethlehem's history. Not, however, the city's whole past. Although Uncas, "the last of the Mohicans," lies buried in the Moravian cemetery, the native American Indian background of the region goes otherwise unnoticed. And there is precious little on public view of the Old World tradition that was not Moravian, something representing the vital cultures of Eastern and Southern Europe, for example, which contributed so many immigrants to Bethlehem.

Probably it is expecting too much of the inhabitants of a city that they be aware of the many forces that shaped and continue to mold their social lives. Yet to be only partially informed is to be vulnerable, as illustrated by the circumstances of my classmate Lee Fraivillig. Lee was already working around his father's engineering office at Broad and Main streets, the corssroads of the downtown North Side, when I met him at Liberty High School in 1949. He went into the business full time after his graduation from Lehigh in 1956. When the federal funds flowed, Fraivillig Engineers worked for the Redevelopment Authority. Lee described those times with his customary enthusiasm:

"We would get sixty properties to survey. Then we were told to see what it cost to relocate the utilities in other blocks. There were bucks there to spend. I was surveying to beat the band. When $10 million is put into Bethlehem, it should be spent. We heard of plans— steps going down behind Orr's [a department store also located at Broad and Main, backing on Monocacy Creek], an overpass, an underpass, symphony halls, Hess's and Sears and a Master Store.

"There must have been thirty-five little businesses in that area. It was humming. We watched out for each other. We were proud. Parades came through. One day John F. Kennedy came into our office—stopped his caravan, hopped out, came in, and said 'Hi.' We were in the middle of things but in the way of redevelopment—and we were working for them! How would we know, as one particle of sand, that the whole beach was going to go? We were simply told, 'You fix up your block here. Something's going to come in.' We heard rumors of a convention center, hotels, Bethlehem Steel putting a dome over the city.

"Shortly thereafter they came to our building. They told us we had to be out within a year. 'Here's a check for your business, here's a check for your building. Go!' We came out here on West Broad, just pushed our cabinets up the street. It took the steam out of my father, out of a lot of older people. Yet here we are. I'm happy—but what happened to Bethlehem? Where is it? Where's the intersection? Right now, at quarter after four, I'd say there are three people at Broad and Main. That's our city.

"I think we were all naive. There was no foresight. Now they blame people that are gone. You can't do that. Ten or fifteen years ago, we didn't know. Things were happening here. Lehigh was building over the mountain, Steel was putting in its basic oxygen furnace, people were making lots of money. Now—one theater, no shopping, no restaurants. The high school is half full. Every high school student in this whole area school district would fit into Liberty. Then you could have a good old strong school again—powerful teams, powerful glee clubs. There's nothing like this.

"I had no idea but to stay here when I came out of college. It's a wonderful place to live and work—Church Street's beautiful, downtown's beautiful. But my kids aren't here. Jill went to Lehigh and now is in Rochester with Eastman Kodak. Jimmy went to Princeton and is in Wilmington with DuPont. Judy's at Penn, and I'm sure she's looking at California; my brother Johnny is out there and never comes home. I couldn't afford to employ my kids—they're too high-powered and expensive. Even Bethlehem Steel can't hire good engineers anymore; who wants to come to a company that's saying, 'We're hanging in there'?

"I'm almost fifty. Why should I stay here? I bought a condominium in Sarasota last June. I've never been through the Moravian buildings [Lee was a member of the Moravian Church] or the Kemmerer Museum. I don't appreciate the gas lights or the Sun Inn or the Mill. I don't know what Historic Bethlehem does. There's not a block, *not one block*, in this city I haven't worked in. I know all the zoning codes and subdivision ordinances. But I don't know what Historic Bethlehem does. I guess I'm not interested. It's sad."

Lee, a lifelong Bethlehem resident, attributes his naiveté about urban redevelopment to his never having been told what was happening and not having the curiosity to find out. Jim Howell's situation was entirely different. He could not wait to leave Bethlehem; a month after he graduated from high school he was on the road to Oregon and a job he expected to get in one of the lumber mills of the North Bend-Coos Bay area. He got his job and was welcomed into the community.

Three classmates who accompanied Jim returned to begin college, but not Jim himself. "I didn't feel like going back to Penn State and into forestry, especially after I met some people in Oregon who had been in the woods. My dad was upset but said he understood. He didn't try to coerce me. He had always pretty much treated me that way. I went to college [Oregon State University] within half a year, but I did it on my own. Yet I always knew I had my family to fall back on; it's not like I was *really* on my own."

Jim decided he had made a mistake by entering the engineering curriculum at Oregon State and soon returned to North Bend, Oregon, where he apprenticed himself to a sheet metal tradesman. In the mid 1950s he was drafted and shipped to Germany, where he married a native of Koblenz and, upon his discharge, returned to Eugene and the study of architecture at the University of Oregon. When twins arrived, he took a job near the university, and when that fell through, he moved on to Portland.

Jim recalls: "I worked for an architectural firm for about five years after I went to Portland. Then I quit and opened my own office, which I had for about eight years. And at that time I was doing neighborhood planning. It started off as a voluntary effort. Then I was asked by the neighborhood to do it as a paid job.

"I planned traffic patterns, a lot of neighborhood improvement projects, street tree planting, park design, house rehabilitation. It was part of the Model Cities program. In order to get federal funds, the neighborhood had to have a consultant or an advocate. It was a sort of urban renewal project on the neighborhood scale. I think the measure of its success was how little controversy and static it caused.

"Before I started my own office, about 1968, 1969, I had gone over to a friend's house to get some information about back-packing equipment. At that time there was a report just done by the City Club of Portland, talking about what to do with Harbor Drive along the Willamette River, between the downtown and the river.

This report had made several suggestions. But the state highway department had already decided to widen Harbor Drive. The more we discussed, and the more beers we had, the more we were convinced it probably wasn't a good idea. Maybe it would be a good idea to form a citizen's organization to fight the widening of Harbor Drive.

"That's how we created the River Front for People committee. His wife was quite active in the Democratic party, and she egged us on. We had an organizational meeting, where we got another twenty or thirty people. And there we decided to have a couple of picnics down on the river front to illustrate the problems, with all the noise and traffic.

"We had two lunch-time picnics and had a lot of people coming down to see what was going on, a lot of publicity. From that publicity we were able to convince the governor's task force, which was the organization that was going to make the decision on what to do with Harbor Drive, to hold a hearing on the subject—which back in those days wasn't always done; nowadays you always hold hearings on any kind of project.

"They had a public hearing, and most of the people there were against widening the drive and wanted to see it returned to park land along the river. The State Department of Transportation decided that rather than to widen it to just rip it up and plant grass there. Which is the way it exists today—as the Riverside Park. It indicates how easy it is for a group of people, if they have a logical proposal, to get it through.

"A year or so later, when I was doing neighborhood planning, there was a so-called 1990 Transportation Plan for the Portland metropolitan area that had hundreds of miles of proposed freeways on it, just red lines all over the map, which was done by our regional planning office and the City of Portland planners. It was a perfectly ridiculous plan, because no way could it ever be built—there wasn't enough money, and if they did built it, they'd tear up a large part of the city to put it in."

Jim and his friends formed STOP (Sensible Transportation Options for People) "to get rid of these future freeways" and, by taking the state to court, got both the state and the city to cease supporting the plan. Observing that "the bureaucratic machinery can be pushed around very easily," he continued his reflections:

"I don't know why I have a conscience about community. But

working in architecture is not just designing buildings but also designing the environment. A lot of those things interested me when I was going to school in architecture. We had a professor at the University of Oregon who had come from Portland and was active in beautification efforts; I think he might have influenced me.

"At the time I was working in architecture, I was getting involved in more and more planning, urban planning. And from urban planning I got more and more interested in urban transportation.

"It's kind of hard to say where you get interested in things. I mentioned this guy, this architect, when [our classmate] Charlie Cook and I were hitchhiking through New England that summer [1951] — his enthusiasm for architecture really reached me. When we lived in Germany I saw how public transport over there operated, and I was quite impressed with its efficiency and the ability for people to get around without automobiles — the economy of good transit. When I got into neighborhood planning, it seemed that our transit system was so archaic compared to Europe's. I think that's what got me started on it.

"I remember going to the New York World's Fair in 1939 and seeing the General Motors exhibit, 'The World of Tomorrow.' I think the model was to represent the 1960s. They had these little-bitty cars going down these big wide freeways with cloverleafs and all of that stuff — and how the world of 1960 is going to be such a wonderful place because you'll be able to travel by car on these wide motorways. It was very impressive at the time."

I observed to Jim that although he was geographically mobile he always seemed interested in being rooted and part of a community. He responded: "I feel that I've been more rooted than moving. I moved to North Bend, and I bought property there. And when I moved to Eugene I bought property. And when I moved to Portland I bought property. I tend to get myself rooted, maybe more than I should. Now I have no intention or desire to move from Portland."

I was struck by the contrast between the lifelong native of Bethlehem who passively accepted the change imposed on the city's downtown and the immigrant to Portland who actively opposed alteration. The former has become discouraged and plans to leave, while the latter has put down roots. On the face of it, they shared many traits: middle-class WASP backgrounds; university educations (civil engineering and architecture); entrepreneurial inclinations and moderately successful careers; marriage, children, and separation

(Lee divorced, while Jim reconciled). Was the difference between their respective postures toward the community to be explained by some hidden factors in their personal pasts, by chance, by the variant effects of stasis and mobility? I considered this sort of question often as I talked with others from our high school class, most of whom — like Lee — had stayed put.

I too had every reason to remain. Most of my ancestors had immigrated in the early eighteenth century from Germany to eastern Pennsylvania, where they put down their roots and stayed. Both my paternal grandfather and my father, though they spent a few years as teachers, devoted most of their working lives to local businesses. Dad built a road with New Deal funds in 1934, the year of my birth, but did not get into construction full time until 1945, when he became a beneficiary of the postwar housing boom. Building residential dwellings in Bethlehem was symbolic of his dedication to family and place, and he assumed that I would one day take over the operation. The immediate effect of his newly found prosperity on me, however, was an income large enough to absorb the tuition at Princeton University, sixty miles from home. I entered, only to find myself in a new world. Though it had effortlessly maintained its half-serious, half-hedonistic character since the days of Woodrow Wilson and F. Scott Fitzgerald, Princeton was populated by young men who let me know they were "going somewhere." I would have been ashamed to graduate and return to the family business.

Instead, I went off to the University of Pennsylvania, another Ivy League school but one which was having a harder time than Princeton maintaining the status quo, what with urban Jews demanding admission and street crime in West Philadelphia disturbing its genteel serenity. Yet the traditional curriculum at Penn remained largely intact, the scholarly atmosphere somewhat reminiscent of that of the nineteenth century, when American historians, Anglo Saxon and upper class, felt that the country created by their ancestors — Pilgrims and Founding Fathers — still belonged to them.

Of course, these men were no longer in the classroom, and the occupants of the chairs named after them were less patriotic and elitist. They conceded that the Pilgrims were religiously intolerant, that the Founding Fathers framed a Constitution preferential to their own economic interests. My professors were good twentieth-century historians, able to turn from the biographies of great men to an examination of social forces, to the influence of the frontier, for example, with its democratic and egalitarian characteristics, its typification of vitality and growth, adaptation and change.

I took the required courses, passed the necessary exams, and entered the ranks of college teachers, thinking I was ready to settle for quiet respectability close to home. Then I was offered a position in California. Though I had studied the restless westward movement that vitalized the frontier, it never occurred to me that I could still be part of it. I doubt that I had ever considered my own life in the context of the American history I was examining. I accepted the challenge in a fit of foolhardiness: I decided to leave home.

In the summer of 1963 my wife, son, and I jammed sleeping bags, a tent, and some personal belongings into our late-Eisenhower Chevy and pointed toward the sunset, leaving behind our teary-eyed families who waved their goodbyes and wished us luck. We gasped at new scenery, camped on plains and in forests, visited Indian reservations, and watched rodeos. Finally, on a bright September morning, we sped across the Golden Gate Bridge to my job as assistant professor of history at San Francisco State College.

We brought several cartons of books and incalculable cultural baggage; pioneers are resistant as well as open to the new environment. Teaching the history I had learned at Princeton and Pennsylvania, I found myself reinforced in outlook by most of my colleagues. But I was bewildered in a department meeting when our two radical historians — a farm boy from Indiana and a city kid from Brooklyn — opposed my teaching a course on the influence of great personalities in American history on the grounds that it was elitist. Never had I heard the case for a new social history put so bluntly. I was still unprepared to listen.

Meanwhile, my wife started work on her master's degree in English literature, and our son began his rapid progress through the public schools. We wore tweeds and ties, visited "the East" or Europe in the summers, and made friends with other émigrés. Our backgrounds and our academic inclinations shielded us from the San Francisco of popular legend. We joined no consciousness-raising groups, smoked no pot, seldom ventured into the Haight-Ashbury district with its hippies, or listened to rock bands. We knew of the existence of these things, knew people involved in them, and were tolerant of them. But we were unable to make them ours.

To the extent that we created a new life, we put our liberal values into practice. We did live in an integrated neighborhood, attend civil rights benefits, and march in peace parades. More important, the enticing atmosphere of San Francisco State drew me farther and farther into a new social milieu. To have black friends was at first a novelty, then a way of understanding. I was suprised that a graduate student, whom I thought I knew well, deeply mourned the death of Malcolm X; I knew the Muslim leader only through the white news media, and I considered him a rabble-rouser. Yet when the same graduate student asked me to be the faculty sponsor of an experimental seminar on black nationalism, I eagerly accepted. Every Saturday morning in the spring of 1966 I met with ten to fifteen black students, many of whom held me in contempt. They set the subject, and I listened. Did I say I never joined a consciousness-raising group? This was it.

Still, I was unprepared for the demonstrations and student/faculty strike at San Francisco State a few years later. The trauma began for me in December 1967, when a dozen Black Panthers entered my classroom and ridiculed me, a profoundly different experience from living in a mixed neighborhood, parading with Negroes for civil rights, or even being the minority member of a seminar. I was frightened as I sensed the vulnerability of my academic haven.

Looking back at those times today, I have to admit that I had hardly considered the potential consequences of my liberalism. I had approved of the campus being used as a launching pad for civil rights demonstrations and, later, antiwar protests. It had not occurred to me that eventually the university would be accused of complicity in "the system." Why did it not have more black students? Why did it fail to meet the special needs of minorities? Why did it accept government funds targeted for research that could aid in the production of the instruments of war? Why did it tolerate military officer-training programs?

The university was accused—and convicted. Students revolted. As the campus upheaval occurred, I did not consider that the disruption could well be temporary and some of the consequences healthy. Rather, my strongest feeling was the anxiety of being caught up in an irresolvable conflict. I reacted almost viscerally against the disorder of the protest movement, especially after I received anonymous, middle-of-the-night phone calls accusing me of being a scab for not going on strike (I was conducting my classes in my home). Yet I could not support the forces of control, directed by the perverse S. I. Hayakawa, later a United States senator, and brutally carried out by the San Francisco Police Tactical Squad. I searched in vain for a reasonable middle road, but my liberal values were not applicable to this situation. I was a painfully confused historian who could not understand the dynamics of social change.

Instead, I used my sabbatical to retreat from the battle, finding a haven in eastern Pennsylvania where I researched a book on early America. I did not return to San Francisco State for a year, by which time the situation had been transformed. The life had been squeezed out of the college. Bitter feelings existed between faculty members who had been on opposite sides of the struggle. Students seemed beaten and apathetic. The atmosphere said: "Teaching cannot take place." Yet the classroom was where we worked.

To meet the challenge I had to drop some of my cultural baggage. One of my first acts was to shed my coat and tie. Later my son would tease me by referring to my attire as a barometer of the social climate, yet the change I displayed in the early 1970s ran much deeper than style. The events of the previous decade had affected my perception of reality. I was less a captive of my past, more open to dealing with the present on its own terms.

I was capable of letting go the history I had been taught and embracing a view of the past that fit the realities of my classroom, realities that had both psychological and social dimensions. For whatever reason—call it the need for a sense of immediacy produced by watching television—students were uninterested in the slow, gratification-deferred process of reconstructing history. Yet like all young people, they were striving to come to terms with themselves, to forge identities, and here history could be relevant.

Suppose students were asked to become acquainted with their own families over several generations, ever mindful that a recognition of family continuity could aid self-understanding? My new responsibility in this process would be to provide a social history of America that would include their ancestors—black slaves, Asian immigrants, Eastern European steelworkers, Mexican laborers, American Indians—and include them not as "problems" in the American past but as respectable actors.

For the state universities and colleges of California threw their nets far and wide, as was increasingly the case with higher education everywhere, thanks largely to post–World War II prosperity. In 1950, with the returned veterans of the war still crowding the colleges, 14.2 percent of the American population between the ages of eighteen and twenty-four attended some institution of higher education. In 1960 the figure had risen to 22.2 percent and in 1970 to 32.1 percent. I was not teaching the same people with whom I had gone to Princeton.

Furthermore, this vastly expanded college population faced a new kind of professor. To meet the market demands, the sources of supply had expanded. Old graduate schools grew in size, and new ones were created. This history profession, once a closed circle of the elite which expanded only slowly, now embraced many more outsiders. When I reached graduate school in 1956 the first Jew on Penn's history faculty had been there only five years. But the situation was changing. That was evident from looking at my fellow graduate students, who also were not the upper-class WASPs I had known at Princeton. While I pursued traditional research topics, many of them studied such foreign (to me) subjects as immigrant and labor history. It took the leaven of life in San Francisco to jar me out of old patterns. Yet after I started assigning family history to my students, I found that colleagues of mine across the nation were making essentially the same classroom requirement.

The colleges were changing—but so was the rest of the country. Twenty-five years after high school graduation, when I was giving a public address in Bethlehem on the subject of this book, a former classmate whose father had been a junior high principal arose from the audience to ask, with a strong trace of anger in her voice: "Are you going to reveal that the Presbyterian Church is the center of wealth and power in this community?" The question not only revealed where the Bethlehem Steel officialdom prayed but also—and more importantly, I think—that resentment lingered about an issue that was never raised above the level of gossip, was never (so far as my questioner knew) honored with a page in a history book.

I see my classmates, like me, groping for more accurate understandings of the world we live in, trying to achieve what I have earlier called a balancing act of past and present, wanting to be at liberty. They have contributed generously to an enterprise of sharing outlooks. What we previously shared, most obviously, was a community. That is still possible. The remainder of this book will concern them in the context of topics we never studied in high school.

2 | *Family*

"How are your parents?" The question came up time and again, asked by former high school classmates who, I was certain, had never met my mother or my father. That was not the point. Rather, they were telling me how much they valued family. It was not a message I was used to hearing in San Francisco, where my friends are likely to be separated by hundreds or thousands of miles from the relatives with whom they grew up. The focus on family in Bethlehem was a concern I had to accustom myself to, an adjustment which reminded me that I was not yet on intimate terms with the town.

Before I ventured back to my old haunt to talk to members of the Class of 1952, I had sent them questionnaires — and the message was already spelled out in their responses. Ninety-six percent of us married, myself included, showing that we came away from home with a high regard for the salutary effect of matrimony. When I attempted to elicit information from a recalcitrant classmate, she informed me quite matter-of-factly: "You wouldn't be interested in me. I never married." Marriage — and family — are seen as giving meaning to life. A wife wondered, in the midst of our exploring the problems of the younger generation, "what it would have been like without children." "I don't even think about not having children," her husband immediately responded.

Not only did we marry, but 80 percent of us stayed with our original spouses, and of the 13 percent who divorced and 3 percent who were widowed, over half remarried. The 1980 census revealed that 73.2 percent of households in the United States are headed by married couples, widows, or widowers, but for the Class of 1952 the figure is significantly higher: 90.1 percent. The age at which my classmates married is virtually the same as the national average, which in 1950 and again in 1960 was 20.3 for women and 22.8 for men.

Only 7 percent of the married couples had no children. The parents of Class members grew up in large families (usually, five children) but produced smaller ones (three children), a decline typical of American families in the Depression. Class members appear to follow their parents' examples, for they spawned still fewer children (2.6 on the average) when the national pattern was for their generation to produce more babies than the preceding one. (Interestingly, there is no correlation between the size of a Class member's family of origin and the number of children he or she produced.)

Most Class members demonstrated their respect for family bonds by marrying fellow residents of the Lehigh Valley, and most remained in Bethlehem and its environs. They thus forged a kind of continuity in family life by staying close to their parents.

Bob Henry, a quiet and studious boy as I remember him, crossed town from Liberty High School to Lehigh University, then took an engineering job with the Bethlehem Steel Company, married the younger sister of one of our classmates, and raised two children on the far west side of the city. I had coffee one evening with Bob and his wife, Jeanette.

BOB: My dad comes to visit with us almost every Sunday. My mother's dead now. He remarried, and his second wife died. He lives in Bath in a trailer court—very nice trailers, individually. He comes to visit with us on Sunday morning; we go to church together.

We sat around the late breakfast table one morning, going over your questionnaire. I told him you had written and I didn't know all the answers. He said, "Well, I'll be darned. I probably won't know 'em either." "Well," I said, "They're not difficult questions, just questions about family." It's the sort of thing you don't really consider until somebody does raise the question. But one thing that helped us is that he has a cousin that years ago decided to write a family tree of his side of the family. That made it fairly simple on his side.

On my mother's side, her brother's still living, but there are not too many people on her side. On my father's side, the men are very long-lived people. And on Jeanette's side, the women are very long-lived people. We'll have a long happy life together.

JEANETTE: My mother's up in Bath, but I'm originally from Bethlehem. I'm a Schumacher, with seven brothers and three sisters. I don't speak Pennsylvania Dutch, but my parents did — when they didn't want us to know what was going on.

BOB: In my family, my grandmother spoke German; she was from Germany. My parents spoke the language. I took German in high school so I could talk to my grandmother.

JEANETTE: I see my mother once a week. But as far as my sisters and brothers — I have some in town — I see them every three or four months.

BOB: Before my mother's death, our family got together more regularly than it does now. I have a brother who's only eighteen months younger than I am. And I have a brother who's thirteen years younger than I am; he's almost like a son to me. I'm too quick to give him advice. That relationship doesn't exist too well.

We go out socially with some of Jeanette's brothers. Her brother John is close to us. With a large family there's quite a bit of sibling rivalry, and that shows up quite vividly in later years.

JEANETTE: We were close until my father died six years ago.

BOB: My father was the patriarchal type, kind of ruled the house. Pop said something, everybody came together. Things have changed now.

Bob's father died in 1983, three years after Jeanette's mother. For the moment there are only two generations. Daughter Debbie lives at home, works as a waitress, and has just graduated from Allentown College. Son Bob went off to the Culinary Institute of America, married, and holds a job as a chef near Philadelphia, less than fifty miles away. The family remains very much intact.

Jim Placotaris almost broke away. In high school, we recognized him as the strong, silent type. First-string end on the football team and runner-up heavyweight wrestling champ of the state of Pennsylvania, he was there and he was dependable. He still is, as he sits

Table 1. The Class of 1952 by Residence

	1952		1976	
	Number of persons	Percent of total	Number of persons	Percent of total
Bethlehem	462	84.0	186	33.8
Ward 1	24	4.5	9	1.6
Ward 2	26	4.7	6	1.1
Ward 3	9	1.6	3	0.5
Ward 4	33	6.0	4	0.7
Ward 5	23	4.2	2	0.4
Ward 16	19	3.5	2	0.4
Ward 17	25	4.5	9	1.6
South Side Total	159	28.9	35	6.4
Ward 6	14	2.5	2	0.4
Ward 7	16	2.9	2	0.4
Ward 8	24	4.5	5	0.9
Ward 9	55	10.0	14	2.5
Ward 14	41	7.5	47	8.5
Ward 15	54	9.8	21	3.8
North Side Total	204	37.1	91	16.5

Table 1. The Class of 1952 by Residence (*continued*)

	1952		1976	
	Number of persons	Percent of total	Number of persons	Percent of total
Ward 10	9	1.6	3	0.5
Ward 11	16	2.9	0	0
Ward 12	23	4.2	11	2.0
Ward 13	51	9.3	46	8.4
West Side Total	99	18.0	60	10.9
Lehigh Valley (excluding Bethlehem)	88	16.0	135	24.5
Pennsylvania (excluding Lehigh Valley)			59	10.7
Northeast (excluding Pennsylvania)			69	12.8
New Jersey			13	2.4
New York			13	2.4
New England			19	3.5
(Del./Md./D.C./Va.)			24	4.5
Southeast			16	2.9
Midwest			16	2.9
Mountain States			1	0.2
Southwest			4	0.1
Far West			16	2.9
Outside U.S.			3	0.5
Unknown			46	8.4

in his small office at the rear of Placky's general store and bakery. Solid but gentle, not handsome yet physically attractive for qualities that radiate from within.

JIM: I graduated from Lehigh in 1956 and went to work for General Motors Acceptance Corporation. Whaley Barber [another classmate and the other end on Liberty's starting eleven, he grew up a few blocks from Jim] told me about the opportunities there. But I had a military obligation, so soon afterward I entered the Navy Air Force, where I spent over three years. I enjoyed it immensely, saw a lot of the Far East, and had a strong inclination to stay in — but the career possibilities were limited. And GMAC was holding my job for me.

But I couldn't go my own way with any peace of mind. Not with my mom and dad and brother and sister struggling back home with a business they couldn't sell. All I saw was them going down the tubes. So I came back and pitched in and we pulled it up. I couldn't do it any other way.

When I came out of Lehigh I didn't want any part of the business — a mom-and-pop store with a bakery on the premises. I could have done so many other things with a lot less headaches. But I decided to come in.

I married a local girl, younger, Mexican. I always have had a strong sense of being Greek. And there has always been tremendous pressure on Greek children to marry other Greeks. A lot of marriages are arranged, though it's harder to keep the boys in line than the girls. I just decided I would marry the girl of my choice. My father did the same; my mother is Italian. My mother picked up the language, the customs, the food. Our family ties are very strong.

I grew up on the South Side of Bethlehem, on Vine Street near the College theater, a great area. I can't think of a more ideal place to grow up. It's not that way anymore, but it was then. Nearby was a playground, a baseball field, the Lehigh University campus. When we got bored with playground activities, two or three of us would go hiking in the woods. Or we'd walk out to the Heights, through Morton Street, Fifth Street. And other kids, who were strangers, would never bother you. When we were older we got to meet them through the Boys' Club or the schools.

There was never a dull moment when I was a kid. I was never under my mom's shoes, hanging around the house. And it was safe. My parents didn't have to worry about us kids being out, though we had to be home by nine. They never asked where we were going to be, they knew we were around the block.

Now my kids don't have this. I've since moved to Center Valley. It's beautiful out there, residential, I have a lot of ground. But they don't have any of the things I had: sports, a playground, just the general area. I think if I could have given them that I would have. But it doesn't exist anymore. If I could have moved right back to my parents' old home or nearby, and everything was the same as when I was a kid, that's where I would have raised my kids. If things were the same. But things are not the same.

I wouldn't trust my kids out at night. There's too much going on. There's dope going on, there's young punks riding around in cars.

Maybe some people on the North Side felt the South Side was a rough place even when I was a kid. But the distinction between the two places was income. We knew the North Side kids were in a higher income bracket than us. They seemed to have a little more culture, were not so raw, so earthy as South Siders. But I never felt intimidated, nor did I make any remarks to anybody.

I never planned to go to college. I was in the commercial course in high school; that was no challenge for anybody. My parents felt, when I was a senior, that I ought to go on. But I was unprepared—and scared of Lehigh. It was rough all the way through there. The best I could do was C+. My wrestling record helped me get in, not football. But since I had no scholarship, I decided not to get into athletics. I didn't go back to my twentieth reunion at Lehigh.

Lehigh bought my parents' Vine Street home. They moved out here near the business. I lived near here for a while. But as our family grew—we now have three sons—we wanted a bigger home with some land. I often talk to the boys about the way I was raised and how it was. They can't understand. We live in a little suburban neighborhood—no playground, no movie theater—the kids are under our feet. We chauffeur them; the oldest goes to Little League in the summer, wrestling in the winter, and so forth.

My kids don't think of themselves as Greek. We're getting absorbed into American culture. I spoke Greek, and my wife spoke Spanish—we talk to each other in English and that's what the boys speak.

Today Jim is still managing the family business, but now with the help of his two older sons, who were the beneficiaries of commercial courses at the local community college. The business expanded when Jim qualified as a ticket agent for the highly successful Pennsylvania lottery. As the American economy slumps from its post–World War II zenith, the prospect for employment in a family business brightens—and helps bind the generations together.

———

In traditional society, of course, the family was commonly a business venture, engaging not only blood relatives but apprentices and servants in one productive household. The distinguishing characteristic of the modern family, however, is not economic but romantic.

I remember Jo Marino and Don Bittenbender walking down a school corridor hand in hand, not an easy accomplishment given the fact that he, a basketball star at Nitchman Junior High School, was at least a foot taller than she. They were voted the class sweethearts in 1952, and on the summer evening I visited them in 1976 I was immediately struck by how close they had remained. Don, shirtless and tan, solid and trim, looking every bit the athlete he was and the steamfitter he is, dominated the conversation, his confident, Pennsylvania-Dutch-accented voice continually modulated by a warm acknowledgment of Jo's presence. "Isn't that so, Jo?" he would ask, rhetorically perhaps, but obviously hoping for her confirmation. She, petite and shy, almost hiding behind the flow of his words, would smile and agree, occasionally adding a few sentences. During the evening their two children, with friends, casually came and went.

DON: I took your questionnaire down to Mom and Dad for some help. But once Dad starts talking about the past there's no stopping him. The area where we're living now was his playground. He used to hitch a dog up to a wagon and ride around here. To hear him talk, it was a different world. He thinks those were the Good Days.

My mother is English, Irish, Scotch. My dad is Dutch. There's not too many Pennsylvania Dutchmen anymore; that's a thing of the past. At one time this area, Rittersville [now on the western edge of Bethlehem], was ruled by them. And they wouldn't allow nothing to go wrong; everything was on the up and up.

That's where I grew up. I went to Nitchman [Junior High School]. Have you seen Jimmy McGovern? Hank Durkop? I'll tell you, during seventh, eighth, and ninth grade the three of us traveled all the time together. Football. Basketball. Then in high school, everything just faded away. The people weren't the same, we didn't have that closeness anymore, all different faces. There wasn't that personal interest to push you in athletics.

The guys from South Side got the breaks. Believe it or not. Those from the west end, over past Pennsylvania Avenue, we were the people they didn't care for in sports. The basketball coach favored the kids from the South Side, thinking maybe they were rougher, or tougher, or better athletes because they were in the street. But we were raised in the street also. And we didn't live in a bed of roses. We had to come up the hard way. You had to work your way out.

I met Jo in Miss Bustin's English class. She sat in front of me. We had to do a book report, and I actually did it! Jo didn't show up for class.

JO: I always did my homework. I just forgot all about it, and I was scared to death of Miss Bustin to start with. So I just skipped class.

DON: So I threatened her—if she didn't go out with me, I'd tell Miss Bustin.

JO: That's where we started.

DON: Well, we began walking home together. And she said I ought to be doing better in my classes than I was.

JO: He wanted to quit school. I said that if he quit school, it was off.

DON: Yeah, it was getting too tough. All I had been interested in was sports, and when I lost interest in that, well, what was left?

And in the back of my mind I knew at the end of it all I was going to end up over there anyway, in some sort of war. If you remember, that's what was on our minds ever since we were kids, from the second war.

But I stuck it out. From high school I went down to the Steel. Everybody went down to the Steel. Soon I was in the service. I don't know if I ever discussed with Jo how I felt about it—war. That's a heck of a thing to be hanging in the back of your head. And I saw fellows I had grown up with go over there [Korea], come back wounded. What nonsense! Policing the area, that's not a war. Same with Vietnam. Far as I'm concerned, that was big business playing the role there.

This kind of turned you off on a lot of things, the way you're treated. When I came back I felt I had put my time in. I might not have been in the thick of it, but I was still there—there was a possibility that I would have been in the thick of it. So I go down to the Steel to get my old job back, because that was the only place we had to go, really. There was no other place you could go for work.

At that time, you recall, the [Hungarian] Freedom Fighters were here. I call them the ones that had the money to come to the United States. They left their country to come here. If they were so patriotic and wanted to do their thing, why didn't they stay and do it? But they came over here and I'm standing in a job, and they took me from the front and put me in the back because there's four others who are refugees. They were getting the job and I'm sitting back.

So, I started working for my dad. And then, finally, again through people you know—it's not what you know, it's who you know—her father got me back in there. He got me to go through apprenticeship school down there. It did a lot for me, gave me that *bounce back*, you see? And I felt that I'm going to do something. I didn't have the education I should have had, but I'm still doing what best I know how to do, which was what I took up and what I did in the service— pipefitting. Well, I got finished with apprenticeship there and I got bumped off, in '57, the first time in twenty years they ever did something like this, and I was down again. She had to go to work.

Don Bittenbender, his father, and his son at work on the family garage. (Photo by JEI.)

You're thinking, "What's this all about? What's this all about?" Sure they have privileges, but don't we? We have the same privileges. Well, anyway, everything turned out right. Her father again got me a job—at Western Electric.

But I had been out of work for a year and a half. I figured it was a waste of time to try to buy this house. We're going to lose everything we got. But she saved constantly. To be quite frank with you, I gave up the whole situation and I took off. Saturday afternoons I'd go with the boys, play basketball, do anything. I hadn't grown up. I couldn't face the music. Then after the first two or three years, things got better—"You can do it." She kept pushing. Everything we have today, the credit goes to her.

I do the work. It's bullwork, and I'm no spring chicken. You got to use your head too. There's gas in the lines; it's dangerous. But all you are is a number. Still doesn't mean anything. You don't get recognized for doing a good job. Ah, I've been in the ditch since I was fourteen. Some people are meant for some things, some for others. I'm a producer.

I get tired. We make the kids come in early compared to their friends—at 10:30, sometimes 11:00 P.M. They can stay here later, if they want. Even at nineteen, Mick has that limit. I put it this way to him, "When your mother and I were younger we stayed up all hours of the night—when you were sick, as a baby. If you think now that we're older we're going to stay up all hours of the night—waiting for you—again, you're out of your mind. We want to go to bed when we're tired."

Our son came home from class at the community college just this morning and said the professor told them that parents were making slaves out of their kids. I went in a rage when I heard this. I said, "What does he know about getting up every night, on the hour every hour, changing you, feeding you. When you were sick your mother and I sat with you in the hospital, we worried." This is a younger group, twenty-five, twenty-eight, telling these kids eighteen, nineteen, twenty, what is happening.

The kids today could care less. They just want to go out and smoke joints and have pot and raise royal hell. They think in several years the earth's coming to an end anyway, so they want to live it up now. Their philosophy is that they're going to die young and they're going to do their thing. And this is why everything's getting rearranged—living with people, don't get married, don't believe in marriage. And the parents are caught in between.

The kids are doing their thing—let them pay for it. That's my philosophy. You know that from fourteen to seventeen, eighteen, nineteen, nobody could tell you what to do; if your mother and dad said, "Do this," you turned around and did the opposite. This is the way Mick, our nineteen-year-old son, was, too. But amazingly enough—we were talking about this on Sunday—everything we told him about different things in life. He says, "You know, Dad, you were right, but you've got to be hurt before you realize."

Now, Donna's in the same situation. She's fifteen and has a boyfriend. You try to talk to them the best you can. It's not the way it was with our parents, when you hid behind the covers and they threw a book at you and said, "Now read it, see what it's all about." It's not like that today; it's all out in the open.

The younger kids today don't have the meaning we had, *I* think. It's not that love anymore. It's what they can get, what they can have, what they can do. It's not like before, when your mom and pop said, "This is it. You're not changing nothing." You obeyed them, you did what they told you, you didn't argue back or you got it across the kisser, and if you asked why you got another one. Today you've got to talk to them. The brute stuff is finished. And it's hard, sometimes. We start out slow, talking clamly, and end up yelling. I finally say, "This is the way it's got to be and that's it." Then he'll laugh it off and walk away.

Our kids don't go to church as much as I'd like them to. When I was going to school, from the time I can remember, I didn't miss. It was fifteen years straight.

Jo: When the children were younger we always went. And we still go in the winter. But now we have this place in the mountains where we go weekends. Sometimes we attend services up there.

DON: You see, that's the problem today. My dad says it in this way: "Don, this is a faithless nation and you're going to get punished for it." You can see it, it's happening. People are fighting amongst themselves, here and overseas, the blacks against the whites, the Puerto Ricans are fighting and taking over parts of the cities for their own. You can't go some place without being mugged or robbed. I don't recall this when I was a kid. I wasn't there, then. Today it's here.

You warn your children not to do this, not to go here, don't go unescorted, don't walk the streets like they do. They walk down the middle of the street, hitchhike with everything hanging out. You know what I'm saying? There's the problem. So maybe I'm wrong. Our parents were strict. The kids will tell you today, "We have a mind of our own."

In the upper class they blame the middle-class people; those are the ones who are on dope and stuff. Well, we're the middle class. Both my son and my daughter saw dope being passed in the school halls. They just said, "Well, if that's what they want."

I guess you see all this out in California too. We have a

friend in Arizona who left here because of health problems. He's bugging us to come out. And to be quite frank with you, I was ready to go. We discussed it. Jo's brother is in California, but she didn't want to leave. In a way she's right, in a way she's wrong. Our ties are here.

When I told Mother and Dad that we were just talking about it—of course, mother instinct—she said, "If you go, I'll die. Wait until I die and then go." That just cuts it right off.

JO: I feel it more strongly than he does. Our family was always closer than his family, right?

DON: Well, in a different way. I got to say this, and she is going to agree with me. Their closeness is if their family is in trouble. Italian people aren't real affectionate outwardly. I'll go down and visit and before I leave I'll kiss my mother on the head or pat my dad on the back. Where her family will talk and laugh and leave it "as is." They don't go in for that kiss goodbye, or whatever. But now there's a different thing that comes here. If there's trouble within that family, man, they'll flock together. And they're very emotional if something happens, more so than our group. She had her problems in life. Remember her sister? She passed away when my wife was sixteen and she was twenty-five. And her brother had a tragedy with his son.

JO: It's not only family. I don't like traveling. We go up to the mountains, that's far enough. It takes an hour and a half, ohh.

DON: I can't even get her to go anyplace. I would love to fly, and I've had opportunities to fly when they had this free flight to Arizona, free flight to Florida, all these places, then they show you around, three days, two nights, then you come back. She won't budge; she's afraid. She's afraid to go up a four-foot ladder. I would go by train, car, *anything*, just to go.

I noticed Jo looking a bit nervously at the clock, so I said I had to leave. She breathed a sigh of relief; she was due to take her mother to the shopping center in a few minutes. Don asked me to stick around and have a beer on the back porch. As Jo left and we settled down to enjoy our drinks, Don turned serious. "What do you think of it?" he inquired, and before I could come up with an innocuous answer he continued. "Not the house, *life*. Many is the time I have sat back here and tried to figure it out." Inside, Don had said that the credit for getting through the tough financial times must go to Jo. Now, without changing the story, he presented a different perspective.

Yes, Jo had gone out and worked when Don was out of a job for over a year. Baby-sitting had not buoyed his confidence as a man, but they were happy to have the children, indeed had had problems having children — a situation I could empathize with. Yet Jo had had some difficult times. Don astutely connected her depression at twenty-five with her older sister's death at the same age. And he saw the importance of finding a retreat in the mountains so as to escape an intense family environment that was not healthy as constant fare. While sometimes he could barely suppress his anger — at South Side athletes, Hungarian Freedom Fighters, glib college professors, to-day's youth — he also had a very thoughtful and nurturing side. He cared enough to understand.

On a later visit to Bethlehem I called Don to arrange another meeting, but he couldn't fit it into his busy schedule. "I'm taking care of houses — mine, my father's, my two kids'. They're married and we're grandparents. The only time I could see you is during my lunch break at work." Although we couldn't arrange a meeting, I had found out what seemed most important: Don continues to weave the web of family. He isn't flying off to Arizona.

_____

Don consciously recognized and accepted a situation: his parents and Jo's cherished their children's nearby presence, the feeling was reciprocal, and it was passed on to the next generation. But it was also possible that parents — or a parent — saw virtue in a child's mo-bility, certainly the case with another high school couple I visited, not in Bethlehem but on the outskirts of a beautiful old Connecti-cut village where they had recently settled in a large, new house. It was their fourth move, and their two older children (then twenty and eighteen) had remained in the area where they last lived, several hundred miles distant, while the two younger resided with them.

In high school they had been known simply as "Buzzy and Sally"— no last names were necessary. Sarah Noll lived somewhat in the shadow of Warren Richards, since he was one of the most promi-nent members of our class. The son of a South Side steelworker, Buzzy joined the elite high school fraternity yet held the allegiance of students from his part of town and was easily elected president of the student council in his senior year. Both Buzzy and Sally were chosen for the prestigious singing group Liberty Twelve Plus.

He qualified for Anapolis but dropped out after two years to attend and graduate from Lehigh, then entered the management of General Electric in marketing and finance. She went to nursing school, worked part time in a hospital until their third child was born (1959), and re-entered the profession through a refresher course a few years ago.

BUZZY: [On being told that Jim Ramberger, a classmate, said Buzzy played the most important role in helping him out after high school.] It was really my mother. Jim and I had an unspoken understanding. There was something he and I strived for. I wanted to get out of the South Side. I was pushed to feel that, especially by my mother. She was a very strong woman. She told me: "You got to get ahead; you don't want to work in the Steel Company all your life, shoveling slag." She wanted the finer things of life. She wanted her kids to succeed.

SALLY: Your mother was Catholic and she became an Episcopalian. Maybe deep down she wanted to "get out" that way.

BUZZY: The people I met and associated with in high schools, like you and John St. Clair, showed me how the other half lived—and Jim and I shared the feeling that we wanted it.

That river between the North and South sides really divided the city. I can remember my older sister growing up, there were family arguments, she would want to do something and argue: "All those West Siders can do it, those North Siders can do it." But I didn't let it stand in my way. I guess I was successful in bridging the gulf.

Many kids just accepted the division. They resented it, but they didn't want to bridge the gap. Who wants to join the enemy?

The Boys' Club played an extremely important role in what's happened to me. There was an older man there, John Betts, who talked with me when I was thirteen, fourteen, fifteen years old—discussions I could never have at home.

Since I've gone into business, I've changed my mind about moving around. General Electric's president, Ralph Cordier, was a great believer in layers of management, moving people around, exposing them to different businesses; if you were a manager, you could manage anything. That idea is much less accepted today, and there's less movement than there was fifteen, twenty years ago. Of course, it was very costly for companies to move people. I no longer feel all that movement is necessary, but my reasons are more personal.

We started corporate life in Pittsfield, Massachusetts, and stayed there six and a half years. Then we went to Columbia, South Carolina, for four years. After that we were in Schenectady, New York—actually in a little community called Burnt Hills—for ten years. G. E. was really predominant there. We came to Newton, Connecticut, just recently.

You lose roots by moving so much. It's hard on the kids, moving so much, especially at the high school age. It's unfair. We've been through it several times, and it's family-wrenching. Why does this society insist that this has to go on? There's been a lot less movement lately, but I'm not sure the slowdown is in recognition of the effect on families.

Our son walked out I don't know how many times in his junior or senior year, left home for a week at a time. One time he just stayed with a neighbor, a shattering couple weeks for us, before he came home to the fold. Then his senior year he moved out, lived with some other young guy, and worked nights in a restaurant. He kicked around for a year before he decided he was going to go to college. I don't really comprehend, don't really have much faith in what our relationship is—his and mine. Sally has a better relationship with him.

SALLY: Yes, I do. I think the key is listening. I think it's tough for Buz to listen to the kids without jumping up and saying, "That isn't right," or "You should have done this," or dealing with them the way our parents dealt with us. If the kids have someone to listen while they're telling a problem, they can often solve it themselves.

When we talk about the future, we talk about personhood. To my girls I never talk about marriage. Rather, we discuss working to the best of your ability. We explore different possible careers.

Something that my kids have missed, that I had, was someone else to go to. There were aunts and uncles, grandmother,

Sally, Buz, and Amy Richards at home in Connecticut. (Photo by JEI.)

grandfather—someone else to be on your side or at least listen. And there were special holidays with the relatives there. We always had each other.

BUZZY: The family as an institution, which maybe has an overly soft spot in my heart, I see it going to hell. Maybe it's just the times, maybe it will all turn out for the better. But kids don't seem to be tied, not that they should be tied.

What I see in today's kids is a freedom completely lacking in discipline, feeling without much care about consequences, unselfishness without thinking or caring about what happens to themselves.

I know it's hard for me to put myself in the shoes of my own kids. They got all kinds of different pressures, certainly. You [Illick] have a very unique luxury. You're able to take the time—your work is in this area—to think about what's making things evolve the way they are. I have impressions and thoughts and feelings which are pretty fleeting which might prove irrational or illogical or contradictory. I think the typi-

cal guy like me—the businessman—really doesn't have time
to sit back and ponder.

I experienced one week of an encounter group where G. E.
sent its executives. It was an intense experience, twenty-four
hours a day. It can be shattering. I saw one case where an
older guy started to go off the deep end, and I've read of
such things happening. Now a lot of this approach has been
discarded—it's expensive and time-consuming. In the final
analysis, it doesn't make a profit, it doesn't show up on the
bottom line. That's what matters in the business world.

Buzzy and Sally, like their classmates back in Bethlehem, have
a high regard for marriage and parenthood. But mobility robbed
their children of the cushions family can provide: cousins to play
with, a grandmother to talk to, a gathering of relatives to face the
world with, a sense of continuity and rootedness. Many of these
functions became the parents' by default. Sally, who has spent much
of her time with the kids, knows that their problems must be heard.
Buzzy, necessarily tied to his work, is more apt to admonish them.
His ideas on the meaning of family were framed in the past.

When Buzzy and Sally left rural Connecticut for Cincinnati only
Mary, the secont-oldest child, accompanied them. Her schizophrenia
prevents her from holding a job, but the supervisors of her mental
health program believe she is ready for her own apartment. Peter,
the eldest, remains in upstate New York, the scene of their third move,
working as a chef. Amy graduated from the University of Connecticut, married, and moved to Texas where her husband is in the Air
Force; she works as a nurse in addition to raising a daughter and
was visited by her two Bethlehem grandmothers, eighty and eighty-
four, during Easter 1985. Ann attends photography school in Boston
and works in a pizza parlor. The family network is maintained
as Buzzy and Sally pay close attention to the activities of its members, older and younger. But it is a network dependent on modern
technology—telephones and airplanes.

―――――

Which is not to say that proximity always maintains the best in-
tergenerational relations. Parents, if they are doting or controlling
in some other manner, are able to make life unhappy for children,

even if the offspring do not recognize the source of the problem. This seemed very much to be the case with Henrietta Diefendorfer.

Although Henrietta was a friend in high school, and we may even have dated once or twice, I did not at first recognize her when we encountered one another by chance in a parking lot behind the church where a funeral service was to be held for the father of a high school classmate. Yet I certainly felt her embarrassment when, as we entered the sanctuary, she nervously murmured an inappropriate "Best wishes" to the wife of the departed. Afterwards the two of us went for coffee. I asked her how she remembered our school days.

HENRIETTA: When you watch "Happy Days," that's supposed to be the fifties. And that just doesn't look like what I remember high school. I loved high school, I liked everything. And I hated college. And I was going to transfer, through my first year and part of my second. And I decided it wouldn't do me any good to transfer, that I would just have more problems, I would take the same problems with me. So what I did was just sort of exist until it was over. I don't know why, though, why I didn't like it, except that I was such a big wheel in high school, and I was nothing in college.

At Denison, I just did not fit into the social life. I was too straight. I didn't fit in socially at all, although I was in a sorority. But it wasn't the best sorority. The first time around I wasn't even picked up by anybody. The second time around I was picked up by this one that was not the best sorority. However, it turned into the best sorority. The year I was in there was nothing but lemons in it. I really didn't care for the girls in my sorority class.

Yes, college was like high school with alcohol — and sex — added. Sometimes, nowadays, with the new morality or whatever the term is, I wonder if it really is that much different than it was back when we were in college. Hal [her husband, a teacher] says it is a lot different. The sex and the drugs make a big difference. But he feels I'm too sheltered; I don't know what's really going on.

After Denison I came to Bethlehem and lived at home and worked for a year. That's when I met Hal. I had always wanted to marry a man who had strong religious convictions. I had a whole list of reasons. I wrote them down once. I probably threw it away. They all made sense to me at the time. The reason I wish I had the list was they probably would sound very silly now.

They probably were like I thought maybe you could get into heaven better—maybe. Or maybe I thought that someone religious would be a nicer person, nicer husband, more considerate, something like that. Or maybe I thought he'd be a better father. I wasn't very religious, but I was leaning that way. And I'm not now. I have admiration for people that I feel are religious, and I don't feel that way about myself. I don't really have the personal faith that I'm sure a lot of people have.

Like, for instance, I forget to pray. Day after day I forget to pray. I think that God should be so much a part of my life that I would talk to him. Not a formal prayer but just talk to him in my mind at least once a day. But it can go for days and days and days and aside from—right now, I'm all tied up in wanting to move to some other part of the country. I want to move so desperately, and it's so frustrating, that if anything, I'm just——I get very annoyed with God and wonder if He is ever doing anything about it. I say, "What's going on? Aren't you interested in making us happy?" It's not us, it's me, though.

I wouldn't dare say that to Hal. Hal's getting fed up with me, really fed up. You know, every once a week or something we have some kind of a to-do about if I don't get less anxious and if I don't settle down, he's going to take the first thing that comes along, whether it's right or not. And then I say, "No, you can't do that. You've got to wait until the right thing comes." And he says, well, he can't live with the way I'm acting and that kind of thing. So that's what my problem is right now.

I'd like to get away from my parents. They're still the bosses, and if you go against them—wow! That's one of the big "hurry" things. And the other thing is, I feel we really should have moved before this. Our oldest daughter started high school, and I really thought that this summer was the last time that we should have moved as far as education is concerned, you know, disrupting their education. By the time she starts high school, then the rest come every two years. And I think it's hard to move when you're in high school. I think a lot about the kids.

I get terribly annoyed driving them places to their lessons. On the other hand, I'm the one that tells them about things that are opening up, or encourages them to take a lesson. I want what's best for them, what I think is best for them. And I don't necessarily think that doing all this stuff is best for them, but that's what I do anyway. Last year I said, about halfway through the school year, I said, "I've had it, I'm sick of driving people. I'm just sick of the whole thing. From now on we're going to cut down on activities, and it's just we're never around at the same time together." And all that kind of carrying on I did. But it isn't any different. This year it's worse than last year. And every year it is worse than the year before.

The other thing that bothers me is that I really can't see why I get so disgusted with Easton and can't wait to move. I really, I cannot say why I want to move. I think the schools that my kids are in are very good schools, and so I really hesitate to move because of that. You know, this really bugs me, that I want to move so bad, and I think that they probably won't get as good an education as they are getting in Easton.

And, as Hal says—he's much more relaxed about things—if they're bright they're going to get something out of any place you go. So he doesn't think that the educational set-ups are that important. So that sort of gets me calmed down education-wise. But I really want to move. But if I'm just going to take my problems with me to wherever we move to, then nobody's going to be better off.

I'm not trying to be snooty or anything like that, but the people in our neighborhood—we have no professional people. We have one doctor who we never see, but other than that, we have a nurse or two. The rest of them are factory workers from the different plants that are around our neighborhood. And I really have nothing in common with anybody, really, in our neighborhood. Which in a way is good, because I don't think it's good if people know too much about your personal life.

But you ought to have somebody to talk to. So in that respect it seems ideal because I'm always back to town, and I've got Ruth. And Ruth always was my best friend, and she still is. I can tell Ruth anything. So, in that respect, I do have somebody. Plus a few people here and there that I knew occasionally.

The thing is I think I'm just bored. We've been here ten years, and I think I'm just tired of it. I go to an awful lot of clubs and stuff like that—Women's Club, my sorority has an alumni club, study groups, PTA. I go to everything there is. Because I am just so all the time complaining, feeling like I have to have a social life. So this is my social life, I go to all these things.

Hal and I started a group—these four couples go to each other's houses for dinner. And then the men play pinochle. We started that last year. These were three neighborhood couples. Because I'm really desperate for social life. And I talked to Reverend Hanks about it once—you know, he was my minister—and he said that part of my problem along this line was my parents had such a fabulous social life. And they still do, even when they're home—they're away six months of the year—I don't see how everybody knows that they're home and they start going out. But he says I've just always assumed that that's the way it should be, and it isn't that way for most people. And he said that my expectations of social life are more than is really normal. So that's one of my problems. And I really wish that I had more things to do. I like to go out where people are.

And we don't get invited to things. I have dinner parties a lot in wintertime, like February or March. I plan like one after another. And out of the people we invite, we hardly ever get any invitations back again. And those are like formal dinner parties. And then in the summer we all the time have back-yard barbecues for the families. And there again we hardly ever get any invitations back for anything.

I carry around a big inferiority complex anyway. But this is really one thing that bugs me. And I figure it must be me. I think Hal's so great, that he doesn't make you feel like he's a schoolteacher or anything. So I can't see why we wouldn't get invited back because of that. I think he fits in with any kind of person. So I think it's me.

But I keep trying. Like I'm the one that always organizes, every May I organize about two big parties. I start in Febru-

ary. One is some kids from our class. We try to get together
once a year, and I'm usually the one who starts that. Well, anyway, we would get together, either couples or families or something, but it was usually me who organized. And I would organize one or two schoolteachers' groups, either from the area
where we lived before or else Hal's college class or something
like that. They worked out okay, they were fine, except people didn't let you know if they were coming or not, people
didn't invite you back or do it again. So at that point a couple
years ago Hal said, "Give up, stop it." Because I'd get upset
about this, and I'd get mad at them before the party. I didn't
forget it; I just stopped doing it.

I think the women's movement has got me thinking about
it a lot, and to some respect upset, because on one hand I feel
that I should be going out to work and I should be doing something, and on the other hand I don't see how I possibly could
because I'm so disorganized. I'm sure my family would suffer.
Or else they would not get to do the after-school activities
that I drive them around to. But I don't really feel women have
been put down. And I don't really see what all the fuss is
about either, aside from equal wages.

I went to a psychiatrist for about a year after our daughter
was born, the first one. And I felt it was a waste of time and
money. I was not discharged. I was pregnant with the second
one. And I was told to come back after I had it, and I never
did. I have a lot of problems, I feel, emotional or something.
Which I've been told a couple times I ought to work out. I
haven't done anything about it. I think I need the help, but I
don't want to spend the money.

I would think that I would be always this way. Except the
year that we lived in England was so different, and it was so
fabulous, and I loved it so much that I have been searching
for that ever since then. There must be some place like England. We have discussed seriously going back to England. But
that's so far away.

For Henrietta, the bonds of family weighed heavy. She seemed
unaware how important it was to become independent of her parents.
Yet she succeeded admirably as a mother: her children have left home
easily and have been successful academically. Hal, meanwhile, ac-

cepted a position in California, and Henrietta appears very pleased with the new situation.

———

As I reflect on these stories, all of them different yet all of them telling something about the lingering presence of childhood and the pervasiveness of family, I wonder what I lost—or gained—by moving three thousand miles from my own mother and father, not to mention my brothers and other relatives whom I once saw all the time.

For I, too, was born in this city, although 13 West Church Street, my first home, is no longer a Bethlehem address. The three-story, painted-brick building which my father remodeled into an apartment house was torn down to make way for the Civic Center. Where my mother used to read me my favorite book—*Ferdinand the Bull*—now stands the public library. I was born on November 15, 1934, the first child of Margaret Flexer and Joseph Edward Illick, Jr. I remained the sole focus of their parental attention for a year and a half, until my brother Flex (Arthur Flexer) arrived. Our little family of four, alone in the first-floor flat, moved easily out into a sea of blood relatives. In fact, an aunt, uncle, and cousins were only one flight up in the same building.

My mother's parents, the Reverend Arthur George Flexer and Jenny Griffith Flexer (whom I called Papa and Nana) lived a few miles away in Allentown, the place where they had both been raised. Papa, born in 1874, was an only child and doted upon by his parents. They sent him to Muhlenberg College in Allentown, after which he entered Princeton Theological Seminary to prepare for a ministry in the United Evangelical Church. But most of the time at Princeton he was homesick. In Allentown he had left behind not only his parents but also Jenny Griffith, the youngest of seven children of Welch immigrants. Two years Papa's senior, Jenny was a schoolteacher whom he had met while a student at Muhlenberg.

He was encouraged to leave the academic halls of Princeton early and enter the pulpit directly; the elders of the United Evangelical Church found theological training suspect, believing that a true Christian received inspiration from God, not from books. Papa returned to Allentown, married Nana in 1903, and took on the first of his many charges in the remote country village of Herndon, Pennsylvania. The parsonage was a few rooms in a parishioner's home. Three years later the young couple located in Lancaster, where Sara

Elizabeth was born and died in her father's arms at six weeks of age. Margaret, my mother, arrived on May 29, 1907.

The family continued to move—next to Reading, then Mauch Chunk—and to add daughters—Mary in 1910, Winifred in 1914. Papa loved Mauch Chunk, nestled in the mountains at the head of the Lehigh Valley. When his nephew, Edward Barney, visited from New Jersey, they would spend whole days walking through the countryside—not the sort of outing Nana could enjoy. Indeed, Papa's and Nana's preferences differed markedly.

Though Papa was a sociable man who adored and waited upon his wife and daughters, never neglected his pastoral duties, always showed the greatest courtesy to others (on the street he would bow and tip his hat), and never let an unkind word pass his lips, he had a solitary side, which manifested itself in hours of private devotion. Without making an explicit issue of behavior, he seemed to expect his family to accept religion as an integral part of its waking life, just as he had.

Prayers were said before meals, and everyone attended church on Sunday, both morning and evening, as well as mid-week prayer service. The girls went to Mission Band on Saturday afternoon and Christian Endeavor before Sunday evening worship. Alcohol and tobacco were considered not necessarily sinful but alien, and to the end of his days, Papa was a devotee of health foods. His children and his grandchildren, witness to more worldly behavior, saw him as a saint—quiet, kind, tolerant, serene, totally at peace with himself and the world he chose to see.

Nana embraced innocence in a different way, by allowing those around her to shelter her. They thought she needed protection from the world, since she appeared to be always anxious. She was not, in fact, well-prepared to face life, a malady common enough to middle-class women of her time. Overwhelmed by the burdens of housekeeping and child rearing, she depended on her husband and servants to pitch in. Papa prepared breakfast and sometimes other meals, as well as helping to care for the children. A maid cleaned the house and kept an eye on the girls, who were not expected to assume major chores. A parishioner was hired to do the baking.

Infrequently, Nana went grocery shopping, though she never ventured out alone nor carried more than a dollar, the sum she thought she would need in case of an emergency. She overspent on clothes for her daughters, toward whom she was generally indulgent—though

Peg, the eldest, recognized her mother's weakness and usually felt too guilty to exploit it. Holidays and anniversaries, with secrets and surprise gifts, lifted her spirits, as did games and the late hours which tired her husband. She could become engaged by society, being both witty and acerbic in company, yet she dreaded visits from the New Jersey cousins who (perhaps because of their proximity to New York City) could make her feel dowdy, unsophisticated and, hence, miserable.

The family was, naturally enough, provincial, always preferring smaller to larger towns. Papa's favorite charge was tiny Shamokin, where the Flexers lived happily from 1913 to 1918. Reading (1909–10, 1926–31) and Harrisburg (1918–21) the family looked upon and remembered as less than desirable. Among the cities, only the return to Allentown (1921–1926) and kinfolk was an enjoyable experience. Throughout these many moves the family remained a close and loving unit, though as the girls grew older and sensed the difficulties of acting within the confines of their parents' unworldliness, questions of right behavior arose. Papa's saintliness and Nana's anxiety were not sure guides to getting on in the world.

No one felt the strains of propriety more acutely than the eldest daughter, Peg. Yet she managed to enjoy her high school years in Allentown and the collegiate atmosphere at Albright, an Evangelical institution in Myerstown. She was now regularly dating the young man she had met at a church camp when they were both seventeen, Joe Illick.

Unlike the peripatetic Peg, Joe had lived nowhere but at 239 East Goepp Street in Bethlehem, only ten blocks from my birthplace on West Church, and in view of the construction site of Liberty High School, where his sister Caroline and he would be members of the first and third graduating classes in 1922 and 1924. The Illicks had moved into this three-story double house in 1902, five years before Joe was born.

His mother, Clara, was a native of nearby Shoenersville, a hamlet since then obliterated to make way for the Allentown-Bethlehem-Easton Airport. His father, Joseph, born a year earlier than Clara in 1863, was raised in the household of an aunt and uncle due to his mother's premature death. At sixteen Joseph began teaching school, a job which brought him from Monroe to Lehigh County, where he met and married Clara Huber when both of them were twenty. The couple's first four children — Beulah, Stanley, Esther, and William (who died at birth) — arrived while the family lived at a grist mill Joseph owned and operated on the outskirts of Bethlehem.

After the move into Bethlehem, occasioned by a change in Joseph's business location, a third daughter, Caroline, came along, and eighteen-year-old Stanley died of diabetes during his freshman year at Lehigh University. On March 7, 1907, Joe was born, the darling of his mother, his older sisters ("He is second only to St. Paul," the husband of my Aunt Esther once growled to me), and perhaps his father, too, though that man was so silent his thoughts on most subjects are unknown.

When Joe was growing up in the Goepp Street house, with all the other children but Caroline departed, there were bedrooms and sitting rooms to spare. But family life centered on the kitchen. There Joseph and Clara, who always spoke to each other in Pennsylvania German, began the day early, at 5:00 or 6:00 A.M., reading the Bible and saying prayers before breakfast. Caroline and Joe did not appear until it was almost time to leave for school, grabbing a quick bite and bolting out the side door. The front was always locked, save for that rare occasion when company was coming. Lunch and dinner, both ample meals, were of course prepared in the kitchen, where Clara did most of her work. And it was here that Joseph did his reading — the Bible and the local paper.

In front of the house sat one of the many automobiles Joseph owned from time to time, perhaps his sole concession to modernity. In the alley behind the house was the barn where he stabled the horses used in his flour and feed business, situated near the railroad tracks by the Lehigh River. He carried on this enterprise with his son-in-law, a great salesman who, unfortunately, died an early death in the influenza epidemic of 1918. Joseph then helped support his widowed daughter and her three children, the youngest of whom had tuberculosis and was in need of continuing medical care.

Death was not a stranger to the Illicks. Joseph and Clara's tubercular granddaughter died, as had two of their own children, their son-in-law, and — in a runaway horse accident witnessed by Esther and Stanley as children — Joseph's father. But for God-fearing people there was another life, they believed, salvation from the sadness of this world. Joseph and Clara never missed church or prayer meeting. Joseph frequently was called upon to use the preacher's license he had been granted from the United Evangelical Church in 1897, and every Sunday afternoon he taught Sunday School at Shimer Station, always taking Joe with him.

Clara supported the Missionary Society and quilted with the church ladies. She also moved outside the congregation to serve as president of the Bethlehem Women's Christian Temperance Union: drinking she considered a sin, like gambling and dancing. Emmanuel Evangelical Church, which Clara and Joseph attended faithfully, was full to overflowing when an evangelist came to preach on the subject "From the Ballroom to Hell." Joe was not forbidden to join the chorus line of the Liberty High School senior vaudeville show, but Clara refused to sew his costume (his sister Beulah consented). Nor would Clara attend the movies with her children when the family visited Esther and her husband, Warren Seyfried, in New Jersey. Even Joseph weakened and went! He suffered few such lapses from the moral regimen of his faith.

Nor were there many temptations. Joseph and Clara had no social life outside their home, save for church activities and visits to their married children. In their own parlor they entertained relatives who came to call. With such strong focus on family and church, community involvement was rare. Of course Joseph's work took him into the non-familial, secular world. But by 1920 he was withdrawing from the flour and feed business which had for so long supplied Bethlehem's bakeries and stables. A combination of having to move his warehouse to make way for construction of the Hill-to-Hill Bridge and his son-in-law's death were apparently responsible for his decision to close down, though age—he was fifty-seven in 1920—may also have been a factor.

Joseph had for some time owned, and on occasion operated, farms in the outlying areas, and he had also remodeled and rented homes and apartment houses on the North and West sides of Bethlehem. He traded one run-down property for another with the same zest that he acquired and disposed of used automobiles. He renovated on the cheap. Not at all ungenerous with his family, he looked on business as the place to economize at every turn. Perhaps his behavior reflected a sense of the difference between dealing with people and handling materials. He was not above the hope of striking it rich or, at least, ensuring against the future.

Consequently, he made disastrous investments in a furniture factory, a tire and rubber company, and Florida real estate. Yet he continued to tithe to his church while supporting his family: Beulah was able to send her daughter to a sanitarium (to no avail), Caroline went to Albright College, and Joe became a student at Lehigh University. And these investments did pay off, in a sense. When Clara died in 1939, Beulah, Caroline, and Joe still lived close to Joseph, and he saw them and their children regularly until his own death three years later.

By 1939 young Joe was raising a family. He had met Peg Flexer in the summer of 1924 at Waldheim, the United Evangelical Church's family camp outside Allentown. They courted through college — Joe graduating as a civil engineer, Peg taking a degree in English — and were married a year later, on September 12, 1930, at a small gathering of family and friends in the Flexers' Reading home with Papa officiating. After a short honeymoon in New York City, the couple moved to nearby Pottstown, where Joe was employed by McClintock-Marshall Steel Company. A year and a half later, when McClintock-Marshall was absorbed by the Bethlehem Steel Company, he was transferred home.

The routine in the structural steel department of Bethlehem was unchallenging to Joe. He found time to teach an occasional math course at Lehigh, where he had taken an M.A. in civil engineering. He also, following in Joseph's footsteps, began looking around for old buildings to repair. By the time I was born in the late autumn of 1934, he had bought, remodeled, and moved into 13 West Church Street. Mother's sister Mary, her husband, and their daughter lived immediately above us, while her sister Winnie, a student at Moravian College for Women down the block, boarded part time with us. Dad's sister Caroline, her husband, and their son, resided in a house across the street. His sister Beulah and her grown children all lived nearby.

In 1938, two years after my brother Flex was born, Dad decided to leave Bethlehem for the country. Twenty-three hundred dollars was enough to get him a dilapidated house, barn, mill, and twelve acres of land which included a brook and a wood lot near Coopersburg, Pennsylvania (1,700 people), on the edge of Bucks County. And so, in January 1939 — two months before my brother Kit (Christopher David) and three years before my brother Tom (Thomas Griffith) arrived — we became exurbanites, just a bit ahead of the national trend. The barn was renovated for Nana, Papa, and Aunt Winnie on the first floor, and for Aunt Mary, Uncle Shube, Winnie, Johnny, and, later, Marty on the second. The nine-mile move from

The Illick Family at Coopersburg (Walley Wista, Stone Fences), Summer –1939. *Standing:* Uncle Shube (M. S. Walzer), Papa (A. G. Flexer), Uncle Bob (R. Kuss), Uncle Warren (R. Seyfried), Aunt Mary (M. Flexer Walzer), Daddy (J. E. Illick, Jr.), Aunt Beulah (B. Illick Fluck), Grandpa Illick (J. E. Illick), Aunt Esther (E. Illick Seyfried), Aunt Caroline (C. Illick Gramley), Nana (J. Griffith Flexer), Warren (W. Seyfried, Jr.), Aunt Winnie (W. Flexer), Roger (R. Fluck). *Seated:* Aunt Gene (E. Fluck Kuss), Susan (S. Kuss), Barbara (B. Kuss), Johnny (J. Walzer), Winnie (W. Walzer), Billy (W. Gramley), Flexie (A. Illick), Hughie (H. Gramley), Digsie (D. Gramley), Joey (J. E. Illick III), Mommy (M. Flexer Illick), Kit (C. Illick).

Church Street to R.D. #2, Coopersburg, did not disrupt the family but gave it a different focus, a new place to gather.

Although our relatives in Bethlehem and Allentown referred to it as "the farm," my parents felt it deserved a more distinctive title — or titles, since they expressed their proud attitudes about the property in revealingly different ways. Dad called it "Walley Wista," and he printed that name in crayon across the bib of his overalls. Springing from good Pennsylvania Dutch stock, where a "V" was pronounced as a "W", and half embarrassed about aspiring to the wealth and pretention that might have depicted the view from our lowly hill as a "valley vista," he needed to mock his own upward mobility.

Mother, who turned a deaf ear whenever her father or her husband spoke Dutch (she regarded it as the patois of loutish farmers), designated our place as "Stone Fences" on stationery made to order. This may have been a tribute to the many dry walls her energetic husband built on the edges of the property, and of course it had the ring of genteel stability. But considering her distrust of the outside world and the fact that her own family was established within the ramparts, "Stone Fences" neatly captured a point of view.

Dad looked out, and Mother looked in. He joked, and she fretted. His constant admonition to her was, "Don't worry, Peg." As we were growing up my brothers and I assumed that Dad's confidence was founded in his ability to do anything and do it well or, if he wasn't the best, to shrug off his minor inadequacies with yet another joke—which he always did do well. He certainly was capable of a lot. During the war, when lumber was unavailable for the building business, he resumed teaching for a while, including a course for the Air Force in navigation. Since we boys knew he had never set foot in an airplane, our view of his omnicompetence was only reinforced.

As a builder, Dad was in his car and off to work early in the morning, sometimes home for lunch, always on the move from one construction site to another. His size, a bulky 6'3" frame mounted on feet that prompted his workmen to refer to him by his shoes ("Here comes number 12"), added to his assurance—or the perception others had of his assurance—as did his imperturbability. On the job he mixed easily with the men, being at once comradely and pitching in on the work while simultaneously giving directions and assuming complete responsibility. He provided a model of mastery for his sons to imitate, at least in a career.

At home it was a somewhat different matter. He was never unwilling to wash the dinner dishes or bathe the kids and tuck them in while spinning out long stories and complicated math problems. He deeply loved his children and his wife. But he could not understand, much less empathize with Mother's incapacitating worries, which often sent her to bed after supper with a splitting headache. Like his father-in-law, though, he brought others in to help.

I always regarded these few "servants" as family once removed. Katherine Frantz, who had begun work in an Allentown knitting mill at thirteen before marrying Martin Troxell, raising four children, and working for Nana, now rode to our house on the Liberty Bell Limited, an interurban trolley that swayed through the countryside from Allentown to Philadelphia. She did the washing, ironing, and cleaning. And on the rare occasion that Mother and Dad went away for the weekend, she would stay with us for the duration since Mother never quite trusted Laura Dornblaser, who lived in the back of the house with her common-law husband, Edward Patrick Berry, the hired hand who milked the cow, fed the horse and whatever other animals were around, plowed the fields and harvested the hay, stoked the fires in Dad's Bethlehem apartment houses, told us stories, sneaked us cigarettes, let us drive the truck, and—whenever he had the opportunity—got easily and totally drunk.

Sam Fishburn, Dad's business partner and our sage, would observe: "I paid for you guys, and Eddy raised you." Mother never visibly took offense at this statement, but there was no doubting that she carried out the major child-rearing chores, servants or not. She did the chauffeuring expected of a middle-class, suburban woman, taking us to medical and dental appointments, on shopping expeditions, to swimming pools, tennis courts, and ballgrounds. She prepared most of the household meals for a family which, after her mother died in 1943, often included her father and sister Winnie as well as her husband and four ravenous sons. She did the marketing not only for these meals but also for other household needs, for birthdays, Chirstmas, and whatever special events arose. Most community affairs and organizations lay outside her round of activity.

Her children demanded most of her energy. From 1934 to 1948 she always had at least one son at home with her, and in the summer she had four, not to mention our three cousins across the way who had free access to the house. Our doors were never barred (indeed, they were without locks), and no room in the house was out of bounds to any of us, nor was there a piece of furniture, stair banister, chair rail, or counter which could not be variously climbed, slid upon, upset or walked over by the children. Outside we roamed and rode our bikes around the countryside, swam in the brook in summer and skated on the pond in winter. There were few other children in the vicinity, so we invented or adapted games accordingly. Johnny, Flex, and I knew as much about three-man football as any trio in the nation.

Our city relatives, mostly Dad's, visited for Halloween parties, Christmas celebrations, picnics, christenings, or on no pretext at all. When Uncle Warren lost his job in Florida during the late Depression, he and Dad's sister Esther moved into the guest room for an extended stay, and their children spent summers away from college with us.

And thus my childhood pleasantly moved on into adolescence. I was happy in the bosom of family, witness neither to divorce nor untimely death. No turmoil, nor even passion, troubled the easygoing flow of events. Family provided a sense of continuity, strength, and tradition, all of which was reinforced by strong religious faith and the seeming timelessness of life in rural Pennsylvania. World War II came and went; we were hardly affected. Family was protection from the outside.

I cannot say that by leaving Bethlehem I gave up this sense of protectedness. Rather, it is part of my emotional baggage, carried everywhere, but in some times and places temporarily lost. And, of course, its meaning changes with time.

Older, perhaps wiser about myself and my relationship to the past, and curious about the way in which my contemporaries perceived and faced the issues of adulthood, I returned to Bethlehem to find out. My discovery of the durability of family ties — I never doubted my own and had never investigated others — is in conflict with modern fears or rejoicing concerning the death of the family. Neither the handwringing on the Right nor the clenched fists on the Left, one pleading for an enforced dependency and the other demanding a greater freedom, are attuned to reality. The persons I judge to be at liberty have consciously achieved personal independence within the context of familial love.

Still, an issue remained for me. I did not follow Bob Henry's inclination to remain in or near Bethlehem, where I grew up nor did I, in the manner of Jim Placatoris, join the family business as Dad wanted me to. Unlike Jo and Don Bittenbender, I moved to the Far West, despite my parents' obvious displeasure with my leaving. Was I motivated, like Buzzy Richards, to get "up and out" of the Lehigh Valley in quest of a success that seemed more important than close family ties? Or did I sense that remaining there would subject me to the sort of parental manipulation that Henrietta Diefendorfer suffered? I found I could resolve this issue only by examining my life as its context enlarged to include neighborhood and school, work and marriage, and rearing children of my own.

3 | *Neighborhood*

Skip John and I were sitting in his office behind the bus maintenance shop, which he supervises for the Bethlehem School District. He was smoking a cigar and reflecting on the South Side neighborhood where he grew up. "When I lived on the Heights," he recalled, "that was the League of Nations. We had Mexicans, we had colored, we had the Italians and Hungarians and the Slovaks and the Russians and all that. It was mixed and yet it was a real good community at that time. I never felt, as a Hungarian, that I was separate from the others." Skip spoke only the Magyar language when he entered first grade, and he had to learn English quickly. He resents the efforts of the newly arrived Puerto Ricans to have classes taught in Spanish. Gil Huertas, the Puerto Rican-born husband of our high school classmate Rosemarie Andre, wondered whether Skip simply resents Puerto Ricans, period.

No one could doubt Skip's accuracy in referring to the South Side as a League of Nations. Over half the grandparents of members of the Class of 1952 were born outside the United States, a quarter of them in Eastern Europe, another 15 percent in Western Europe, 10 percent in Southern Europe, and a scattering from north and south of this country's borders.

And Skip was hardly unusual in his skeptical view of the newer immigrants. Davy Salgado, another classmate, heatedly stated: "I've never been discriminated against. We made our way as Mexicans, so did the blacks." When on a local television show Puerto Ricans claimed to be victims of intolerance—what we historians call "nativism," the opposition to a minority because it is foreign—Davey phoned in to say they were imagining things. He plays softball with Puerto Ricans but seldom socializes beyond the athletic field. He is married to a woman of German extraction and spends a great

Table 2. Class Members and Relatives by Birthplace (%)

Class members & relatives:	Bethlehem	Lehigh Valley	100-mile radius of Bethlehem	Elsewhere in U.S.	Mexico, Canada	Western Europe	Southern Europe	Eastern Europe	Other
Paternal grandfather	8.6	13.7	7.9	17.3	1.4	13.7	11.5	25.2	0.7
Paternal grandmother	7.6	13.7	6.1	19.8	0.8	13.0	12.2	26.0	0.8
Maternal grandfather	8.8	10.2	13.9	14.6	1.5	16.1	9.5	24.8	0.7
Maternal grandmother	7.4	12.5	11.0	16.9	1.5	15.4	8.8	25.7	0.7
Father	30.4	11.5	9.9	23.0	1.0	3.7	5.8	9.4	0
Mother	25.7	19.9	15.2	19.4	1.4	13.7	11.5	25.2	0.7
Class member	70.4	11.7	7.8	10.2	0	0	0	0	0
Spouse of Class Member	39.8	18.4	7.7	29.1	0	2.0	0	0	3.1

Table 3. Ethnic Composition of the Class of 1952

Parents of Class Members	Number	Percent
English or Irish	14	7.5
English or Irish/Pennsylvania Dutch or German	35	18.7
English or Irish/Italian	1	0.5
English or Irish/Hungarian	1	0.5
English or Irish/Other	2	1.1
Pennsylvania Dutch or German	30	16.0
Pennsylvania Dutch or German/Italian	3	1.6
Pennsylvania Dutch or German/Eastern, Western Slav	11	5.9
Pennsylvania Dutch or German/Hungarian	7	3.7
Pennsylvania Dutch or German/Other	14	7.5
Mexican	2	1.1
Mexican/Other	1	0.5
Italian	8	4.3
Italian/Greek	1	0.5
Italian/Hungarian	4	2.1
Italian/Other	1	0.5
Eastern or Western Slav	10	5.3
Eastern or Western Slav/Southern Slav	6	3.2
Eastern or Western Slav/Hungarian	3	1.6
Eastern or Western Slav/Other	4	2.1
Southern Slav	6	3.2
Southern Slav/Hungarian	4	2.1
Greek	4	2.1
Greek/Hungarian	1	0.5
Hungarian	5	2.6
Hungarian/Other	3	1.6
Other	6	3.2
	187	100%

deal of time with his nephew and former classmate, Gus Romero, who points out, "I've never had any problems because I was a Mexican, though some of my uncles who worked at the Steel said they had problems."

Excepting the Indians, all Americans are immigrants, but some of us arrived more recently than others. Skip, whose father was born in Hungary; Rosemarie, both of whose parents came here from Portugal; Davy and Gus, whose parents were natives of Mexico — all are usually labeled "second generation," a category that includes at least a quarter of the Class of 1952. Third-generation Americans, those people whose parents were born in the United States but have at least one grandparent who began life outside this country, make

Table 4. Linguistic Heritage of the Class of 1952

Languages spoken in home	Paternal grandparents		Maternal grandparents		Parents	
	Number	Percent	Number	Percent	Number	Percent
English	44	28.0	48	29.8	120	80.8
English & German	40	25.5	41	25.5	30	15.2
English & Spanish or Portuguese	0	0	0	0	1	0.5
English & Italian	2	1.3	6	3.7	6	3.0
English & Slavic tongue	9	5.7	9	5.6	13	6.6
English & Hungarian	2	1.3	2	1.2	2	1.0
English & Other	2	1.3	1	0.6	1	0.5
German	11	7.0	11	6.8	1	0.5
German & Italian	0	0	0	0	2	1.0
German & Slavic tongue	2	1.3	2	1.2	3	1.5
German & Hungarian	4	2.5	0	0	2	1.0
Spanish or Portuguese	2	1.3	2	1.2	0	0
Spanish or Portuguese & Italian	0	0	0	0	1	0.5
Italian	11	7.0	6	3.7	0	0
Italian & Greek	0	0	0	0	1	0.5
Slavic (east, west)	7	4.5	8	5.0	0	0
Slavic (east, west) & Slavic (south)	1	0.6	0	0	1	0.5
Slavic (east, west) & Hungarian	1	0.6	3	1.9	1	0.5
Slavic (east, west) & Other	1	0.6	0	0	0	0
Slavic (south)	4	2.5	6	3.7	2	1.0
Slavic (south) & Hungarian	2	1.3	2	1.2	4	2.0
Greek	5	3.2	3	1.9	1	0.5
Hungarian	4	2.5	8	5.0	2	1.0
Other	4	2.5	3	1.9	0	0
	158	100%	161	100%	194	100%

up a majority of the members of the Class of 1952. I belong to the "old stock" Americans, simply because all of my grandparents were born here.

These distinctions have had special meaning for historians ever since one of us, Marcus Lee Hansen, convincingly argued that second-generation Americans emphatically rejected their Old World heritage while those of the third generation attempted to recover it: "what the son wishes to forget, the grandson wishes to remember." Hansen himself stood as an exception to this rule since he, the son of Scandinavian immigrants, undertook an intense study of his parents' past.

Apparent proof of Hansen's law resides in the person of Frank Donchez, whose grandparents migrated to the steel plants, cigar factories, and knitting mills of America from Slovenia, now a province in northwestern Yugoslavia. Fully a quarter of the grandparents of the Class of 1952 hail from Eastern Europe; Slovenians are referred to as "the Windish" in Bethlehem. Frank's father was head of the detective bureau of the Bethlehem Police Department. Frank went to Lehigh University, joined the management of the Steel Company, and lives in a comfortable new home on the suburban fringe of northeast Bethlehem with his wife Rose, also a Slovenian. Both of them converse in Windish with their parents.

"We were keenly aware of ethnic backgrounds," Frank recalled of his childhood. "We knew who the kids were who were Italian, we knew who the kids were who were Hungarian. But the background didn't make any difference to anybody. And there weren't any ethnic jokes in those days. It didn't mean anything to me to be Windish. I would like to have my kids aware of that background, though. I think it's sad that people lose sight of where they came from. I think it's nice to know where your grandparents came from, if possible, even your great-grandparents. Even though you really may not care so much about ethnic background, it's good to know where you came from, who you are."

Members of the Class of 1952 recognize their ethnic backgrounds, but that recognition is not proof of Hansen's law. From the second to the third generation there has been not a revival but a decline in the importance attached to the Old World heritage. The use of foreign languages in the home has dramatically dropped (even Frank and Rose speak only in English to their children), as has membership in ethnic organizations. The child-rearing methods of the first generation, rejected by the second as Hansen would have predicted, are not even considered by the third generation. Martha Marcinko, whose mother was born in Czechoslovakia, observed: "I try to keep an ethnic background, but I feel that I have lost it entirely." Then she added, a little lamely: "I tell the children about our customs on Christmas Eve."

"The different groups on the Heights, well, it just didn't matter that much," said my friend Skip—and I believe he's correct. "The same with religion," Skip continued, "it didn't matter, it never entered our minds." Here he is wrong. Members of the Class of 1952 almost invariably worship in the faith of their parents and grandparents, either Roman and Greek Catholic (33 percent), Protestant (almost 60 percent) or Jewish (less than 1 percent). Only 7 percent of the class has renounced religion.

Parents have passed their beliefs on to their children. Skip probably erred in his observation because he is an exception; having grown up in the Hungarian Reformed Church, he wed Rose Marie Fondl, a German Catholic. Ethnic groups often intermarried, but religious faiths seldom did. Nick Begovich, Martha Marcinko's husband, recounts a situation that must have been typical: "I went to Catholic school. And my [Croatian] father always said about girls to marry, 'Go up on South Mountain and get a good Slovak.' So I did. He said, 'Marry your kind.'"

———

Who was not "your kind"? To some members of the Class of 1952, the answer was easy, since they felt like outsiders from the start and were probably regarded as such by others. Norma Rajeck, for example, was unfailingly cheerful and an enthusiastic participant in school plays and musicals. But she was also assertive, a stance that seemed incompatible with her friendliness, and a bit baffling. In the yearbook she expressed interest in being a social worker or a musical comedy star, two careers unimaginable not only to me but, I'm sure, most of our classmates. I never thought of her as one of three Jews in our class, but she recalls living with that label.

NORMA: My father, Max Rajeck, came to Bethlehem in the late 1920s. He managed a silk mill owned by his cousins and at first lived in the mill alone with a bed and a piano.

Norma Rajeck, as she appeared in *The School for Witches,* Krannert Center for the Performing Arts, Urbana, Illinois (University of Illinois), September 1974. (Courtesy of Norma Rajeck Marder.)

He took singing and piano lessons and sang in the Bach Choir. Eventually he became a part-time cantor and Hebrew teacher at the Brith Shalom Community Center. He worked in the mill and the temple for thirty years. My parents were both singers and my mother, at seventy-two, still performs Yiddish folk songs. There have been singers in every generation of my father's family, as far back as the Levites who were singers in the first temple in Jerusalem. It was only a few years ago that I realized I was part of this pattern. I felt I had not chosen my career.

My father and mother grew up in the same apartment building in a small town in Poland. They fell in love when my father visited her in New York to pay his respects to my grandmother. My mother never fully adjusted to Bethlehem and when my father died she moved back to New York. My parents' best friends were the Blindermans. Every Sunday in nice weather the Blindermans drove us out into the country. I still remember their license numbers.

My first home was at 312 Hanover Street. Teresa Zulli lived next door, and since I was an only child I loved being part of her family. They had ten children. In her house the shades were always drawn against the sun and the smell of home-made wine rose from the cellar. Teresa's priest pressured her to convert me and one day, when I refused to bow my head while saying "Jesus Christ," she stopped speaking to me. For three years we walked to school on opposite sides of the street.

Bernice Blinderman was my closest friend. We were like sisters, drawn together by the accidents of age and our parents' friendship. Though different in many ways we shared our lives for eighteen years. In the temple we sang duets and Bernice stood on a box behind the pulpit so that we wouldn't look like Mutt and Jeff. When we went to college the bonds loosened and the friendship dissolved.

I lived in three social worlds — school, the Jewish community, and the music community. In school I was an outsider. For six years, in elementary school, I was persecuted for being Jewish; called names, beaten up, made to feel like a freak. From junior high on I never experienced any discrimination, but the feeling of being an outsider remained. Even in the Jewish community where I "belonged" I felt different. Like other girls I was interested in boys and clothes, but my attitudes and values were different, and I couldn't explain them to anyone. I read a lot and didn't discuss books with anyone. Consequently I developed a private vocabulary in which some words, learned in the wrong context, had private meanings. In high school I felt much of the time that there was a fish bowl around my head and I couldn't breathe. My way of being part of a group and aloof from it was to become a leader, to be president.

At sixteen I spent the summer at a music camp and for the first time met other people like myself. Toward the end of my senior year I realized that being Jewish didn't stand in the way of having school friends. I felt close to Gertrude Lutz, Audrey Vollman, Mary Chris Sideris, and Carol Schrader and wished that I had allowed myself to be open to them sooner. But I was happy to leave Bethlehem.

I arrived at Brandeis University when it was only four years old. [Norma discovered it in *Look* magazine!] Many of the roads were still unpaved and the future of the apple orchard was a hotly debated issue. I was in a production of *Trojan Women* directed by Eliot Silverstein, who later went on to Hollywood and directed *Cat Ballou*. I had a scholarship for voice lessons and sang pieces written by student composers. I enjoyed the work and pleasures of the Brandeis community. After graduation I became a voice major at the Manhattan School of Music. I always felt at home in New York.

My work has been in experimental music. I perform pieces that use the voice in unusual ways and require a high degree of improvisation. In New York I was a soloist for two chamber ensembles, performing Baroque and avant-garde music. John Cage gave me his tape recorder and I did one concert with Yoko Ono. In 1965 my husband, Herbert Marder, and our two sons, Michael and Yuri, moved to Champaign, Illinois, where Herbert and I soon joined with a few other people and converted an old railway station into an experimental theatre.

This lasted eight years. During that time Herbert's work and mine began to draw closer, his writing and my singing merged in the formation of an improvisation ensemble, the New Verbal Workshop, a group of six people who jointly compose and perform pieces that use the human voice in all possible ways. The work is a blend of music, poetry, and theatre. For the past few years we have been turning in still other directions. Herbert, a writer, has been painting. I, a singer, have been writing. I am still a loner. The lessons of isolation learned in Bethlehem are always with me. But I am also part of a community—my family, friends, other artists. I teach voice for a living and am writing a book of short stories. Some of them are about Bethlehem.

I pressed Norma to say more about Bethlehem. She has visited me twice in San Francisco, and I felt I could take advantage of our friendship to plumb her feelings.

I grew up Jewish in the Christmas City, in a Protestant and Catholic working-class neighborhood where little boys rubbed thumb and fingers as I passed by and sneered, "Money-money-money-money." At home, the only child of immigrant parents, I was adored, a prodigy in the Promised Land. In Fairview School I was a pariah. During the years when Nazis slaughtered Jews in Germany and Poland, children hit and ridiculed me on the playground. "Hitler is a Jew who's killing all the Christians in Europe," one of my tormentors used to shout while kicking my shins. Not only was I the only Jew in school, I was brainy, tall for my age, and brought dried fruit to recess instead of Hershey bars. Perhaps I had other defects as well.

In retrospect I believe childhood experiences of security and rejection balanced each other nicely in forming my character. I am a confident person who is generally prepared for the worst. But if I were to go back to Bethlehem today the old self-consciousness would flood over me, and I would be once more the clumsy girl who wasn't certain, until nearly the end of her senior year in high school, that she was accepted by her Christian classmates.

Norma does not return to Bethlehem ever, but travels in the circle of her academic and artistic friends. Her last communication, from her summer home on an island off the Maine coast, describes the wedding of her son Michael in the foothills of California's Los Padres mountains: "I sang and Herbert read poetry."

———

If religion was a divisive issue in Bethlehem, race was more so, if only because in the early 1950s Afro-Americans were burdened with all the imagined qualities that had stereotyped them for centuries. The black community in Bethlehem was even smaller than the Jewish congregation. But Dorothy Lewis did not feel so isolated — segregated, yes! — as I would have guessed. We reminisced in the living room of her home on the upper-middle-class periphery of Washington, D.C.

DOROTHY: We had our clique, clan kind of thing. We experienced — I have to put it on a personal basis, but I am remembering many conversations with classmates—kind of a coldness. It wasn't possibly because we didn't want to venture out, but our venturing many times proved to be one that had us against the wall.

Now there were those of us who did choose to get into the school orchestra, the glee club, but those were the kids who had special little talents or someone just had mercy on us or something. I was very pleased and surprised to learn that I had made the school orchestra; it was a real treat. But as far as other organizations within the school itself—I'm trying to think. Even though we were a part of a situation, there was still a kind of feeling, at least in my experience, that you're sort of a little part of it, you're there but you're not there.

So I remember having very, very few friends, Liberty-wise, other than neighborhood friends. We lived on Second Street in Bethlehem. It was the old Heights, as you remember—it's long since been gone. And our friends, other than black friends, were the kids up and down the street.

You know my granddaddy founded our home church there, St. Paul Baptist church. Oh, my gosh, you talk about really good times. We were totally involved with life, real community living. We were Sunday school involved, Sunday school orientated, church orientated. We involved ourselves with things like the Y dances. You talk about going to the Y, *now* kids don't even know what you're talking about. But that's where we received much joy. And of course, the Scouts—we were involved with programs with the Girl Scouts and other, well, mostly Y activities.

Yes, we had boundaries, but I'm wondering now if they were self-imposed boundaries. I kind of think so, because really I find now that people are what they are. It's not so great to be thinking that someone is keeping you right here because you are black or Jewish or whatever. It's how *you* meet people that makes the difference.

I have been in Washington twenty years this coming August. But I'm still very naive and very sheltered. The Lord has blessed us. My situation in Washington is almost like it was at home, because there I was sheltered, living in Bethlehem. I married, came here as a bride. My husband was able to put me in a home so I don't have to be bumping elbows with this community in Washington that's totally black and totally unlike what I'm used to.

And then of course, I dove right into teaching. Yes, then I'm confronted with black children and their needs, but for the most part, I wondered if I could really relate. When you're trying to put over a lesson to children who are hungry because they are living in despair, then you soon see. But can you really feel?

When Malcolm X died—I've not ever been one to not feel compassion because a life is lost; however, I didn't know what was going on. In many situations, I still don't know what's going on. Again, because my life style is completely different, has been and will be, certainly now.

I went to Chaney State Teachers' College [an all-black institution in Pennsylvania]. I had a scholarship to Penn State, and Daddy refused to allow me to go three hundred miles from home with even a short cast on [as the result of a hip operation]. So I stayed out that year and became interested in getting a little closer to home and Chaney came up as an opportunity, and I loved it.

It's amazing now, to me, as we sit here and talk about it, how far removed I was, as a being, as me, from so much that other blacks seemed to be totally caught up in. Again, I don't like violence, maybe that's why.

Dorothy described her first visit to Walnut Cove, North Carolina, the home of her husband, Ernest Hairston. It was 1958. She and her Philadelphia cousins entered a drugstore.

My husband and his brother were outside waiting for us; we were going to get ice cream. It's kind of hard to shimmy in between bars or counter stools, so, certainly not thinking anything, we sat down, I being the first.

We had asked the woman already for ice cream, so she was scooping and, as she scooped, I thought I heard her murmuring something, and so I said, "What did you say?" She said, "I said, 'You can't sit here.'" I said, "I beg your pardon." "He said you can't sit here." I said, "Who said that? What's going on?" And he came along, he said, "You're not going to come in here and start any trouble." I said, "My dear sir, I am Dorothy Hairston, my mother-in-law is Judy Hairston, my father-in-law is Dave Hairston. They live right around the corner. I don't know what this is about. I'm not here to do anything but get a cone of ice cream. Now if you choose not to serve me, fine, but . . . " Well, he became flustered: "Oh, ma'am, I'm so . . . "—my in-laws are much, much respected in their community—"Oh, I'm so sorry! You're George's sister? Who's wife are you?" I said, "Ernie's, from Washington, D.C." "Oh, I'm sorry." His name was Steve, they all grew up together and they knew each other. But again, the uprising that was going on across the country, we being strangers, he thought, "Well, here these women are going to try something: I'm not going to have it."

I don't know how I bypassed it: I just haven't been caught up in it. I suppose, had I been, I would have . . . Joe, I don't know, my thoughts and viewpoints, even back there, as I remember, were different. I never thought that anyone owed me anything because I was black or had a handicap, a quote-unquote hip problem. I didn't have that kind of inner burden, inner thought, right up the line. I have never had, again, perhaps it's me, my attitude, personality, I'd walk up to a bear and say, "Hi, how are you." So when you're like that, you're not looking for anything, things work well, I would imagine.

Our family has been one, but all I can say is God has blessed us over the years. My grandmother had property, real estate, and if there was anyone in the minority, it was our neighbors who were white, if that's how you want to look at the situation. They knew Grandmother as Miss Kate, who had these homes here, and she lived in the big house over there—that kind of situation. So we didn't have that kind of pressure that even my close friends had.

Dorothy married Ernie Hairston, a graduate of North Carolina A & T and the University of Maryland. Now working as an aerospace engineer at NASA, Ernie has provided well for his family. Their son Michael, a freshman at Hampton Institute when I first talked to Dorothy, shielded her from his high school experience, as he openly admitted: "Mom, I could tell you things that would stand your hair up on end, but I guess I'd better not, 'cause I don't think

Dorothy Lewis in her home in Washington, D.C., 1976. (Photo by JEI.)

that you could handle it." Their daughter Crystal was totally para-
lyzed by encephalitis at three and a half, but the brain damage was
motor only, and she recovered enough to attend a special school.

Dorothy and Ernie had gone back to our fifteenth high school
reunion and had a marvelous time. "Feelings came out that I didn't
know existed. One young man, I can't even think of his name, told
me in front of my husband that he always had a crush on me." Not
surprising, perhaps, because Dorothy is attractive and vivacious.
She also loves parties — or did, too much. Although raised a Baptist,
she was drawn into the social whirl of the nation's capital: "Too
much food, too much drink, too much everything."

Her behavior at one party in particular, followed by a warning from
her son to take care of herself, and most important of all, her daughter's attraction to a born-again Christian on their block combined to
give her a jolt. "It was the fact that all of a sudden I came to the reali-
zation that I needed help to get through life, and I'm very sincere when
I say that. So I made up my mind that I was going to confess to
my Father, who was in Heaven, that, yes, I was a sinner and really
making a big mess of my life, and Father, if you'll come and help
me right now get through this in your Son's name, fine. *You* guide
me, since I thought I was such a smarty cat before, trying to do this
and do that and ending up having maybe people mad at me."

Feeling that she had been living "a double kind of a standard,"
Dorothy stopped smoking and drinking and turned to God for help.
She then recalled the most difficult trial of all — Crystal's encephalitis
attack:

> And I'll never forget my minister . . . yes, I cried . . . Ernie
> and I drove home from the hospital, and we looked at one
> another. They made us go home because they said, "You've
> gotta have strength for whatever is to be." My minister came
> and he said words that were very encouraging.
>
> "Father, you know, you see us here and I don't know
> what's going on, only you do, but you know you put Chris
> here for a purpose and if she has fulfilled all that you want
> her to do, if she's done everything that you want her to do
> for you since she's been here, then we want you to take her
> with you right now. And we're happy because we've had her
> for these three years." And I understood. I said, "Hey, that's
> it, that's really it."

And, needless to say, she's going to be fourteen New Year's Eve. One day I was walking around here and it was like the Lord said, "Call somebody and tell them Chris is going to be completely healed." She is healed, but we're going to see the full manifestation of her healing, in other words, the arm's going to drop down to normal because Jesus still does heal. He is still in what we call the healing business. That's the kind of ministry they have at Christ Church. Gosh, if you could get up there tonight it would do something for you.

I knew I wouldn't go to Dorothy's church. But I remembered that Jesus extended a similar invitation to his disciples, promising: "I will make you fishers of men." I took a picture of her under the marlin she had caught in Chesapeake Bay.

Dorothy remains steadfast in her faith. It has carried her through a serious hip operation and, more recently, her mother's lingering illness and death. And she has been given signs of the Lord's blessing: her daughter Crystal has been living on her own for several years; her son Michael has enjoyed some success in the art world as a painter; and NASA honored Ernie by inviting him to witness a Cape Canaveral launching into the heavens.

———

Dorothy's associates are mostly black. Norma Rajeck married a fellow Jew. Racial and religious boundaries were seldom crossed in Bethlehem, and class barriers loomed large, too. I recall wondering, back in high school, why it was that Charlotte Cole, a German Catholic from a working-class neighborhood, was dating Lloyd Rensalier, whose Protestant family belonged to the Saucon Valley Country Club and sent him to Yale University. Her situation was close to unique.

CHARLOTTE: I led a very, very interesting life that I think sometimes it's a shame my children did not. I'd go to a Russian Orthodox marriage, and then I'd go out to Lehigh University to one of their cocktail parties, right? And then Lloyd might take me down to the country club. And I might come back for a wedding the next day at another place. I shifted in that society. I don't know how to explain it. Because I was smart enough to be in classes with some of what we called "richer kids" from the North Side, I would get invited to some of their parties. By the same token, I happened to enjoy dancing and a lot of the music. So I really enjoyed some of the very traditional things there in Bethlehem. If you'd ever seen a Russian wedding and danced to the Russian songs and seen the people! Then I'd go to a Lehigh dance—you just cannot do that here [in the suburbs of Boston].

My kids just die when I tell them I used to go motorcycle climbing. I did. And then in the evening I'd get all dressed up and go someplace else. I had friends in both spheres. Unless you lived in Bethlehem you can't understand. Some people just stayed in one area, in one group. And sometimes at the country club I felt like I didn't belong. But now I can have this feeling that just because people don't have a lot of money—well, where I grew up they were honest, and they were hard working, and they had a lot of fun. I'd come back from the seashore just to go to the polka dances. Then I went down to those country club dances. I had to learn how to eat. I came a long way.

I enjoyed both worlds. But I don't think I'd like to stay in that world. The people were very different sometimes—superstitions and traditions. But my father was always "education, education," and he did an awful lot of reading. He probably had a college education by the time he died.

I didn't go to college because of marriage—and also because they wanted me to live at home and go to Moravian. I wasn't spending four years someplace I couldn't even become an airline stewardess with, right? The kids who went to college were the rich ones.

Also, I got a very good job. I worked for the director of city planning, and I was secretary of the zoning commission. This was very interesting. But I wouldn't work while my children are still at home.

My mother worked, which was quite typical. I wouldn't do that to my children. I want to be here—and go out and see them perform; my family's pretty athletic. I was a lonely child, and this is why I bounced around so much. Don't forget, parents worked three shifts. And I was an only child. I often didn't care what people thought; I could do what I wanted to.

We lived in San Diego. I like California. I don't mind moving the children. Young Lloyd was in three kindergartens and
three first grades. If you're smart, you're smart. But sometimes I think the moving is bad. My son is studying psychiatry—our principle unit, the mother-father-sister-brother relationship, is stronger than in Bethlehem, where I was alone
and could go to my aunt's. I think the reason my mother and
I don't get together is she's still South Side, she still carries
the superstitions. I always fought with her about going to the
country club—she didn't think I belonged there. My father
would always say, "If she can handle it, let her go."

My father and I had a very good relationship. Going to a
Yale weekend was like—hell. Fight all week. What did I do
when I went down there? Everybody thought I was pregnant
when I got married. I really surprised them—it took us five
years to have our first baby!

Charlotte's babies are now grown. All were active in sports, ex-
celled academically, and attended prestigious private universities on
scholarships, studying engineering or science. She proudly observes:
"My chidren never cease to amaze me by their wonderful accomplishments, and best of all, they seem very happy. We really have
enjoyed all the years, and I never regret not working. I have had a
back fusion of three discs so working anyway would be most difficult. So I paint, wallpaper, garden, take care of our Great Dane,
and manage to read a book a week."

Although Charlotte regrets that her children could not sample
the rich variety available to her in Bethlehem, the fortunate consequence of her moving into a new world was her ability to pass it
on to them. Nor does she idealize the life she left behind. She believes that the traditional beliefs and practices were too confining,
and she is quite happy to live at some distance from her girlhood
home.

———

The more usual pattern for Class Members was that they neither
crossed class lines nor left the Lehigh Valley. But to remain subor-
dinate in a nation that preaches equality and worships success may
engender feelings of resentment. Margaret Crosko, when I saw her

after a quarter of a century, was living on the South Side—which, she claimed, was still looked down on by the North Side.

MARGARET: You still have it, the kids in junior high, it's awful, band-wise. Now we have a very good music director down in Broughal [Junior High School], Mr. Hawes, and he had built that band up. He really has this band going beautifully. But when it comes to doing anything together with the junior high over on the North Side, they kind of look down on Broughal. Once they get over to Liberty, I think they do better. My daughter just had a birthday and she had girls from the other side—better sections—that I had never met before. So in the band I think they get together.

With me, because my husband was Protestant and Irish, and I was Catholic, he came in the house and asked maybe four times and that was it—he was no longer welcome in the house. That's how we dated: I never told them he was coming, I just went out.

Oh, he wasn't good enough—it was all kinds of excuses, that he wasn't good enough for me and so on and so forth. It was really religious. And yet my father was not a religious man. Like they say, funerals and weddings he'd go to church and that was about the extent of it. My mother, yes, she'd go to church, but I don't know, to put a son or daughter through hell because of it, to me it just isn't worth it.

I'm prejudiced up to a point. I'm not going to kid about it now, if my daughter, one of the girls came home and said, "I want to go with a colored fellow," or marriage, that would be quite hard for me to take. I don't think I could accept it. Now maybe you've been brought up different, otherwise.

Now you probably remember those twins, what the heck were their names? They were colored. Yeah, the Lewises. They were like night and day. The bigger girl was as immaculate—she was in my history class, she was as immaculate as you could get. I'd bring food, something to eat during class, we had lunches made. I'd bring something to eat, she'd bring something to eat, we'd share it, you know? Like I say, if she'd go to the ladies' room, she'd wash her hands and wash them, as if she was trying to wash the black, you know, the

dark, off or something. But the other sister, that is what I remember about her—I forgot who had said, her sister said it—
when her socks got dirty, she just turned them inside out and
wore them the other way. And they were twins, they weren't
identical, they didn't look alike, but I believe they were twins.

I think what the people in this area really resent are a lot
of Puerto Ricans that came in. And I think what the people
really resent is a lot of them are on welfare. There are so
many people struggling to keep their heads above water to
make ends meet, to care for their kids properly and this sort
of thing, and they come up, they're on welfare, some of them
go back to Puerto Rico, they're still on welfare, they're getting checks that are being sent down to them. And I think
this is what it is more than it is nationality or the ethnic
group they belong to.

Hey, you probably remember as well as I, like when my
grandparents came here, and there were so many people who
say it, when their parents came, or grandparents, they
couldn't speak English. They talked the best they could, they
worked, like at Bethlehem Steel. They went down there and
they worked for their money and to keep their families supported as best they could.

Like I said, the Puerto Ricans just come up and go right
on welfare. Some of them work, I'm not sure, but it seems
like there's so many that just want to sit back and live easy.
And my husband and all the other husbands go to work and
put their time in and maybe work overtime to get a little
extra, whereas *they* could care less.

Well, today I would say religion is minute compared to
what it was, but race, I think, is—well, that's being torn
down, too, to a certain extent, but I'm not ready for it. I tell
you, you'd be surprised, the colored fellows, I would say
more so, and white girls, than the other way around. They
go to football games, you see them at band concerts, things
like that, and even shopping and wherever you go. You see so
much of it.

Margaret's house is on upper Wyandotte Street, perched on the
side of South Mountain. Her kitchen window overlooks the borough
of Fountain Hill and beyond. I observed: "In San Francisco, real es-

tate is sold by the view you have, so that the most expensive houses in San Francisco command a view of some valley, the ocean or something like that. I guess that's not really true here."

No, I think the section is what dominates around here because you've got your Saucon Valley, which is very elite, and the East Hills over there are supposed to be the better class of people. Around here I think it's sections.

I think you kind of separate. You've got someone who's an office worker and he's got a position—well, hey, he wants to do different things. Now she [her daughter] had a friend, her father is something over at Bethlehem Steel, and they're the type, he come home, they have a few cocktails before dinner, with dinner. I said, "Hey, I couldn't do that." I have one cocktail before dinner, and I'd be flat on my face. I couldn't keep up with that sort of thing. We live a different life than they do. I wouldn't want to live like that, and I'm sure they don't want to live the way I live. Financially, I couldn't keep up with them either.

Maybe it's just our imagination, but it seems today our ministers here will favor people that have the money and the position. You can work as hard as they at—well, we have a church fair in November—but it seems like sometimes you get the feeling that they pass you by. Well, you see it: they'll walk right by you and put out their hand for someone that you know has position and money, and you've worked as hard if not harder doing something. It's a little bit discouraging, it really is.

We've been wanting to get out of this house, and then. Oh, my husband's just up at Mack Trucking about seven years now, so, when you're kind of between jobs—hey, you know: we move and got payments, monthly payments. The kids are pretty small, suppose this job falls through? He gets laid off? And then she went to high school, she didn't want to move, she wanted to stay at Liberty. Well, she's in the band—I kind of felt that Liberty meant a lot to her, she worked real hard with her music to get herself where she is, and I just couldn't see taking it away from her, so we're okay for a couple of years. But every year the houses get more expensive. I'd really like to get out of here.

A few years after they talked, Margaret moved off South Mountain to the flatlands of the countryside, where she gazes at goats, cows, and guinea hens from her kitchen window, a bucolic setting comfortably removed from the social inequities of the city.

———

The South Side is being deserted by the children it nurtured, yet it remains a well-fixed memory in their minds. George "Skip" John grew up there, the eldest of six children. His father came from Hungary to work at Steel, his mother was for many years employed in a factory. He distinguished himself in high school as "lineman of the year" on the victorious 1951 football team. He now runs the Bethlehem School District's bus maintenance shop from a building overlooking the Liberty High School stadium. Impatient for football practice to begin in mid-August, he never misses a game during the regular season. His own trim athletic frame is now hidden by new pounds of flesh, but his three sons have carried on the family tradition. They, his daughter, and his wife Rosie form with Skip a tight unit. He does not fail to remind them of his past.

SKIP: Yeah, you know when we were kids, down on the South Side—well, it would be Washington or Broughal Junior High Schools—we were always known as tough characters. We took all the championships in football, basketball, wrestling. We referred to the kids on the North Side, whether it be at Franklin or Nitchman [Junior High Schools] as the cake eaters. Naturally, when we got over here to high school, it was always "who was going to be on the teams?" I have to say with all honesty there was more South Siders on the teams. But we never went into tennis—that was for you.

Now I live on the North Side—and I often tease my kids: "You guys are nothing but a bunch of cake eaters." Yet we couldn't stay over there. The Heights is no longer; now it's the B.O.F.—Basic Oxygen Furnace. That's where I originally was from. But I can't honestly say my kids are cake eaters. Let's face it: all our type of people that lived down there, we've moved all over the city. Most of the fellows that were from Broughal, too, they're over on this side now.

After high school I went in the Navy, and when I got out we lived three years in South Terrace. I saw it getting bad. So

George John at work, 1976. (Photo by JEI.)

we moved to Ninth and Montclair, right above Broughal. I
rented, but the price wasn't right to buy. We heard about this
place on the West Side, and the price was right—so we took
it. What we always thought of the West Side was that they
were a higher class.

When I lived on the Heights, that was the League of Nations. We had Mexicans, we had colored, we had the Italians
and Hungarians and the Slovaks and the Russians and all
that. It was mixed, and yet it was a real good community at
that time. I never felt, as a Hungarian, that I was separate
from the others. The difference at that time was class. We
were supposed to be of the lower class; anybody on the
South Side was that way.

The different groups on the Heights, well, it just didn't
mean that much. The same with religion—it didn't matter, it
never entered our minds. I remember in seventh grade at
Washington Junior High School, a fellow came in from
Portugal—Cicero Bronco—who didn't speak a word of
English. And we had a teacher, Mrs. Hallihan, that poor
woman, she'd speak with him and just make him repeat

words. And today he has his own business by the coke works, he has his own bar, and he can speak English like anybody else.

Today we have Spanish-speaking classes for Puerto Ricans—I can't see it. They want to come here; they should speak English. Everybody else learned how to speak English. I'll never forget I was a "greenie" in the first grade: I spoke only Hungarian. I still speak a little, but Rosie is German, and our kids speak only English.

Out there on the Heights, we didn't have a Boys' Club like the Broughal kids. Washington Junior High School was our playground, summer and winter, all outdoors. If it snowed, we'd just shovel our way out to the key and say the snow was out of bounds—no matter how cold it was. That's what we did, all the time.

Athletics brings out a lot of good in all people. That's what I tell our children. I don't care what you are or anything else, sports really knits you into the thing, and you really get to know a lot of people. I attribute all my friendships to athletics. Anybody who goes to school should get tied up in sports—it's about the greatest thing you can do. My kids are in sports.

I started football at Liberty at 135 pounds. I was the smallest kid on the team. All the big boys on the line protected me at center. I never got hurt. I played sixty minutes of the game.

On, jeez, take me back to my high school years, I'll tell you, they were wonderful years, wonderful years. I never played football again. I coached for a while over at Nitchman. But I would have had to stay in the Navy longer to play. I wanted to come home.

I guess it paid off. Rosie and I are still together. We have a happy marriage. I met her ice skating—we were twelve and a half—and I never looked at anyone else. We have four million dollars invested in our four children. We have a good home. The only club I ever belonged to was the Hellertown Legion, a place to go on New Year's Eve or on Dollar Night and have a nice time. Now we just go out maybe once a month to some place to eat, have a nice meal, and that's it. Most of the time the children go with us.

We've spent many summers in Wildwood, New Jersey,

together. Young Skip told his mother not so long ago: "You know, we never had enough money, but we always had lots of fun." People don't do that anymore.

Tonight is shopping night. We'll go out to the store together, then come home and relax. We have a good family.

When I visited Skip at his home on the West Side in 1983, his wife Rose was there. She had been a member of the Class of 1952 who left school for work in order to help support her family. Now the two of them talked proudly of their grandchildren who lived close by, but they did not forget the other generations.

ROSE: My mother came here from Austria when she was nineteen. My mother is eighty, and she still speaks with a heavy Austrian accent. Her friends are German, and Holy Ghost Church is German. I understand the language, but I can't speak it well.

Skip and I met at an ice skating rink; I had just gotten new skates. Now the rink isn't there anymore, or Washington School. We never got on North Side except to go to high school and go to the Boyd Theater. I could cry when I go through the Heights — everything's gone.

SKIP: It makes me sick. It was a real community. We never locked our doors. The playground was the central thing; we always went there.

ROSE: Our kids did the same at Fairview School. It's a shame they did away with neighborhood schools. They brought the parents together, too. But I guess times always change.

We've been here for twenty-three years. Skip, our oldest, started kindergarten here. Now he's twenty-eight and married, a schoolteacher and assistant basketball coach at Liberty. His first demand is education — first you're going to be a student, then an athlete.

Crouched beside Skip on the Liberty High School football team was guard Gus Romero, who with his uncle, Davy Salgado, grew up in a small house just off Coke Works Road — on Princeton Avenue, but a long way from the Ivy League. As they went through high school

together, Gus on the gridiron and Davy playing soccer, and both
of them varsity wrestlers, it did not occur to them that they ought
to be studying as well as playing.

They now live in new ranch homes along Revena Street on the
edge of the city, as do other members of this extended family headed
by Helen Salgado (Davy's mother, Gus's grandmother). Davy has
labored all his life in the Bethlehem Steel Company plant, both as
a welder and a millwright, but Gus was laid off by the Steel and
went to work for the post office a few years ago. Davy only recently
ended his soccer career and still plays softball; Gus's athletic activities are now limited to bowling.

They recognize that a few, but only a few Mexican-American
families "push" (Gus's word) the old culture onto their children.
And although Davy still speaks a lot of Spanish, both men realize
they are losing a cultural inheritance and speak as though they regret
it or ought to regret it. Yet neither has made any move to arrest the
decline. No family member in their generation has married another
Mexican-American: Gus's wife is Hungarian by background, Davy's
spouse is German. They belong to the Aztec Club, but it has become
just another drinking establishment with no special ethnic character.
Older family members have returned to Mexico, but the land they
held was lost in the 1930s. Both Gus and Davy proclaim that they
are Americans, nothing else.

GUS: When the Mexicans first came here, they were in the
"labor camp" with the Slovaks. They had the piñata at
Christmas, that sort of thing. When the Steel started closing
that camp down, the Mexicans spread out, first through the
South Side and then throughout the city.

The South Side was poor. At that time it was the poor
against the rich. I was lower class. I've never had any problems because I was Mexican, though some of my uncles who
worked at the Steel said they had problems.

DAVY: I've never been discriminated against. We made our
way as Mexicans, so did the blacks. I recently saw a TV program with Savy Pasqualucci [president of the Class of 1952]
on it, and other people on the panel were Puerto Rican,
black and white. Those Puerto Ricans were telling everybody
that they were discriminated against, so were the blacks. I
called in and said we got the same opportunities as everyone.

GUS: The Puerto Rican community is much larger than the Mexican community, lots of people in one house, often lower class, often without jobs and collecting welfare. The working class resents this, and resents the ghetto atmosphere. I'm not saying it's the Puerto Ricans' fault.

DAVY: We started our married life in South Terrace. All nationalities got along there. Then the Puerto Ricans began settling on Third Street. You couldn't walk there without cat-calls. It's better now. I'm playing baseball for the Puerto Rican Club, and I'm having a ball. We never had any problems. I played soccer with the Italians in Easton, with the Germans, with Hungarians after 1956. I never had any problems in athletics. I can go in almost any club in Bethlehem and get along. People get along better through athletics. Sure, boys mixed better than girls in high school, due to sports. I just quit playing soccer after twenty-six years. I'm still playing softball.

Davy and Gus agree that athletes had a pretty easy time of it in high school, that there were teachers who pushed them through. Gus took the scientific curriculum, while Davy was in the general curriculum—"which was nothing," in his estimation. Gus, who was a football player, recalls going to Rutgers University as a high school senior and being rebuked for not having "college grades." He did get an offer from Colgate, and his father encouraged him to go, but Gus refused. In Davy's family, where there were several children, college wasn't an option.

GUS: I remember biology class, if you didn't have a notebook, you couldn't pass. And I simply didn't bother to make a notebook. It's a lot with the parents. I know I'm lenient with my kids: I don't push them, I never threaten them. My father always let me loaf. Your father, maybe he said: "You're going to go to college so you'd better work," and he pushed you. I'm more lenient than my father was; so is Davy. I often tell my wife that I think I let my son down.

DAVY: Gus's father and mine worked hard at the Coke Works. And they gave us the best they could afford. And we want our kids to have something more than we had. But if you don't push, they stay at the same level—my kids are at the same level I was. Sometimes they don't give a damn. My four sons don't have good jobs.

When you see your kids struggling to get out of the hole, it makes you a little irritated, and you got to get down on their backs a little bit. I got four guys, and we sometimes almost come to blows. These kids don't obey as we did.

If you don't give them something to look forward to, they're just going to stay where they are. I went to high school, and I've had a pretty good life. I went to work and climbed up the ladder. Hell, I'm ahead of guys I went to high school with in terms of money and job responsibility. I want something like that for my kids—or better. Ten years from now I don't want to see one of my sons still a laborer. It's human nature for me to want them to have something better. I don't want to go to my grave and not see them have something good!

GUS: My son was all set to go to college. Then suddenly he says, "Dad, I've had it with studying." Next thing I know he's enlisted in the service. Davy lost two of his kids to the service at once, the older drafted and the other by enlistment.

My son's studying while he's in the service. Why can't he stay home and do that? I didn't give him the incentive he needed, just like our parents didn't give us the incentive we needed. The difference between generations is that our parents used a belt on us. And my dad could punish Davy.

Our family is very close. One thing we always gave our kids was love and stuff like that. After my son Johnny left for the service, he called home all the time—we told him not to worry about the expense.

DAVY: Our family has been together for years. The kids all visit their grandmother, get along with each other. We're always in each other's house. We've all had our problems, we work them out. My oldest son, though, he's got a good enough deal in Pittsburgh, and he'll stay there.

We have a two-year-old in our house now—she's from my wife's side of the family. Her parents can't seem to make a go of it, so we're trying to adopt her.

I was out in Wyoming a few years ago. Miles and miles of nothing. That was my first trip away from home. I was never in the service. I was away for two weeks and I felt lost. I damn near cried when I walked out of this house. I drove out there with my buddy. And when I got there I said to myself, "What the blazes are you doing out here?" I sat in that tent and got homesick right off the bat.

GUS: There's so much to see in this country, I don't feel any need to go to Mexico. My father has gone back. We took him to the Philadelphia airport—he looked so pathetic getting on the plane. When he came back he was wearing this huge Mexican hat and carrying twelve bottles of tequila.

When people ask what we are now, I say I have a Mexican background, but I'm an American first.

DAVY: That's what we all are! I always felt that way. When I started school, I always said I was an American. When I didn't go to college, I never felt it was because I was Mexican. It was *my* hard luck.

The kids, when they look back, they sometimes realize we were right in telling them to get ahead. Sometimes they give you a big surprise. I hope they surprise us and get somewhere.

Boys like Skip John, Gus Romero, and Davy Salgado had little trouble shedding the ethnic labels that might have been affixed to them if Bethlehem had had ghettos. But the South Side itself was a mixture of nationalities, and during the high school years boys from all parts of town mixed easily in the free-for-all of athletics.

While participation in sports was a privilege pretty much denied to girls in the mid-twentieth century, otherwise they had most of the opportunities for assimilation enjoyed by their male counterparts. The assimilation process was speeded up by the fact that few of Bethlehem's immigrants and their progeny maintained close contact with the countries from which they had come. Katy Trivanovich is a striking exception to this generalization.

KATY: My mother is Serbian, but from Hungary. I speak Serbian and Hungarian. When I started first grade I only knew Hungarian. My mother went to Europe when I was three to study nursing there. She didn't know enough English to go to school here. And she took me along. So I went to Hungarian kindergarten, and I started first grade here. I traveled in eastern Europe before I got married—I was there in '39; I was there in '47, right after the war. That [1947] was an experience. I was twelve when we went there for six months. We went to see my grandparents in Hungary.

I can still remember as a child during the war, how people moaned and groaned about ration stamps. When I saw over there—when we were on the Hungarian border, they had these trains, regular cattle cars, and they were herding people in to take them to Siberia. Kids with no clothes on, little three-year-olds with ankles like this [makes a gesture with her hands], big pot bellies from kidney trouble and—oh!—it was something. I was just at the age where it sunk in, and I could remember. This country never felt war. They don't know what war is.

I traveled there since then. My father lives here six months then goes back to Yugoslavia. I spent a month with him there. My husband finally traveled two years ago—we went to Vegas!

I speak Serbian with my father. And now my little one, I'm trying to teach her Serbian, but she's picking up the Hungarian. It seems to be easier for her. When I was young I spoke Greek and Italian. My great aunt knew seven languages, and she spoke Greek to her friends when they would come, these Greek ladies, and I would pick it up. Today, when my mother comes here, we speak Serbian. In school I learned English, then I came home and spoke Serbian and Hungarian. And that's why my mother has a hard time picking up English; then she went to night school. My father never bothered. Oh, he killed the English language something terrible.

There are very few Serbians in Bethlehem now. There were about six, seven families when I was a child. We all went to the Russian Orthodox church. We didn't have our own church; our church is in Elizabeth, New Jersey.

In first grade Skippy John, and I sang Hungarian songs in front of the class. For that I got A's.

I've signed my daughter up to go to a farm outside of Emmaus, where they're teaching children Hungarian on Sunday afternoons. Have her learn the proper way.

Did you ever see the Tamburitzans from Duquesne University? They come in every year. They do Croatian singing, dancing, Slovenian, Serbian, Macedonian. You should see how they crowd them into Liberty High School—two nights, you can't get in—they sell out! They're a bunch of American college students; they have to be straight-A sutdents to get in-to that, because they only spend half their year in school, and half they travel all over Europe and the States. If my kid is smart enough, that's where I'd like her, where she can keep up with my side of the family. I'm teaching her how to dance.

My ethnic background was never an embarrassment to me. I never thought much of it in high school. I was very proud in nurses' training, because they'd ask me to interpret Hungarian and Serbian. We'd get a lot of people in who couldn't speak a word of English. Whenever I was asked, I would always say, "I'm American, of Serbian descent." Nobody is ever going to talk against the USA to me. There's a lot of good and a lot of bad here, but there's no place like this! I don't care what crook you have in the White House. It's still a good place to live.

No matter how hard I have to work, no matter how much taxes I have to pay—I moan and groan about it—I saw mid-Europe under Communism. I saw it right after the war, and I saw it in '65, and they haven't gotten ahead one itsy-bitsy bit. My mother's village where she was born was exactly in 1965 like it was in 1939. And I remember it in 1939. The same ruts in the road. They still go out to the well for their water.

Katy, who had worked at Bethlehem Steel Company as a nurse since her graduation from St. Luke's, struggled just as conscientiously to become pregnant. Her daughter arrived after fifteen years of mar-riage. She was intent on passing the Old World heritage to the new generation, as well as her USA patriotism. But she found, as she informed me seven years later, that loving America and having an Americanized child were not exactly the same.

I was in Yugoslavia in '79 again. I spent a week with rela-tives in Hungary, and three weeks in Yugoslavia, but my fa-ther was ill at the time so we didn't get to see much. I was going to take my daughter all over. Nine days after I left he died—and he was buried there. Yugoslavia was great; their standards were like ours in the fifties. My cousins were living well, everything modern in the house. They had cars, good jobs. They enjoy their life there. Not hectic like here. They live from day to day.

I tried to teach my daughter Serbian—she just didn't want to learn. She covered her ears, and that was it. She studies French in school. She takes after my husband's side of the family. They have relatives here, and they're not close. But I wasn't brought up that way. Our type of people—second, third cousins—they're like first cousins here. Close. My cousin in Yugoslavia, she took my father in like he was her own father. Took care of him, kept him there. You wouldn't find anybody around here doing something like that. It's the way we're brought up.

To this day—I'm going to be fifty—I still wouldn't think of talking back to my mother. I'll have a friendly argument with her if I think I'm right—not like the kids today. Even my own child. I tried to bring her up that way but they get out in society; she does what the other kids do. Any elder in Europe commands respect. You ask a child, only once, they'll do it. "Aunt Katy." You don't even hear that here. Everything is first name.

I've come to the conclusion that our kids have everything today, which we didn't. I didn't. I was an only child, but my mother didn't hesitate to say "no." Today, I don't know, I guess I'm just as bad. After hearing her moan and groan about it, I'll go and get it, which I guess is wrong too. She's thirteen years old now, and she—you name it, she has had it or has it. We were talking the other day, we don't know what to get her for Christmas. Stereos, organ. She ice skates every day. Anything her little heart desires, we gave her.

I'm still a strong American. I'm a little disappointed the way things are going. There's still no country like the USA—it's the freedom. In Hungary in '79 they're still afraid to talk, you have to watch how you talk. I couldn't live under a system like that. Now Yugoslavia was different, they weren't afraid to speak their minds. They're not under the Russian rule, they're under their own Communist rule, but still it was more socialist. You're allowed to own your own property.

What surprises me there is everybody's up to date on

politics. That's the main thing at the supper table. They're very interested in what goes on in the world. I bet you go up and down the street here you wouldn't find two people that could tell you—skim over the headlines. They're bringing all their little ones up to remember the Second World War. They weren't in it, they weren't even born at the time, but they know all about it. And my daughter's in eighth grade, and she doesn't even know the history of the United States. For me to take her to Washington, D.C.—she doesn't know a thing.

You have to raise your kids with the times—to a certain extent. I'm still not going to let her do like a lot of these things—date at thirteen and that. Like her girlfriend down the street.

My daughter is in ice-skating competition. She went in a meet in Philadelphia—back and forth every day. She'd like to pass more skating exams, teach skating—she's good with children. She skates from quarter of six to quarter of eight every morning. Then gets the school bus at twenty-five after eight. Comes home at four, does her homework, practices her organ. And every Monday, Wednesday, Friday, she skates from six to eight. And some Sunday mornings she goes. Though now she's in confirmation class, and I want her to go to church. A lot of activity for me, but I like it—it keeps her off the streets. The class of children she skates with— they're really wonderful kids. There's no smoking, no dope, no cursing. They all come from good families. And she skates ten weeks during the summer from twenty of seven until twelve-thirty.

She's keeping her marks up—between an A and B student. I told her, "You don't keep your marks up, we're going to cut down on the skating." That's all she needed to hear. I skate too, and I play the organ. I'd scrub floors if it was necessary for her to go to college. We bought a computer for her last year.

For centuries foreign observers have been appalled at the liberties American parents grant their children—liberties that American children *take* for granted. As someone who came to parenthood late in life and has but one child, Katy shows more than the usual concern for her daughter's future. Her attitude is reinforced by the fact that she is both European and American in outlook; her offspring is not.

———

The relationships among generations, as well as "new" ideas about such time-honored subjects as family living and education and religion, were topics of discussion in my conversations with Martha Marcinko, whose grandparents and mother immigrated from Slovakia, and her husband, Nick Begovich, whose grandparents and parents were born in what is now Yugoslavia. Martha, whose mother and father were factory workers, was torn between being a secretary—the job expected of a young woman with her background—and studying art. She finally opted for the latter, in addition to raising four daughters in a suburban tract in northeast Bethlehem. Nick, the sone of a shop owner, trained to be an auto mechanic but works as an electronics technician. When I stopped to see them Martha, a youngish looking blonde in sweater and slacks, appeared very hip beside Nick in his old plaid shirt and stocking feet. An odd couple, I thought, but Nick explained (as though reading my mind), "We are two individualists." They appreciated each other.

MARTHA: I'm into a lot of different things. I haven't had a Sumi show—or Oshibana. But I would like to. The two things are so related. I began by using Sumi ink drawings as a method of teaching children. In order to teach it I had to learn it; I taught myself from books. It's done on the basis of Zen—less is more. And it's a good philosophy as you paint into other things—subtract and see more when you show less. There's also a lot of symbolism in it. Then I got into Oshibana.

Nick's very nice. He's never hollered at me that I've got to stay home, got to stay in my place. I was always free, as much as I could, to get out and do my own thing. Which struck me as a whole lot more sensible than staying home and doing dishes. Housework doesn't bother me. Windows can stay the way they are—if you see light through them, that's fine. There's so much more to do, to fulfill yourself, than windows, eech!

NICK: These things you don't plan. They happen. You don't say, "I'll liberate my wife." A lot of guys I know, their

Martha Marcinko and Nick Begovich at home, 1976. (Photo by JEI.)

wives have the freedom to do as they please—and a lot don't. I think the women themselves determine it, pretty much.

MARTHA: I know women who don't know how to drive and won't learn, who never leave the house. A friend called me up last October; I hadn't seen her since she was married. She says, "Talk to me." She's in a real poor state. "I don't go anywhere. I don't know how to drive." She wants a part-time job, but she can't get there! Her husband is always saying, "You stay at home" and "My wife doesn't have to work." She gradually slipped into that role.

NICK: Naturally, when a couple first gets married the wife does throw her support behind her husband at some sacrifice to herself. It's a financial thing. His job, their house, their standard of living are more important. This particular guy, he was pushing for a living standard. She backed him, but he never let her out from underneath when they got to what their goals were. He uses her a lot as a showpiece.

MARTHA: She was used, physically and mentally, in a bad situation. I call her from time to time and ask her how she is. She went into hypnosis. "Oy," I said, "get into a group." I was in a terrific TA group last year. I told her a couple of things she might do. The thing is to get out, get away from that house and husband. Start to get independent.

The first group I was with started with the Adult Evening Courses, sponsored by the Bethlehem Area School District. I stayed with it until it disbanded, after about seven months.

My kids think that I am far out because I'm into Yoga and meditation. My Margie talks about her mother who is weird. She means it like a compliment. My relationship to my children is so different from my mother's to me. I've just been thinking about how different our childhoods were.

NICK: I think the trouble is today that we parents, we adults, get too involved in the kids.

MARTHA: No! No! Our neighbors were involved. All the Italian ladies would come out while we were playing stick ball in the street, and they'd holler. Everybody was involved.

NICK: As spectators, not as managers. Today very little is left to the kids' imaginations. I think our school system pro-vides this. How many counselors were in school when you were there? Two, one for boys, one for girls. What were their qualifications? None. Now you have one for every fifty students—or some ridiculous ratio—and it's a doctorate in psychology. They're helpful in some sense, but they're over-domineering.

Before, you got your information from a teacher or several teachers, from friends—you got it. Now you go in to a counselor and get all his views, that's it.

Our parents sent us to school for an education. And in the process you were not exposed to a very large environment so they had a very high influence on your conduct. They didn't relinquish too much, sending you to school.

MARTHA: But my father was always overwhelmed when he had to go to school. He was a laborer in the Steel. He took a bath, dressed in a suit and a tie, to see a play or whatever. We didn't have counseling with the teachers then. My mother worked nights at a silk mill. So if there was something doing and he wasn't entirely bushed, he would come. And he would have to go down and take public transportation. He was awed by this experience. He didn't graduate; he only went to the third grade.

NICK: Well, you take your immigrant parents, or the first generation—they were very insecure coming here. They moved from a place they were familiar with, and they came here insecure. And they also found hostility here. So therefore there was hostility to their children, too. So they did keep them close. And the environment *was* hostile.

MARTHA: When I was young, it was a shame to date a Protestant boy. You kept it real quiet. You didn't bring him home to sit in the parlor. Now a parent doesn't even care what kind of religion it is. I remember dating a boy from Lehigh once, he told me his name was Barry Cohen. My mother is giving me the old third degree because I'm going out with him a second time. So I tell her his name. "Cohen? Going out with a Jewish boy?" I didn't know you could tell all the Jewish people by their names. We didn't see each other after that.

I try to keep an ethnic background, but I feel that I have lost it entirely. But I like old linens, and I tell the children about our customs on Christmas Eve.

NICK: I went to Catholic School. And my father always

said about girls to marry, "Go up on the South Mountain and get a good Slovak." So I did. He said, "Marry your kind." He didn't say, "If you marry someone else you'll have problems."

MARTHA: My father's mother, who visited us from the coal regions, she was prejudiced—and she would always back it up with a sound reason. The Italians were wild, unruly people—stay away from. The other thing was Johnny Bull— any Englishman—stay away from him. Another one was Swedes—"Oh, you'd better watch the Swedes." The Slovak people were okay, but the rest—watch out.

NICK: I have to feel my parents didn't want me to be ethnic. They never spoke anything but English to us children. Yet among themselves they always talked Croatian. The only time my father said anything to me in Croatian was when he was cursing at me, when he was trying to get hold of me to give me a good licking.

MARTHA: The only time my parents spoke Slovak was when they had a secret. If someone would suggest they teach us the language, my mother would say, "No, they're American." You were backward if you spoke Slovak at home.

NICK: The immigrant parents made us Americans. On purpose. The Jews, they never made their kids American; they made them around the Jewish religion. When I say American, I mean look, act, do. They're still good American citizens. But their religion is very active, and their life is around their religion. Protestants don't have it. Catholics got their bingo, not much more.

MARTHA: We go to church. We take the children. But we are not churchy Catholic.

NICK: I think religion has a place in everybody's life, regardless of what it is. Psychiatrists cost so much more. No, really. There's times you find something in religion that tides you over, that serves a need for a human being, that prepares you. If I ever studied psychology, I'd say, "If I ever have a problem in this area, I'll know how to handle it." I think, basically, that's what religion is.

Religion has its place. Sure as hell our government can't teach us the Ten Commandments. We know that government can't teach morals. Religion will do it. All religions teach the fundamentals of life and living in society. I don't think you have to apply all the little rules and regulations.

This one Sunday the priest goes on about why do you worry about your food, what you're going to eat or drink, does not the Lord take care of the birds, are you not more important to him than they are? And I sit there and I think about this—and really, really—how am I supposed to take that? That if I do what a bird does and don't worry about these things about work, that they tell us are the pleasures of life—central heating, sanitation—will I be taken care of like that bird?

Religion is strongest in the nations that are poorest. You've got the famine in them—all religions, not just Catholicism— you've got the unsanitary systems, you've got disease. That's where religion is strongest. Is the religion holding them down? Could very well be. Religion tells them not to worry, the Lord will take care of your physical being.

What does a dictator do the first thing when he takes over? He has to belittle his people. In order to control them he has to take certain things away from them, in order to have them as his followers or at least not to resist him. I wonder sometimes, is South America what it is because the religions are making it that way? Having them forever dependent on the churches' way?

I continue going to church to get my own religion, to get what I need out of it. Maybe you don't believe in everything that's going on, but you should be there to influence the organization. I think you're obligated to go to your local town meetings and school board meetings, even if you can't get a word out. Just your body there is a certain influence. Imagine what they would do if *no one* showed up!

Kids should be taught that there's such a thing as religion. "Here's one—look at it." The same way you send them to first grade and to second grade.

MARTHA: When you think back to how persuaded you were under your parents' rule; you'd do things without question. Now the kids say, "Ha, I won't do that." They don't care what you think about it.

NICK: You have a heck of a time persuading kids. The

influence of the environment is so much to overcome. I send my kids to school, and some of the things they're for giving them in school are turning right around and countermanding my thoughts. But by the time I realize it, it's too late. It's hard to undo something once it's done. You can't just pluck it out of the mind.

MARTHA: You don't always know what's going on with the kids. They have the same rules that we did. There were things that you talked about with your girlfriends, and there were separate things you talked about with your boyfriends. And none of these things you ever talked about with your parents. "How'd your day go?" "Fine." "Where are you going?" "Out. I'll be right back." Like my mother, I'm not in on anything. What I find out surprises me, but I find it out by accident.

NICK: Occasionally, I say to them when they're doing something I don't like, "Do you see anybody who's sixty years old doing that?" When we'd sit at the table, my seven sisters and my brother and me, my father would sit where my brother and I couldn't get out from our seats. There was no way in hell you were going to get out if he was going to preach to you about something. You just sat there and took it. He often did it for half an hour, forty-five minutes.

He did it when I was nineteen. I didn't think very much of his awareness or anything else. But as I get older I think of the things he had told me and find out more how much smarter he was than I thought he was. He really had some wisdom of life. Maybe not formal education, but life—what it's about, what experiences you could expect. And he gets smarter now as I get older—and yet he's not going back to school, that's for damn sure. He was worldly wise.

I don't think you have a right to take difficult problems to your parents. You kick away your parents and say, "I'm free." If you're going to make adulthood for yourself, well then you have to go and make your decisions and live with them.

But if you're going to counsel with them, then you must accept their recommendations. The kind of problems you got to talk to your mother about, you know there's nothing nobody can do about them. Something time will take care of, or something you got to solve yourself.

MARTHA: My mother taught me where I belonged. Foremen lived on the North Side, laborers on the South Side. Protestants lived on Center Street—Germans. We were taught that right away. "Your library is down here, that's where you go. There's no reason to go over there." [The main building of the Bethlehem Public Library was on the North Side, and there was also a South Side branch.] My mother didn't want me traveling that far, but I guess she was also trying to keep me in my class.

NICK: I didn't use the library. But I know this: you'll always have that social class difference, although they're trying to get away from it by busing.

MARTHA: You should hear what some people say about them, the Puerto Ricans, especially when there was a controversy about the free lunch progam: "What nationality coming over here got anything from the city or state?" I remember some of our neighbors on the South Side, very poor, who never got anything. Why do they [the government] feel now such a responsibility to provide?

NICK: Numbers. So many have today, it's assumed there are few who don't have. At that time, so many didn't have. So what difference does it make?

We have every year a Halloween parade. Invariably the Puerto Ricans will have a float in that parade. They are showing their ethnic background; they have their social clubs. They have everything any Croatian, and Slovak, any Pollack, Windock, any South Side immigrant did—churches, social clubs. The Puerto Ricans are in the early stages of doing the same damn thing. The people that put the floats in the parades, these are the ones that are going to find their place in America. The Puerto Ricans that are bums are just like any other bums.

Our conversation turned to an aspect of the Begoviches' own Americanization: how they happened to be in a suburb.

MARTHA: I knew when I went over to the North Side I was in a different territory, out of my class, because that's what my mother said. But I didn't give it much thought when we bought a house here. And then I'd go back on the

South Side. Oh! It was real trauma to me for a while. I couldn't stand to look at my neighborhood, how dumpy and little it was. I can't think of any real nice neighborhoods on the South Side.

NICK: It didn't have longevity in my mind. It was economics that brought us here. And there weren't stratas. There are about 130 homes here. I think there's four of us don't have a college education.

Seven years later I had dinner with Martha and Nick, along with their youngest daughter, Diana, a fourteen-year-old who spoke with great authority about drug use among teenagers. After she left we discussed their four girls and the difficulty of turning children into independent adults, and especially how to deal with the parental desire to be helpful on those occasions when the child couldn't or shouldn't be aided. They had had to face the divorce of one daughter ("I accepted the divorce more than the marriage," observed Nick; "It was hard," answered Martha), and even young Diana had gotten into trouble in an incident involving alcohol and the police that, while not an event of her own making, reflected a poor decision, according to Nick.

"Our life is just overwhelmed with children," remarked Martha who claimed to be looking forward to an empty house. "Sometimes I wonder what it would have been like without children." "I don't even think about not having children," Nick immediately responded. "That was my goal way back. I'm aware that there's going to be problems. But I tell you, problems are in everybody's life." Martha reflected. "When the good times come along," she mused, "we should say, 'Everybody take note: these are good times.' Because we know the bad times."

Martha went on: "I've watched my life go through so many changes. Now I'm going through another change again. And I'm wondering. I was into so many things—well, I'm still quilting, doing yoga, painting—that were quiet and reflective. And now I'm into roller skating and bomba—a more open kind of outlet."

I reminded them of when I stopped by seven years ago, and they had described themselves as individualists. They both laughed warmly; they had been speaking the truth, and perhaps they were happy I remembered it. "I think a good relationship is when each one has to give what the other one needs—and gives in that area.

And is appreciative of what that person has to offer," said Nick. "In the areas where you have no needs, neither gives, and these are the areas of freedom that you have."

Freedom in areas where you have no needs — Nick's statement intrigued me. It spoke directly to the idea of being at liberty and, for me, it was clearly relevant to the issue of moving from the familiarity and security of the household to the mystery and excitement of the larger society. In the latter region my role was undefined, my responsibilities were unnamed; I had the freedom (if I wanted it) to explore and carve out a place for myself. Like some of my classmates I viewed the unknown world outside my family as threatening; yet at the same time, like others of them, I found it enticing.

Time and distance give a different perspective: I now judge my early environment to have been tame, homogeneous, and provincial. Center Valley, hardly even a hamlet, and Coopersburg, a town of seventeen hundred people, marked the outer reaches of my childhood experience, though neither was more than a mile and a half from home. In these two places I went to school and to church with other white Protestants of German extraction, most of them the children of farmers, small storekeepers, or other local workers. The black family that moved into Coopersburg in the summr of 1943 for two months could have been visiting from another planet. The polyglot industrial city of Bethlehem, less than ten miles distant, might have been a separate continent.

Rural Center Valley and Coopersburg showed little evidence of economic and social class differences, not acknowledging even a local gentry — though the fact that the Illicks got *The New Yorker* made us suspect in some eyes. There was a small social distinction made between residing in the town and living on a farm — again, my family fell into neither category and, hence, were something of an enigma. But the sensitivity my Liberty High School classmates exhibited to living on the wrong side of the city, being from the working class, not qualifying as an "American" — that sensitivity did not exist in the country. It was not easy for me to leave home for a larger society.

Home was the comfort of R.D. #2, Coopersburg, with its few familiar buildings inhabited by relatives and well-known neighbors, a place where I belonged. Even today it evokes images of swimming in the brook, skating on the pond, and roaming through the fields; playing basketball in the driveway, football in the yard, baseball in the meadow; smoking cornsilk in the shed and gaping at lurid magazines in the hay mow. It was a self-contained world, sometimes including only my cousin John, my brother Flex, and me.

Home was close to the Coopersburg Moravian Church, a red brick edifice, pure white inside, its starkness softened only by a maroon carpet and tinted windows. In the pulpit stood Dr. Charles Rominger, an otherworldly, sometime-scholarly preacher whose sermons were an amalgam of recollections from his midwestern boyhood and Biblical allusions learned in seminary. Our own Papa was also a spiritual person; hence, we tolerated Dr. Rominger, however much he was out of touch with "real life"—unlike Dad, Uncle Shube, and Clint Weight from across the road, all of whom were practical men. The line between the etherial and the material was clearly drawn. Indulgent of Dr. Rominger, we were far less forbearing toward the spiritual musings of the Sunday School superintendent, an insurance agent who (we thought) should have restricted himself to the offering, attendance, and other such worldly details of the Lord's Day.

Between ten o'clock church and eleven o'clock Sunday school the men and older boys stood together on the sidewalk in front of the church, sharing reality—cars, sports, and even some off-color stories. But back in the sanctuary we were devout, and members of the congregation assumed their roles as choir director, organist, usher. Aunt Mary's talent was as a tremulous soprano, which always embarrassed me. Mother functioned as disciplinarian, at least for her own boys, and whenever she coughed everyone turned to see what we were doing wrong. Church was like home, and we were frequently there not only for Sunday services but also at evening socials and Daily Vacation Bible School, prayer meetings during Lent, and youth gatherings during adolescence.

School, too, initially resembled home. At age three I was sent across the street to "The Playhouse," a nursery run by Aunt Winnie and two of her college classmates for the children of their relatives and friends. When I began public school at five, I was chauffeured by Mother or Aunt Mary. But my family could not protect me on the playground or in the boys' bathroom. There I was quizzed about my mother's anatomy, confused by remarks about parental behavior (I knew nothing about sexual activity), and taught words entirely new, which I soon discovered must never be spoken in the hearing of adults. I was flattered when invited to play running games with the older boys and pleased when I could tell a dirty joke that made them laugh. I prized their friendship.

My own sheltered past had not prepared me for their rudeness or their ridicule. I tried to develop a thick skin toward their taunts, and I was willing to fight if necessary. Some of the other little boys were as soft and as sweet as I was. I felt for them when they were attacked and on occasion came to their aid against the coarser, usually older fellows—the first "strangers" I had ever met. Crude, funny, threatening, exciting, ominous, they operated in a youthful society unsupervised by adults.

Theirs was not a world I had been raised to inhabit, much as I learned from it. Nor was I long forced to fit into it. When I was eleven my parents joined the Saucon Valley Country Club, bringing me on the brink of my adolescence into contact with children of the upper middle class. I was ready for the change. Now, instead of being angrily abused for dropping the rare fly ball that came my way in right field, I was complimented for a well-placed backhand or a graceful swan dive. Soon I was attending dancing class in Bethlehem. I embraced polite gentility because I had been prepared for it by Mother and got the impression from Dad that it was useful.

My world expanded to include Bethlehem because my new chums from the Club lived in the city. There also resided Dad's sister Caroline, only a few blocks from Liberty High School, where she had been a member of the first graduating class. Her four football-playing sons, who wanted no part of gentility, would sometimes take my brothers and me to the nearby gridiron to watch Bethlehem's Red Hurricane tangle with Easton, Reading, Phillipsburg or, best of all, Allentown.

Aunt Caroline's family faithfully attended my grandparents' church. Her husband, Dale Gramley, was the son of an Evangelical minister who, as a newspaperman, engaged in the worldliest of professions. He had gone to tiny Albright College, where he met Aunt Caroline and Mother, then on to the Columbia School of Journalism before becoming editor of the *Bethlehem Globe-Times* and one of the most popular speakers in the Lehigh Valley. And because I enjoyed listening to his lectures, always an appropriate mix of anecdote and moral message, gravity and humor, I chanced to be given a lesson about a Bethlehem that was neither genteel nor evangelical.

The occasion was a Coopersburg High School graduation and the scene was the town hall, where Uncle Dale was to conduct a symposium on a most unlikely topic, given the region's homogeneous environment: the melting pot in American history. Most of the townspeople were there, seated in the rows of movable chairs that could be pushed to the walls when a dance floor was needed. On the stage were the six participating seniors and Uncle Dale, seated behind a long table on the front of which was tacked white shelf paper bearing a legend, in large red letters: "THE MELTING POT."

I had no idea what a melting pot was, nor had I ever heard of immigration, though both processes were alleged to be a part of Bethlehem life. That was my lesson, which I remembered but was not prepared to understand. I did have a dim sense of what made a "foreigner." Half a mile from our house lived a woman who spoke neither English nor Pennsylvania Dutch. One day Mother saw her walking along the road and offered her a ride home, in return for which she wanted to give us a cabbage but did not know how to say it. We kids began to refer to her place as "the witch's house" and ran at the sight of her. She was not half so weird as Lotte, who also walked the local roads and would now and then render a hymn in front of our home. In fact, there were several eccentrics who were teased but tolerated around Coopersburg. "The witch" was so named, I think, solely because she was foreign.

I occasionally was driven through the South Side of Bethlehem, where the old women in black babushkas made the place seem strangely alien, *their* territory. I imagined these women entering the dark, mysterious Catholic churches, there to engage in some ritual quite unlike any I had witnessed in our plain Moravian service. Every spring my brothers and I were taken to Refowich's clothing store, in the heart of the South Side shopping district, where my mother might hear from Mr. Klein, the man on the floor, what model suit "they" were wearing to Confirmation this spring. Thus did the Jew and the Protestant conspire about the Catholic. Anti-Semitism I never knew; anti-Catholicism seemed to be in my blood.

It was not a personal matter. Sam Fishburn, Dad's business partner, and Phil Philippi, Dad's old high school pal and a frequent visitor in our house — one Jewish, the other Catholic — were openly fond of us, and we reciprocated. I simply regarded them as two of my father's best friends, no labels attached. But I was unsurprised when Dad laughingly confessed that during his boyhood a persistent rumor among Evangelicals was that in the cellars of Bethlehem's Catholic Churches were arsenals, to be drawn upon for the extinction of Protestants. And I had overheard Katherine, Mother's housekeeper, say that her brother-in-law, a plumber in Allentown, had more than once dug up baby bones under the Sacred Heart convent.

Priests and nuns were another breed. Bing Crosby knew no greater fan than Aunt Winnie, who had to overcome her deepest prejudices to watch him in cassock and collar, film after film. My mother, in an effort to have me read a book, once took me with her to the South Side branch of the public library where I, unwittingly (for my only object was to find the slimmest volume available) chose a story about a boy who became a priest. She made no effort to hide her disappointment and, when I realized what the subject was, I thought she was justified!

One night I went into Coopersburg to watch the high school basketballers take on the team from Coplay, a multi-ethnic, industrial town nearby. At twelve I was a fierce partisan in sports — and in religion, too, as I could not help but notice that evening. A priest sat on the visitors' bench, a sight which stunned me; half repelled, half intrigued, I couldn't take my eyes off him. Then, when the Coplay players crossed themselves before shooting fouls, I was angry. Much as I had fantasized about rituals in the Catholic church, I did not want to see them performed on the very floor where I had my gym class. That was *our* territory. And besides, religion didn't belong in sports, Reverend Bob Richards on the Wheaties box notwithstanding. Religion wasn't supposed to be brought into school, despite the daily Bible reading and Lord's Prayer. Not that religion, anyway.

We were confirmed that evening in our belief that God was Protestant, at least when He was called upon in Coopersburg, for we won a surprise victory. The upset Coplay team retaliated by ransacking the boys' locker room, which prompted me to make disparaging remarks about Catholics in front of my parents, both of whom took offense. Dad, ruffled in a way that I had seldom seen him, reminded me that one of his closest friends was a Catholic.

The abstract and the intimate were not as easily separated when in high school I began dating Catholic girls, who were reputed (though not by my parents) to be more passionate than Protestants. Though empirical tests never proved the truth of this rumor, I did find them more alluring. Perhaps it was the forbidden quality that drew me in. I dated one steadily my junior year, another my senior, while my mother anxiously expressed to me her fear that I would "turn." What she failed to recognize was the meaning of the fact that these young women attended St. Anne's on the North Side or Sts. Simon and Jude on the West Side. They were Catholic but, in a society whose priorities were secular and social, what mattered was not their religious affiliation but their economic class—they lived on the management side of town. (I felt freer in my choice of male friends because, of course, I knew there could be no worry that they would become part of the family).

If my parents passed on to me a parochial perspective for dividing friends from strangers, other mothers and fathers did no less. "I'll show you how times have changed," promised Savy Pasqualucci, president of the Class of 1952, as we lunched in the cafeteria of AT&T Technologies. "When I was in ninth grade, we were given forms to fill out, and one question asked what church we attended. So I wrote, 'The Italian Church.' 'No,' said the teacher, 'that's not correct.' So I turned to Joe Iampietro: 'Joe, what church do we go to?' 'The Italian Church.' So finally the teacher helped us out, and we wrote down: 'Holy Rosary Church.'

"When I got home that night I told my mother what had happened, and she said, 'Sure. We go to Holy Rosary, and the Slovaks go to St. Cyril's, and the Irish go to Holy Infancy, and the Windish go to St. Joe's.' So I asked, 'Mom, are there any churches on the North Side of town?' 'Yes,' she answered, 'two: St. Anne's and St. Simon and Jude.' 'And who goes there?'" His mother's response was swift and to the point: "Americans!"

"But I was an American," Savy exclaimed. "I knew that!" My own puzzlement was different. "Didn't your mother acknowledge that there were *lots* of other churches on the North Side?" I inquired, thinking of my fellow Protestants. Savy understood but waved my query aside. "Everybody else was a Moravian."

"Now, he continued, "my Dad used to say to me, 'That Terry Zulli is a nice girl. Nice family.' My Betty Jane was a Protestant, even sort of Pennsylvania Dutchy. She still reminds me that she didn't become a Catholic for my sake. But she's Catholic—and can cook Italian.

"When our boys were growing up I would tell them: 'Marry any-one. I don't care about the religion. I don't care about the color. I'd prefer if it were a girl.' They said they didn't believe me, but they listened. So Dante met this beautiful Jewish girl from Cherry Hill, and they decided to get married—at the Sheraton Motor Inn. I had to explain to my Dad." (Savy's mother passed on some years ago.)

"I told him that Dante wouldn't be getting married in a Catholic Church [here Savy imitated his father shrugging his shoulders as if to signify his passive role, 'What can I do?'] and that he wouldn't be getting married in a temple, either [another shrug]. I told him that Dante and Francine had decided to be married by a rabbi at the Sheraton Motor Inn." That last bit of news was too much, according to Savy. "At a motel?" his father responded incredulously.

But of course he went to the wedding—as did other family members and friends in a bus Savy rented for the occasion, fearful that half of these insular Bethlehemites would become lost in Philadel-phia if they attempted the long journey to New Jersey in private cars.

Armando Pasqualucci was handed a yarmulkah as he entered the room in the motel where his grandson was to be married. No less puzzled than before, he donned it—as did the other males disem-barking from the Bethlehem bus. At the end of the ceremony he asked the bride's father whether he could keep it. Certainly.

Next day he went to mass at Holy Rosary, knowing he would find his young friend, Father Delrico, in the sacristy. As he entered he donned his yarmulkah and muttered, "Morning, Father." The priest returned his greeting, then noticed the unusual headgear and inquired, "What is that?" "Yesterday my grandson was married in New Jersey by a rabbi, and I wore this during the wedding," Ar-mando answered. "Very nice," observed the Father as he modeled it, then returned it to its owner.

Now Armando had done his duty. He was the first to inform the priest, and the priest in turn had given, if not his blessing, his sign of acceptance.

Nor is Dante entirely lost to his Italian-born grandfather. Though he and Francine have moved to Hollywood, she has assumed the Italian-sounding stage name of Fran Lucci and was employed as an accountant in the production of Sylvester Stallone's *Rocky IV*.

Dante's brother Michael is married to a Southern Baptist. He owns and operates the Pizza Roma, a restaurant in the suburbs of Chattanooga, a fitting occupation since his grandmother prepared

Bethlehem's first commercial pizza for Christie's Hotel under the Hill-to-Hill Bridge.

As we peered outside the family, looking into that mysterious world peopled by multitudes unknown to us, who can say we ignored the messages from our parents—even our grandparents—about the friends we should make and the Americans we should be? Yet at the same time we had to create our own areas of freedom, find our own ways to be at liberty. For some members of the Class of 1952 it merely meant moving across town and settling among the Americans. Others of us had to go as far as California in the search for social comfort.

4 | *School*

"I told my kids that the high school years were the best of your life," Pat Frankenfield observed as we sipped coffee in her kitchen on a bright autumn afternoon. Pat was not a class officer, newspaper editor, sports figure, or member of the high honor society. She quietly worked her way through Liberty, having been raised in a row house around the corner from the school, and she went on to the St. Luke's Hospital nursing program, married, and watched her own two children attend her alma mater. Content now, she recalled the "good times" then, when whe was preparing for a career but unburdened by the kinds of worries that came later.

Similarly, for Joyce Dickson, secretary of the Class of 1952, high school was "a very exciting time in my life, and it ended abruptly." She had prepared for a clerical career, since she recognized that her widowed mother would be unable to put her through college. Quickly bored with the lack of opportunity in Bethlehem, she headed off to New York. She found herself equipped to meet the challenge of the city, but she later made sure her own daughter got a better educational preparation.

Most members of the Class of 1952, in fact, recalled high school with nostalgic fondness. Those days evoke memories of carefree innocence, fast friendships, and demanding challenges. Being at Liberty signified leaving the parochialism of the local junior highs and coming together in Bethlehem's one high school. It was a focal point of the city, and the students responded to that fact with enthusiasm.

That the high school had a broad civic mission was explicitly recognized just a few years before the Class of 1952 entered the elementary grades, when the Bethlehem School Board invited a group of educators from the University of Pennsylvania to examine and report on the city's educational system. In their response was the message that schools were not to purvey abstract knowledge but, rather, social and vocational skills.

> In this city, where raw materials are transformed into steel products, the public schools, and other agencies, are engaged, among other things, in the more difficult task of amalgamating cultures in order to mould a desirable American cultural product. This is the primary responsibility of the Bethlehem public schools.

It was all too obvious to the visiting educators that this responsibility was not being met. They called for a revision of the "antiquated curriculums found in all the schools" and pointed particularly to the high school as an elitist institution which focused far too exclusively on book learning, to the neglect of "household virtues, civic virtues, vocational ability." To prepare students for life in the twentieth century, the high school should be "expected to develop all phases of the personality which are considered important in the citizens of a complex and rapidly changing democratic society."

These phrases have the murky quality of educationese because their authors were unable to acknowledge the dilemma of industrial democracy. In patriotic legend, American society has been and always should be classless, offering equal opportunity to everyone. In reality, job requirements varied widely and job holders were rewarded differently—and all jobs had to be filled.

Without acknowledging this dilemma the educators simply recommended that the "industrial curriculum should be expanded to more adequately meet the employment opportunities offered by the industries of Bethlehem," while simultaneously observing that the presence of several colleges in the city made it "unusually fortunate in its educational atmosphere." Translated, these phrases meant that students would choose their economic and social class position in high school.

When my classmates and I came to Liberty in 1949, curriculum choices were there to be made, but we had no official counseling on their meaning. What influenced students' choices? The answer to this question bears strongly on the controversy among scholars of education today, some of whom argue that public schools equalize opportunity while others assert that the schools perpetuate privilege.

Students in the Bethlehem Public School system were not differentiated by curriculum until the tenth grade, although they were homogeneously grouped by academic achievement in each of the four junior high schools (Washington and Broughal on the South Side, Franklin on the North, Nitchman on the West), a fact of life which could not but affect the choice of curriculum in high school.

A boy entering tenth grade could choose Technical High School on the South Side, where most of its students lived, for training as a draftsman, machinist, electrician, woodworker, auto mechanic, printer, radio repairman, or the like. Vocational training in shorthand, typing, bookkeeping, and so forth, was also available at Liberty High School on the North Side, open to boys and girls, though the latter outnumbered the former in this curriculum almost four to one. Of the Class of 1952, 42.4 percent took the vocational option at either Tech or Liberty, slightly more boys than girls.

For those students aiming at post-secondary education, either college or nursing school, there were academic and scientific curricula; almost a third of the Class took this option. (In the Allentown-Bethlehem-Easton metropolitan area, there were five private colleges — Moravian, Lehigh, Lafayette, Muhlenberg, and Cedar Crest — and two nursing schools — St. Luke's and Sacred Heart.) Here emphasis was put either on mathematics or sciences or on Western European languages: Latin, German, French, and Spanish. No Southern or Eastern European languages were taught, although in Bethlehem there were weekly newspapers published in Hungarian and Slovenian.

The remaining quarter of the Class of 1952 enrolled in the general curriculum, which featured neither a vocational nor a post-secondary orientation. A less demanding course of study, it also promised less for the future. (Of the 210 responses to my questionnaire, 42 percent were from persons in the academic and scientific curricula, 29.3 percent from the vocational, and 28.8 percent from the general.)

Students could hardly have been blind to where their courses were leading (or not leading) them; the question is whether they felt it mattered to consider their choices. The amount of care taken in planning for the future is an index to what an individual expects it to bring. Since the present is the future seen from the past, it is revealing to analyze the precedents which affected the choices made in school.

Those students taking vocational courses belonged to families where there had been minimal contact with formal education: over half the fathers and somewhat less than half the mothers had not attended beyond the seventh grade. Parents of students in the general curriculum had a better record with fewer early drop-outs, although high school completion was unusual: almost three-quarters of them did not go beyond eleventh grade. In the academic/scientific curricula, parents' completion of high school was the rule (67.1 percent of fathers, 55.5 percent of mothers), and college or even post-baccalaureate education was not extraordinary (31.4 percent of fathers and 18.4 percent of mothers had bachelor of arts degrees or more). The reader may remember from chapter 3 Gus Romero's lament: "My father always let me loaf." Then he turned to me and observed: "Your father, maybe he said, 'You're going to college so you'd better work,' and he pushed you."

The correlations between the educational attainments of grandparents and the curricular choices of their grandchildren in the Class of 1952 are not nearly so striking (and the sample is much smaller). Generally speaking, at least 75 percent of grandparents did not complete high school, a figure violated only by paternal grandmothers (71 percent) and paternal grandfathers (59.4 percent) of students in the academic/scientific curricula. (There are no calculations for maternal grandmothers, but also no reasons to think they would deviate from these statistics.) Grandparents did not provide educational models; few of them could, except in a negative sense.

Turning from formal education to occupation, we find the careers of fathers were related to the curriculum choices of children. The most crowded category of jobs for fathers was that of machine operative (32.5 percent of the fathers of Class members fell into this slot), not surprising in a city dominated by the steel industry. Yet two-fifths of the fathers of vocational students ran machines. Only a quarter of the fathers of academic/scientific students were so employed, while a higher-than-average number of them were in professional fields. Looking at mothers we find, as we could expect, that the largest category is housewife (42.9 percent). But mothers of vocational students were far more likely to be found in the home rather than working outside it, probably a reflection of the same traditional attitudes that consigned their children to vocational pursuits.

Place of residence was relevant to choice of curriculum. The academic/scientific students were preponderantly from the North and West Sides of Bethlehem, while the vocational courses recruited more from the South Side, where Tech was located. The general curriculum almost perfectly mirrored the residence patterns of the whole class, and South Siders felt with some justice that Liberty High

School was in alien territory and that their educational backgrounds were inferior to the training of their peers across the Lehigh River.

Ethnicity had some bearing on curriculum choices too. For example, academic/scientific students came at a higher-than-average rate from homes where English was the sole language spoken, while vocational students' homes were more often multilingual. Furthermore, academic/scientific students were somewhat more apt to have a Western European background.

Another relation between family background and curriculum choice seems evident when the size of the household is considered: academic/scientific students came from smaller families than did students in other curricula. (Children with fewer siblings do get more attention from their parents and, therefore, can be expected to be better prepared for school.) Religion no doubt played a part in creating this situation, since Roman Catholics in the 1930s were instructed not to use birth control devices. Only a quarter of the academic/scientific students were Roman Catholic, while almost half the vocational students were (yet only about 30 percent of the general students were Catholic).

It was not, of course, the curriculum alone that shaped the high school experience. Indeed, the student-teacher relationship was almost always a less meaningful one than the interaction between peers. The recommendation by the University of Pennsylvania educators that "civic virtue" be embodied in the classroom work simply missed the point about how students learned. No one expected stimulation from a history session, which was mechanical and boring: read the chapter, answer the questions at the end, and remember your patriotism. Neither international, nor national, nor even local politics were ever discussed.

So how did we learn about "civic virtue"? Through student government. Not because students had power (they didn't) or could be expected to hold larger political office at some future date (they wouldn't), but because student elections reflected the unmentioned class tensions which existed in the community and extended to the school. The two most important offices, president of the class and president of the student council, were invariably held by residents of the South Side. (In the Class of 1952, 31.3 percent of its members came from the South Side, while 52.8 percent came from the North and West sides, with the remaining 15.9 percent gathered from surrounding areas outside the city.)

Liberty Senior Class Officers. *Left to right:* Mrs. Joseph Marx, advisor; Thomas Falcone, treasurer; Joyce Dickson, secretary; Saverio Pasqualucci, president; Edward Townsend, vice-president; John Fuhr, advisor.

Social and economic class solidarity led to victory at the polls, a unity made more recognizable by its regional definition. Students from the South Side nominated one person for one office, while the North and West Sides featured a multiplicity of candidates—after all, people from these areas were taught that they should be leaders. And indeed they were, occupying less visible political posts as well as supposedly non-political but still powerful places where the faculty had a voice in selection, such as editing the newspaper or the yearbook.

Student government, then, was one place where class, ethnic, or religious background was not a disability. Athletics was another. The public turned out in huge numbers for high school sporting events; school board members could be elected or defeated on the strength of their attitudes toward the football team; and athletes were respected. And they were recruited democratically. Both the Lineman and the Back of the Year in our Class were second-generation Americans from the South Side.

Participation in student government and athletics, not to mention literary activities such as editing the school paper or the yearbook, helped students get into college, both because such extracurricular

Liberty Student Association. *First row, left to right:* Peter Haupert, vice-president; Lucille Schneider, treasurer; Earl Evans, advisor. *Second row, left to right:* LaRue Snyder, social activities secretary; Warren Richards, president; Froso Collins, secretary.

undertakings instilled confidence and because they made an impression on institutions of higher education. One of the two major office holders from the Class of 1952 was accepted by an Ivy League university but chose Anapolis, while the other went to Lehigh. Both came from working-class backgrounds and moved on to responsible management positions.

That students were able to overcome economic and social barriers may be attributed to the school's healthy functioning in a society which offers opportunity, or such success may be construed as the way in which education locates and moves potentially dangerous members of the proletariat into the bourgeoisie. The interpretation accepted will depend on the observer's politics. And perhaps only a statistically insignificant number of persons move upward as a consequence of such extracurricular factors. But movement does take place; it is noticed; and that is not insignificant.

Although jobs and career mobility are the focus of the next chapter, it seems natural to wonder here what happened to those persons we had chosen as leaders of the Class of 1952: our president (a boy) and our secretary (a girl, naturally); the best male and female ath-

Class ballot from the *Cauldron*. Biggest apple polishers: Marilyn Castles, Clayton Garland. Most devoted couple: Jo Morino, Don Bittenbender (see chapter 2). Biggest Flirts: JoAnne Olay, John Berry. Largest Smiles: Pat Eddy (see chapter 7), Charlie Hoydu. Class clowns: Marian Wagner, Jim Ramberger (see chapter 4).

SENIOR SHOTS

Class ballot. Most dependable: Gladys Lerch, Tom Falcone. Most likely to be President: Ellen Baber, Buzzy Richards (see chapter 2). Most intelligent: Carol Schrader, Charlie Troutman (see chapter 4). Most typically American: Toni Anthony (see chapter 6), Joe Illick. Best athletes: Pat Rose, Billy Miller (see chapter 4).

Class ballot. Hardest workers: Gertie Lutz, Peter Haupert (see chapter 5). Most talented: Marie Smith, Tom Silvester. Biggest gossips: Ann Leh (see chapter 4), Bill Fox. Contributed most to the Class: Joyce Dickson, Savy Pasqualucci (see chapter 4). Most sophisticated: Lois Cowden, Dick Fryer.

letes; the boy voted brightest in the class; our gossip columnist (another girl, naturally); and the class clown.

————

I began my quest with Class of 1952 President Saverio Pasqualucci. I had not seen Savy since we graduated, almost twenty-five years previously. I phoned him at home, and he immediately invited me over, embraced me warmly when I arrived, and introduced me to his wife Betty Jane, who was part of our conversation. In the course of the evening I met their son Dante, but not Michael (Saverio Junior), boys who are reminded of their heritage by frequent trips to visit families that remain on the South Side of town.

Savy described the most salient feature of his own heritage: the circumstances of his birth. Thought to be stillborn, he was plunged into tubs of cold and hot water, then wrapped up for dead and placed on the living room couch. Here, according to his mother, he suddenly came to life, which he announced by kicking off his covers. In the course of that first evening together, I discovered that in his adult life as well, he had been born again.

SAVY: I will offer this for people who don't have names that fit in with the American kind of thing. Being raised with a name like Saverio Pasqualucci, you tend to be shy about wanting to introduce yourself to people. There was usually some kind of awkward silence. My tendency was to stay with people who knew me. But here I am in tenth grade at Liberty High School—and nobody ever heard of me in junior high school.

But I got to tenth grade and Charlie Navle—who I really didn't know very well—from Broughal Junior High said one day, "They're having elections. I'm going to nominate you." That was one thing I didn't want to be—nominated. Because I was a little bit embarrassed about my name. And Charlie Navle nominated me. I thought, "Who knows me? A couple of guys from Broughal and the Boys Club. I'll get killed." And whatever happened, like the day I was born, somebody voted, and they picked me. Who knew?

That changed something for me. Because my dad would say to me: "It's not the name that makes a man. It's the man that makes the name." So I thought, "I'm going to do this right." Just so my dad would have a sense that his son's done something. Who could aspire to more than that? Well, it meant nothing to him—in front of me. There's something about Europeans, I think—they're proud, but they don't want to let somebody get a big head. About the Bethlehem Steel executives he always said, "They couldn't be that smart to get paid that much."

I found out something in seventh grade—I don't know how, a lot of things in my life are unexplained—most of the kids around me were as afraid as I was. Only I knew they were afraid, and they didn't know I was afraid. So I acted like I wasn't. They were pre-programming themselves to fail. Talking in front of people was the same; if anyone could do any better, they'd be up there.

I used to think that guys like yourself and Jimmy Howell— wow!—I hope I never have to be in the same room and have a discussion while they're talking, because they really know how to say things and put things. Because in our minds— let's face it, we were all at the Boys Club. And all you said was, "I got winner." No big discussion.

Charlie Klein [the principal at Liberty High School] taught me a lot. I found that if you speak slowly enough you can think while you're talking. He sounded like he was so well prepared, but-all-he-was-doing-was-speaking-slowly. And he's still doing it the same way today. Our sons think that's just fabulous.

The problem for young people today is the same as it always was. Nobody knows what he wants to be. I can't think of a guy I know who knew what he wanted to be. I can remember at Lehigh, guys getting ready to graduate, say- ing, "I don't know what I'm going to do." I didn't know either. But it's nothing to be afraid of. I tell my boys not to panic.

I was one year at the Steel in metallurgical engineering. Then I got laid off in July of '58, and for eighteen months I was out of work. If anything gave me an education it was those eighteen months. I found that there wasn't anything I wouldn't do to support my family. I'm almost embarrassed to tell you some of the jobs I had. I think today, though, we're happy because of that experience—I never want to forget those eighteen months. I sold meatball sandwiches at the Allentown Fair; we opened a Hungarian pastry shop; I caddied; I cleaned out the wet pantry at Saucon Valley Country Club. I waxed the ballroom floor, and after the Lehigh-Lafayette game I served my former classmates hot-cross buns in the main dining room. If I was ever feeling a little too big for my britches, that just about took care of it.

Then Savy turned to the issue which interested him the most.

There is a movement in the Catholic Church called *cursillo*. What it is, basically, is a weekend renewal. Have you heard of marriage encounter? It started by sending men away on weekends, and then a week or two later the wives. It basically renewed the tenets of your faith. It wasn't run by priests, it was run by laymen. It had a fantastic effect on my life. I said, "My God, that's what it is I've been looking for. That's what's been missing." I couldn't see what was in front of me. Where is it going? I had not really made any decision — I don't want to sound like Billy Graham — any decision for Christ, for or against or even maybe. Mostly because in our faith, being Catholic, the decisions are made for you. I thought I'd better start living what I professed, or stop professing. It was that basic! We *chose* to profess.

People that I grew up with for years and years, we were all Christians, Catholics. We didn't hear the word of God. With my new friends I have a relationship unlike anything I had prior to that. We have something called the *abrazo*, Spanish for embrace. Men didn't do that. But there was no problem now. My mother was always warm that way. It means a lot of things. *Cursillo* allowed me to take my thoughts and put them into the context of Christian thinking. And I saw that what I thought were my thoughts really weren't at all. Since that time most of what Betty Jane and I have done is oriented by our *cursillo* experience.

We meet on a weekly basis in small groups. We come together and share our thoughts about prayer, study and Christian action. You can ask someone to pray with you and they will. Things really do work out.

I began to *like* church. I began to want to *be* there. When we celebrated the Mass, we celebrated. I began to pray. That's not the right word; I began a dialogue with God. About two years ago the Council of Churches in this area distributed paperback Bibles — *Good News to Modern Man* — to every home in this area. And I began to learn something. Betty would read, I would read, we'd read with these people every week. And talk about God. The priest would sit there and be totally absorbed in what we were saying. The priest admitted to being lonely sometimes. Suddenly the Christian community was there. We loved one another.

Betty Jane and I would talk and pray together. After fifteen years of marriage we'd never prayed together. We still don't pray aloud with each other at all times, but we're inclined to do it. It's not strange, awkward, or embarrassing.

I have seen Savy several times since we resumed our friendship. His two sons have left home, one for the entertainment business in California, the other to set up a restaurant in Tennessee. Savy, too, is thinking about food. His thirty years at Western Electric (now AT&T) will soon be finished and, despite a heart attack in January 1985 — indeed, because of his attack, which gave him time and perspective to plan a future — he is buying a restaurant on the Jersey shore, where Betty Jane has been praying, quite literally, they might move. Both of them see a divine plan in the unfolding of their lives.

Savy and Joyce Dickson, secretary of the Class of 1952, were considered by their peers to have "contributed most" to Liberty High — and were appropriately photographed for the yearbook. At that point their lives diverged. Joyce's parents had left Belfast and Cardiff to settle on the North Side of Bethlehem, but she knew her widowed mother would be unable to send her to college so she chose the commercial curriculum. A cheerleader in high school, she found little to shout about immediately after graduation, a situation she refused to accept.

JOYCE: People in high school thought there was a master plan for life — and with reason! Educators in our society promoted certain modes of living, and there weren't many deviations back in the fifties, that we saw. Probably the people

President Savy Pasqualucci at home with Betty Jane. (Photo by JEI.)

who grew up in the thirties and the forties, they in fact did pretty much follow straight paths. And we, our age group, ran into many segments of society that are spurs. And we had to cope with whether to join, to align ourselves or not.

I definitely thought, as a young girl going into her own life, that there were certain things that I would expect. Of course, they didn't happen. And I had to adjust accordingly. I found it very exciting to be challenged. Terribly exciting. The excitement generally came at a time when things were going pretty flat, and I said, "Wow, is this all?"

When I graduated from high school I stayed in Bethlehem for a few years. Then I moved into an apartment in New York City with a couple gal friends who were there; they were the attraction for coming. It was a bit depressing being in Bethlehem after high school. High school was a very exciting time in my life, and it ended quite abruptly. I really didn't have the structure that a school situation or an organized class had; I just didn't have that structure in my life then. I was very active in school, and I missed that very much. So I really didn't have a good feeling.

I was the product of a very conservative household—and of the society itself. It wasn't often that children just left home and went off on their own. My mother was convinced I was off to the wolves—in New York City on my own.

I went to work for the airlines, which also was rather exciting. I wasn't quite old enough to fly. It was an eye-opener. I did a fair amount of traveling—I went to Mexico and California by myself at nineteen. And many nights up late, an MG-TD—ah! This was a lot more exciting than staying in Bethlehem. But I didn't stay with the airlines very long.

I longed for regular hours, for regimentation in my life. I was working weekends, and friends were inviting me to parties at schools—and I couldn't go. I had made a successful change before, just by moving into the city. So I went to a conveniently located building in New York and asked for a job. It happened to be the American Can Company, and I did get a job. I worked for them for several years and had a lot of fun; work was quite secondary to my social life.

But I began to think that I wanted a job I was more involved with. I finally ended up working with the Chairman of the Revere Copper and Brass Company. I was quite proud of that. It was a very interesting job. I was married, and I left that job in anticipation of having a family. I was going to take some time off before: once you have children, that'll be the end so you better have fun.

And then we did a lot of traveling in our early marriage. Abroad—we skied a lot in Switzerland, Austria. And just did a lot of touring throughout Europe, Scandinavia. My husband was in exhibition work, which he has carried on—now he's a museum designer. Then, he was doing exhibitions for some museums but also for industries. Fascinating projects. But the traveling wasn't part of his job.

We were living on the Upper East Side then. [Joyce took courses at the New School for Social Research, to which she commuted by motorcycle.] When we separated, I stayed in New York for awhile, then Brooke [her daughter] and I moved to Vermont. We stayed there for three years and just last December came down here. I was anxious to come out of my hiatus of the country. I needed a lot more stimulus than Vermont had to offer. I had bought and completely renovated an old farmhouse there over three years.

I'm really anxious and ready to seek a career at this point. I look now at making a choice of an area that I will probably spend a lot of time in from here on. I don't have a need, anymore, for idle time or lots of leisure or things that people long to do. I feel that at this point I've spent a sufficient amount of time in those areas. Now, I'd really like to pursue a career. I'm quite enthusiastic about it.

You have a choice, if you believe the theory that we're masters of our own destiny. I find it difficult to believe that. I do pursue my life with the idea in mind that it can be true. But I know I'm a product of my past environment; it's such a strong factor in my decision-making.

In my search for a career I feel I can lean on a certain pattern in my life. I think that I've been pretty lucky in realizing success in my own pursuits. And though at this juncture I think it may be one of the most difficult and challenging pursuits that I've ever had—and it's going to take a lot more work than anything I've ever done—I think the reason why I'm even addressing myself to it is because I have reached out before, which allows me to do it again at this point.

The first I hear when I go in and talk with any placement counseling is, "You're in the most fantastic spot right now. You're the right age, you've got the right appearance, and they want women. Equal opportunity is right there for you." Everybody is getting really excited about this thing. And I'm saying, "That's great." So I'm really hanging on by the coat-tails and coming along with the women's movement, not having done anything actively at all. I've never been discriminated against because I'm a woman.

Many women my age feel unemployable. And their husbands help this by saying, "What can you do?" They've never worked. Or maybe they worked for three to six months before the Big Wedding. Now they are depressed. They're bored. They don't have anywhere to go. They think of working in a department store! I feel very employable, and I've proven that I am. I have a work background. And I have to say that it has to do with some of my schooling, especially the English courses, that has kept me in there.

Still, it's really too bad that I didn't have more counseling in school. I don't know why that is. My mother raised four of us by herself. My father died when I was in first grade. She had her hands filled and was not a terribly capable person in herself. As a result of it I am the person that I am. I really should have gotten a formal education. I think all I needed was someone to help me along. I was too young to know how to do it on my own or even be aware of how to go about it. I lucked out in that respect. I wasted many years until I really started getting a grasp on what was happening. Maybe I enjoy being a student so much to this day because of this fact.

My daughter's in fifth grade now. And this is the first year that they're having class officers. She has a lot to say about it. She's rather resentful that the brightest boy in the class was *of course* made president. I thought that this might be a good thing to talk about, since that's a whole lesson right there. The teacher explained that each month they'd have a new president. So I said, "Well, would you like to be president." She said, "Yes." And I said, "Campaign."

Joyce is currently the assistant corporate secretary for Iroquois Banks Ltd., a food and beverage company, as well as curator of its art collection, an assemblage of the creations of native American Indians. She is also completing her B.A. at the University of Connecticut at the same time that her daughter Brooke, having spent much of her early adolescence in competitive ice skating but now engaged in the theater, is attending Sarah Lawrence College—where she ran for freshman class president but was edged out by a male!

Joyce led the cheering, but it was Billy Miller who fascinated the fans. His virtuosity on the basketball court was legendary, and rightly so. He was a remarkable play-maker, a dazzling dribbler, a great shot. And he passed so fast and so deceptively that he had to warn his mates that the ball was on its way. For all his individual merit, he was fundamentally a team player. He deserved to be chosen for an all-

Joyce Dickson with the president, 1988. (Courtesy of Joyce Dickson.)

state position at guard, and he was. In the midst of this hoopla about basketball, it was sometimes forgotten that he was an extraordinary all-around athlete, who pitched a no-hitter his sophomore year on the baseball team and lettered in soccer until the football coach convinced him that the Hurricane eleven needed him at defensive quarterback. Through it all he remained modest if not self-effacing.

Under these circumstances no one paid much attention to his academic record until he was ready but unprepared for college. He was not the first Bethlehem High School athlete to go on to Fork Union Military Academy in Virginia, presumably to be prepared for further stardom at a higher level of education. But something more than a patina of learning stuck to Bill at Fork Union and at the University of Virginia, where he played varsity basketball for the three years allowed him.

I journeyed to the tiny southern town of Fork Union to visit Bill and his wife Jell, who graduated from Bethlehem High School a year before us. On arrival, I immediately reminded him that he was voted the best athlete in our class, and that his prowess had never been forgotten in the old home town.

BILL: I think that's probably our own culture — everything's related to athletics. The older you get, the more it's brought up. You don't realize it at the time. When I go home it's the same old thing. "Are you coaching?" "I remember this game, I remember that game." Not "How is so-and-so?" It's just a different world up there, compared to down here.

JELL: It *is* different here. When Bill went to the University of Virginia — we were married, you know, his first year there — we could walk into a basketball game anytime during the game and get a seat. After Bill came there, interest was stimulated because of his play.

BILL: We were backward in Virginia then, the whole South was, on basketball, just like it is now with wrestling.

Our enrollment here — we might get as many as eight kids from the Lehigh Valley, all of whom come without contact from me. As soon as it's an athletic situation, they say, "Bill Miller's at Fort Union. Call him." And I've met people who say, "I followed you all through high school," whether they're from Allentown, or Caty [Catasauqua], or Northampton. It's amazing. It helps us [Fort Union] a great deal. It's strange because it's all people you didn't know at the time — that knew you.

I still officiate, but I dropped the coaching six years ago, after thirteen years. My kids were growing and I wanted to spend more time at home. I still help out a little, because my sons are day students here at the Academy.

I'm happy here. We like the South. Our kids have all been born and raised here. I had a job possibility back at Liberty High School in the 1960s, but none of the kids wanted to leave. And it's the "going back to the old high school" thing that all of us might consider at one time or another: you get back and find you have a good situation where you are. I still get back to work at a sports camp in Allentown.

I'm assistant athletic director here, taking care of the

athletes, trying to steer them straight academically, making sure their courses are set up correctly, trying to help them get into college. And we always have those who are average students who want to go to the University of Penn, for example—a dream. Yet you never know what will happen athletically; it seems everyone has a double policy. They can get in those schools if they're superior athletes.

I came here for a postgraduate year, trying to prepare myself for college. Fortunately, I came out of high school with three years' experience, and at Virginia I played all three years I was eligible. But I had to do other things I had never done in high school, especially against such outstanding ball clubs as Maryland and North Carolina State. One year Carolina won the national championships.

At this point Jell began to list her husband's qualities as a player, while Bill made all sorts of denying hand motions. Finally he intervened.

BILL: I should have had you as a press agent. I never realized. . . .

It all boils down to one thing. Basketball opened doors for me. Without that it would have been back up into Bethlehem Steel, I'm sure. Virginia offered me a scholarship. At that time I was the only scholarship basketball player. We had an All-American, but he was a millionaire. He led the nation in scoring. That was Virginia's beginning in big-time basketball.

But it wasn't the way it is today. It was competitive, but it was more enjoyment than now. The pressure wasn't as great. It wasn't overemphasized; now I think it is. Athletics have to be looked at strongly. It did a lot for me, so I'm not condemning it at all. I think there's a place for everything, but I think it's being overplayed. Now a kid has three hundred on College Boards, a total of five to six hundred on both, and he gets in college, a *good* college! We see it here. And it shouldn't be the case. It's interesting to watch when we came along and now.

What we tell kids here at school is: "You're getting an opportunity through athletics, and athletics are going to end very shortly. You'd better be prepared academically to do

Billy Miller on the court at the University of Virginia. (Courtesy of William Miller.)

something, other than just play ball." Because how many professionals do you get? One out of a thousand—that we never see here. And we find a lot of kids are doing that. A lot of kids are coming here through athletics and leaving here not playing athletics in college. Because they've gotten into college and found they couldn't cut it academically *with* athletics.

I had a long argument one night with Carmen Gallo, Chico. [Chico was a starter with Bill on the Bethlehem High five that won the East Penn League Championship in 1952.] It was interesting along the athletic lines that he was restricting his kids. He's gotten to be a real good golfer. He'd win the championship every year or every other year at the Steel Club. And he has his boys coming up in golf, and that's about the only activity he's pushing. He said, "There's no sense in playing basketball. A white kid's not quick enough to play any more." And he went through all that spiel. And it was real interesting to hear that, because when he was through I jumped on him. Because his job, I think, is like my job: had it not been for high school athletics, he would never have gotten the job he has at Steel in the drafting department. His promotions, I think, were because of people he knew athletically. We had a real good conversation—he didn't believe what I was saying. I thought he was taking something from his children.

We all grew up at the Boys Club—Bob Barber, Billy Maioriello, Joe Hobakus, the Calvos, Pete Carrill [currently coach at Princeton University]. And Camp Mohican was so important.

Our sons are athletes, very much so. And yet the older boy, Billy, who's now in eleventh grade, when he was in fifth through eighth was the outstanding athlete in the whole school. And also the valedictorian of the school. He's been a straight-A student all the way through. And he's playing basketball, football, tennis now—which I'm glad he's doing. And the younger one, Michael, though he's small is very good and plays ahead of his grade.

JELL: And the girls are athletes, too. Patricia made the tennis team at William and Mary the first year she was there. Kathleen plays girls' basketball in high school.

BILL: I look back and feel I was sort of cheated when I was in high school because I wasn't made aware of what was in the future. You took this class because it was an easy way out, you don't have to read too many books for that class, you don't have to write term papers. Then you get in college and find out you're in trouble.

Bill walked me to my car and asked about some former athletes and cheerleaders that were known to have traveled in a fast crowd. He recalled some situations that embarrassed him—accepting an invitation to a "big party" which turned out to be for him, another jock, and two willing women, or a telephone request for homework help in math: "I was just a dummy in class, but I was not such a dummy I didn't know what these girls had in mind." Jell didn't want to return to Bethlehem, and Bill seemed genuinely grateful to her for settling him down. Perhaps, though he didn't say so, she played a role in his turn to the books. And perhaps the seriousness, really the intensity, which was manifest in his athletic accomplishments, inevitably turned to other matters.

Bill and Jell have remained at Fort Union, and one of their two married daughters is there also, the wife of a faculty member and a new mother. Their older son is also teaching, while the younger one is playing college basketball. Bill coaches and officiates but no longer considers himself an active player.

———

Boys' sports were at the center of high school life. But athletics was not viewed as a seemly career for girls, though it was of course assumed that sports would be the casual pastime of any American female. Pat Rose was voted the best girl athlete in the class, a label somewhat like being voted the boy most often seen in the library. But the bookish boy could build a future on his studies. Pat, who lives on the South Side and works at the local Western Electric plant, made it clear that females could go nowhere as jocks.

PAT: Does it bother you if I smoke? My athletic days are gone!

What happened when I got out of high school, and I was still interested in sports? Okay, I went and joined a softball

at Rose (*second from right*) on the court with the Allentown Armorettes. (Courtesy of Patricia Rose.)

team in Allentown, which, again, was a high caliber team—state championships and what have you. And all of a sudden, interest dies again. The home field we had was in Allentown. We had to go through so much trouble just to get a field of our own—men would have priority. Well, we finally got it straightened out, but the thing is, why did we *have* to go through all this?

An amateur men's team doing the same thing would have made out better. There's more done for men. There really is, especially in the city of Bethlehem, a lot of backing for men. You have church leagues, you have *everything*. Even though there are now a lot more sports for women than there had been in high school, it's not as good, it's not as good as it should be. But time will take care of it as far as I'm concerned. It's a lot more today than what we had; it's a big difference.

What makes for the difference is equality. I see every day where I work, discrimination with women. Now the plant, at one time, say the enrollment was five thousand, right? Now they're having a little bit of a problem because of the economy. They only had two women supervisors in a huge plant. So all right, there's been suits against AT&T, right? So now it's tokenism at this point.

All right, the next level below supervisor would be, say, layout. You're lucky if you see as many women layouts. It's again, a matter of time, or if the government keeps pressing. To me it's not right—there are a lot of women up there that are qualified. It's the old story. A man is considered a breadwinner. Fine, I don't argue with that, but what about other people? Regardless of whether they're breadwinner's or not. If you were qualified for a job, why not? Basically, the whole thing is, when you pay union dues, you're asking for protection. I don't think too much of the union leaders.

Pat continues to live on the South Side, work for Western Electric, and not participate in sports. Her response to the recent support for women in athletics was very personal: "It's too late for *me*." A great deal of her spare time is spent traveling, an infraction in basketball but a satisfaction in life.

———

The athlete was a high school hero; the serious student was not. And perhaps for this reason Charlie Troutman, voted the brightest boy in the senior class, entrusted with the editorship of the yearbook, and sent off to Princeton to major in physics, has—and always has had—a casual manner which belies his intellectuality. I have been alternately tempted to regard him as cynical and as unwilling to become engaged because he fears the world will not match his expectations. (His brief autobiography in the Princeton Class of 1956's *Twenty-Fifth Reunion Book*—we were classmates there, as well as at Liberty—supports the latter interpretation.)

I visited him in his apartment on the outskirts of Washington, D.C., where he lived alone, having been married for only a few years in the mid-sixties. He spoke dismissively of his ex-wife and fondly of his daughter. He also discussed his job with the Nuclear Regulatory Agency.

CHARLIE: In '56, as soon as we graduated [from Princeton], I went out to California. My cousin and I used to plot to-

gether when we were nine years old how we would get to
California.

I interviewed two or three places when I was in Princeton.
One of them was IBM—the guys all came in their gray flan-
nel suits and their hats. I said, "I don't want to wear a hat."
And I had this idea I wanted to go to graduate school, too.
What was I going to do—go to a monastery like Wisconsin?
The guys from Hughes came in, and they all looked sun-
burned, right off the beach. And they said, "We'll work you
half time and send you to school if you like." So that's what I
did.

Then after I was there a year and a half, I didn't like it, so
I went to UCLA as a teaching assistant. And I lived happily
ever after—until 1963, when I got married. My wife was
from Hollywood High; her family has an original land grant.
In 1963, they desperately needed people to teach; it was still
post-Sputnik. I went to Long Beach State. But the competition increased—guys were coming from Harvard with Ph.D.'s.
So I went back to UCLA and became another professor's
Ph.D. student. But my five years ran out.

So I went to work for a small systems company in Long
Beach. We did everything: intercontinental ballistic missiles,
health care delivery systems, transportation planning studies
in Vietnam—win their hearts and minds—Navy logistics.
There were only ten people in the company. We didn't do a
smash-up job in anything, but I did have a lot of fun in
Vietnam.

I was there in 1970, doing transportation planning. Travel
in Vietnam was coastal, and the Americans wanted to put in
some roads. We had our own plane, traveled around for a
couple of days, then we went home and started gathering
data. Finally, we recommended what would be the best thing
for them to do. Altogether, we spent seven months or so in
Vietnam. In the morning we'd work on the computer program. At noon we would talk to the American planners, then
in the afternoon we'd talk to the Vietnamese guys. We had
experts on roads, railroads, canals. I handled systems
planning.

The Vietnamese were very interested. The American embassy people, who were also interested, couldn't be there with the Vietnamese. It was decided that if the Americans sat down with Vietnamese, the Vietnamese would not speak out. I got in lots of interesting discussions; there were a lot of smart guys there. It was a pleasant country.

When the missionaries came to Asia in the 1600s, it was the Vietnamese who were most adaptable to Western thought. That's still true. They're a very lively bunch of people. For Southeast Asians they're very energetic and alert. They've been fighting the Chinese for thousands of years. Of course, we went in there with the idea that we were going to save them from the Chinese.

But we weren't political. Everybody was sad to leave their loved ones and go back to their families in the States. I don't remember that we ever lied so much in a proposal as we did in this one — we wanted to stay.

When I came back from that, I thought, "I'm getting out of this small company. I can't stand the guy I work for." The company was not well managed. It lost a lot of money, fooling around with a computer utility. We did have this one Navy contract they hadn't screwed up yet. I worked on that for a while, until I got onto ground transportation, where I thought I'd have more of the work I really enjoy.

While I was there this AEC [Atomic Energy Commission] opportunity came along. It's really been good for me. They had no computers, and they had a lot of foul-ups. I told the guy I had seen that happen, and that I could solve the problems. So I got hired, and he got fired — and I didn't have to make good on anything. Then we had this growth period, and the AEC was split into two parts.

There's the promotional, developmental side of the house, the guys who devise new power systems, new energy systems. Research. But since the products go out in industry — pacemakers, reactors, and so on — there's a regulatory side of it. And the regulatory side was put down here to give them some distance and independence. But Congress decided that wasn't enough, that they needed to be totally separate like the CAB and FAA. So they were made autonomous almost two years ago. And they were made a separate commission.

And the other part, the research and development part, was

made into a NASA-type agency. They're just supposed to go in there with their microscope and test tubes, and build better bombs, etc. But before any commercial usage is possible, a regulatory agency must exist. So we [Nuclear Regulatory Agency] got five commissioners, and I must say they're a very high-toned lot.

I'm an administrator, in charge of computing. Data processing and support division. For these nuclear things a lot of computing goes on, because they haven't done a lot of experiments. They haven't blown up reactors to see how many people get killed. So they make calculations. I've been involved in computers for quite a while. It's administration. We perform a service, like bringing the mail around. We don't usually do the substantive work.

We provide the services: purchase of equipment, running equipment, conversion of programs. Most of the codes, computer programs that analyze what would happen to reactors under stress are developed in the national laboratories under contract—a little awkward for an "independent" agency. Traditionally, the expertise has been at these labs—Oak Ridge, Brook Haven, Argonne, Livermore, Los Alamos, so on. We determine how much business goes to one or to another.

A lot of the work is tied to experimental work, where there's been huge investments—stainless steel pipes and concrete and cement. So you can't replicate these experiments. And Congress explicitly said we couldn't. So the major facilities do the work. We can replicate the theory on computers, to an extent.

If you don't want another drink, let's go over to my girlfriend's. She's expecting us to take her out to dinner.

Years passed before I saw Charlie again, but little changed. He looked as young as ever when he picked me up in his convertible, and at dinner his conversation focused on his daughter, now a senior at Harvard. His job at Nuclear Regulatory Agency was more challenging, but not so fascinating to him as his vacations spent diving for shipwrecks off the Florida Keys.

————

The scene is an elevator in the Nuclear Regulatory Agency, the year 1981, the time 7:00 A.M. Charlie Troutman climbs aboard and is greeted with: "Hi. I bet you don't remember me." It is Ann Leh,

Ann Leh. (Courtesy of the U.S. Nuclear Regulatory Commission. D. F. Dehn, photographer.)

voted "the best source of news" in the Class of 1952 poll for the yearbook Charlie edited. At that time Ann wrote for the school and the city newspapers; now she is turning out the NRA employee newsletter.

I had visited Ann some five years earlier in the cavernous living room of the house she inhabited with her husband, an Anapolis grad and career Navy man, and five sons in prosperous Potomac, Maryland. At that time she was employed by the Bechtel Company.

ANN: I'm editing the Bechtel Company news, and I'm editing the final safety-analysis report for the Grand Gulf Nuclear Station, to be submitted to the NRC [Nuclear Regulatory Commission], which is very much combining the two things that I did in high school: academic emphasis in math and physics and then the gossipy journalism. It's kind of interesting that twenty-five years later I'm being paid for doing what I enjoy doing most, for doing the same thing that I did when I was in high school.

Writing is always something I've enjoyed doing since I was in high school. I wrote a lot when I was in college, and of course, I worked for the *Globe-Times* after I got out of college. But then when I got married I was very much the Navy wife and involved in writing activities as far as publicity for Navy organizations and doing wives' club newsletters and Cub Scout newsletters and that kind of thing.

But it wasn't until about eight years ago that I became more of a professional person on my own, writing for the *Hartford Courant*. And then came down here—it took awhile to get back into a writing job because at the time we came down here the Washington *Daily News* had just folded and people interested in writing jobs were a dime a dozen. So I worked for a personnel agency for awhile and then got into the writing end of it.

We got very involved in town government and in politics when we were up in Connecticut. My husband Dave, as a result, is going to law school at night. I ran unsuccessfully for office when we were up there. I'm nonpartisan. I consider myself a conservative, but in a lot of my views, I'm probably a liberal. I was debating the recognition of Red China on the affirmative side in college, and I firmly believed in it. We are registered Republicans.

For the Bechtel Company, I write the typical kind of in-house thing: interviews with employees and editorials on civic topics like voting. Then also technical editing of documents regarding the final safety analysis report, probably sixteen volumes of maybe four hundred pages that will be submitted to the NRC for their final approval of the Grand Gulf Nuclear Station in Port Gibson, Mississippi. That's why I was interested. I had no idea Charlie Troutman was in this area or with NRC.

There's certainly a need for young people's books about the nuclear industry, which is badly misrepresented in the press. A lot of people believe that nuclear plants can blow up and take whole communities with them, but that's not what's going to happen. [Her statement antedated Chernobyl.] The major problem is disposal of high-level nuclear radiation waste. I judge for the Pennsylvania high school press association on feature writing and short stories. This year there were several antinuclear articles and stories. These kids say some very far-fetched things. It's a concern, because it is detracting from the industry which pays my salary—Bechtel.

You do have a citizen activism today, which is a relatively new phenomenon in American society. I'm not that strong an advocate of the women's movement across the board because I feel it's being very destructive to the American family. I think the family is the important basic unit of society, and I think it is being weakened. Maybe not so much with us but with people in their early twenties today who have an entirely diffferent view, many of them, of marriage and responsibilities and family and so forth. I foresee a problem in this regard.

The danger to the family is the lack of the traditional structure, of the mother being home. I didn't go back to work full time until after Chris was in first grade. And although I leave the house before he does, I usually call him when I get to the office, which is only ten or fifteen minutes from here. There are so many girls today, they take off two weeks when the child is born. I'm not so sure that's a good situation. I think if the wife is working and independent you have a much greater tendency, if you have a fight with your husband, to say, "So leave!" I'm not sure how the family will survive when you eliminate the need for staying together. I don't know whether a shaky marriage situation is a better background than a separated situation.

I enjoyed being a mother and a homemaker very much. I'm not sure but that the younger girls I work with have more misgivings. The girl who is pregnant and giving up her job is much more conscious of "giving up" something than I was.

I think the women's movement contributes to the weakening of the family. On the other hand, I feel that women must have their full rights. To me anything else is ridiculous. By the same token, we must have safeguards for child support, protection for the woman who remains in the home and doesn't work for twenty years, her husband leaves for a chick in the office—what does she do for pension rights or going out and getting a job for which she has no current training?

Bechtel is 90 percent men. Until recently—the last five years or so—most women who worked for Bechtel were not at the professional level. I share an extension with a man; it is assumed, if I answer, that I'm his secretary. One guy in particular is going to have his ears singed one of these days; he is only thirty, and young enough to know better than to ask me to go look for my phone mate.

After being down here, I found I could not go back to being a Navy wife, in terms of mornings of coffees and luncheons and serving for Navy League. I was talking to a friend of mine the other day, and we used to be very, very close. She is a Navy wife. It's just not quite the same. Dave's getting out in June; her husband's staying in and they're moving with a daughter who's a sophomore in high school. I wouldn't do that; I don't think it's fair to the kid. There are lots of things as important in life as promotions and getting ahead. I guess I reached the point a couple of years ago where establishing roots became very important. And I'm satisfied here.

Ann's husband, Dave, did in fact retire from the Navy and, with a law degree, has moved into the private sector. But four of their sons have followed his footsteps to the Naval Academy; the fifth, like his mother, attended Penn State.

Soon after I first visited her, Ann secured a job at the White House, replying to letters that required personal (as compared to formula) answers. "I'm sure I was the only Republican precinct chairman hired by Jimmy Carter—but then we know his staff didn't do its homework very well." As noted earlier, she has since moved over to the Nuclear Regulatory Commission to edit its employee newsletter. "I think this is where I started back in high school," she muses.

———

Back in high school Jimmy Ramberger, who later attended Anapolis with Ann's husband, had something funny for every occasion. His humor was quick, playful, calculated to delight his audience at no one's expense. We came to know one another when we joined the fraternity together our sophomore year, and we shared the excitements of adolescence—smoking when cigarettes were daring, drinking (not a lot) when alcohol was forbidden, wisecracking when sobriety was expected, talking about sex and feelings (but mainly sex) in a serious way that boys did not (then) often engage in with one another.

He lived with his divorced mother in an apartment above a drugstore, his older sister and brother having already made their ways into the world. Neither of us ever acknowledged that there were differences between our backgrounds. Yet toward the end of our senior year, when he held a job at the Ford agency close to the high school, I sensed a bitterness creeping into his words, which said: "All you guys are able to go off to college because your parents will pay, and I'm going to be stuck here." He was voted Class clown, but I can't recall that he attended Senior Class Night, where the award was made. If he wasn't there, it was totally unlike his usual self, for he took part in all activities and was expected to amuse us.

JIM: During the last days of high school, I felt down in the dumps, unhappy because of the ending of an era. I felt quite unsure of where I was going at that time. Most of my close friends were going to college. No one in my family had graduated from college. All my friends seemed to have well-defined goals. I was very unsure of myself and unhappy that high school was ending. I was looking into a pit.

I saw the trip to Oregon [to work in a lumber mill the summer after our senior year] as a way of making some money so I could go to Penn State. The trip wasn't really remarkable, except that we [Jim and three classmates] literally were on our own—and we survived. It was the first adventure of all our lives. Jimmy Howell made Oregon his home, and I planned on going back there. When Buzzy Richards heard that I was "on the loose," he called his mother and other people in Bethlehem because he was worried about me. I was touched by his concern. I moved into his mother's house and got advice from Mr. Klein and Mr. Chiles [the principal and assistant principal at Liberty High School]: "Get an appointment to the Naval Academy, stay in Bethlehem, take courses at Moravian."

I did get a third alternate appointment, and the principal and first two alternates didn't make it. I was working in a bakery, in a meat-packing place, selling Christmas trees—anything. Three days before classes started at the Academy, I was notified of my appointment. Naturally, it seemed like an opportunity. I asked them if you had to work nights there, they said, "no." It sounded like a good deal.

Bill Heske [Liberty High School, Class of 1953] and a couple of other guys and I piled into a car, went off to Anapolis, and reported in. That changed the direction of my life.

I hated the Academy. It was a terrible adjustment for me, I think particularly because I had had a year on my own. Cadets work out better if they haven't had any independence. I looked on it as a government scholarship, but I didn't realize that it was going to be a $40,000 education shoved up my ass a nickel at a time.

The first summer, like any military boot camp, they run you, and sweat you, and indoctrinate you. Then the upper classmen return, and the hazing begins. There's not a man that doesn't think of getting out.

But in the back of my mind I supposed it was really a good influence—who knows? I thought maybe I really wouldn't finish any college or amount to anything unless I stuck it out. After the first year it wasn't bad. You get into an academic and social rut, and you just roll along in it. Bill and I were good for each other, keeping a sense of humor and talking about our survival tactics. It amazed a lot of people—Bill was a rebel, and I was a clown. There were about six or seven others from this town who were more affluent, of better background, that didn't make it. It also astonished a lot of people that we made careers in the Air Force.

There was no Air Force Academy then, and both of us thought lives at sea were confining, potentially damaging to our families. Maria and I have spent seventeen of our nineteen years together. In the Navy, husbands and wives typically spend 50 percent of their time apart. Divorce is common.

I think being around people like you and Jimmy Howell—and your families—helped me aspire to better things. When I was at the Academy, I sensed that if I dropped out I'd become a bum—well, maybe not a bum, but I probably wouldn't get a college degree. Sometimes I thought: "This place is so bad it must be good for me."

And it was. Out of the Academy I got discipline; that's drummed into you. The military talks about "The Message to Garcia"—it finally seems like a cliché. But I believe it. I do what I'm told if I believe in it. Though you don't always have that alternative, as they learned at My Lai.

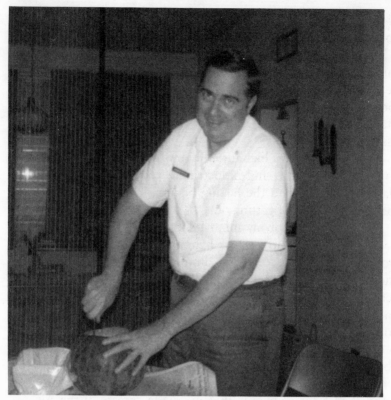

Class clown Jim Ramberger still cutting up. (Courtesy of James Ramberger.)

I also learned responsibility and respect for doing a job well and that sort of thing. But at the same time I've kept my sense of humor, kept my perspective. I'm not a martinet but probably one of the most liberal career officers. I'm a very popular officer. I believe in participatory management, not kick-in-the-ass management, as most of the military does it.

However, I'm not in a purely military situation. I'm in support, not primary mission. In a sense, we're looked down on, seen as low in the military class structure. (I was physically washed out of pilot training). I've been in counterintelligence for nineteen years.

It's a handicap to be a popular officer. It's unusual to be popular among the men. Your peer group and your superiors resent it. A lot of them can get things done only by threatening and punishing. There are options in the military for enlightened management. But I don't believe that I'm typical in taking these options. And I've had only an average career because of my nonconformity. I feel I've never sacrificed my integrity or given up my perspective by abusing my power.

I'm in the Office of Special Investigation. When I'm assigned to a base, I go there as a sort of tenant. I'm not part of the local command but more like an "inspector general." But only part of my job is keeping an eye out for white collar crime. I'm also in the business of catching spies. I'm not really involved in collecting intelligence information but stopping enemies who have gathered information from us.

This is a very touchy political thing right now. Military intelligence agencies are prohibited from collecting any information at all on civilians unless there's a direct threat to our mission. I think that's a good restraint; a lot of my contemporaries do not. During the Vietnam protests, the Army intelligence agents did exceed the restraints—and they were hammered for it. Five years ago Congress passed a law embodying those restraints which, for me, translates to an Air Force directive.

I have to keep a rein on my subordinates sometimes. I'm appalled by the points of view of some of my subordinates— and peers. We're constantly told we are run by civilians. (I'm responsible to the Secretary of the Air Force and the Secretary of Defense.) A lot of military people don't like that, especially among the higher officers. I've never met anybody who thinks of a military coup, but once a guy makes general he thinks that he's omnipotent in some way and not answerable to anyone.

Of course, I exist outside that chain of command by the nature of my job. Even socially, Maria and I don't have to participate. It's the right sort of work for a person like me.

I should add that the jurisdiction of OSI also includes criminal investigation, that is, crimes against persons or property. That's how I happened to be involved in the celebrated Matlovich case. You may recall that he was a Tech Sergeant in the Air Force who surprised his superiors with a letter saying: "I am a homosexual. I have been a practicing homosexual for three years. I know that the Air Force doesn't permit homosexuals. But I maintain that I've been a loyal soldier for twelve years and continue to be and still be a practicing homosexual."

Automatically, OSI was called in. Sodomy is a crime against a person. I was the chief officer at Langley Air Force Base, so it was up to me to run some checks—I interviewed Matt five times, read him his rights, and I interviewed others as well—to see that he was what he purported to be in his letter. We were rather distrustful of the ACLU, as everyone in the intelligence business is. We felt ACLU might be using Matt as a spokesman. But he swore that he had engaged in acts of sodomy while on active duty.

The cause célèbre was fighting it through our courts to say that here is a man who has twelve years of unblemished service, including a tour of Vietnam in which he was wounded and, he claims, it never affected his performance in any way. He fought the battle to stay on for months in court, and he lost.

I believe the military position is correct, that he couldn't function, couldn't give orders to young heterosexual males and have them respond, as a practicing homosexual. I believe the life force gives us sexuality for the purpose of reproduction, and I do consider it deviant or aberrant to seek your own gender. I'm not qualified to judge or condemn someone who does not conform to heterosexual behavior, but I think there's something wrong with them—whether it's physiological or psychological, or maybe a little bit of both. The strongest word I'll use is "unnatural."

Most homosexuals I've known—and I've interviewed a lot over the last nineteen years—really wish they weren't. Maybe you get into social pressures here also. Without social pressure, they might not feel bad about being homosexual.

Maria and I have talked a great deal about getting out of the service. After this upcoming three-year tour [as chief of Air Force counterintelligence in Panama] I'll be eligible for retirement. A lot has to do with whether I get promoted or not. I've reached a medium success plateau of lieutenant colonel. About 10 to 20 percent of us go to full colonel. The odds are against my promotion, and I'll probably get out. I really would like to live in one place for a while, have more stability. I don't really have any well-defined goals, and I'm not trained to do much except tell people what to do. Now there's a market for that. Two of my ex-bosses are with an oil company, and I could go there too, probably at about $20,000 per year. With my retirement pay of $15,000 to $20,000, that would be a living wage. I have one daughter starting college and three coming on close behind.

I have some loosely defined goals, probably not worth exploring. Well, I'll bare my soul to you a little bit. I've always kept my sense of humor. And one of the things I've studied diligently over the years is literature, including grammar and vocabulary. And I really would like to write, principally fiction. I'm counting these first twenty years as a collection of experiences. Some of my favorite writers are Mark Twain and Will Rogers; naturally, I don't aspire to anything that great. But I want to spend my forties, fifties and sixties writing humorous fiction. I've taken a number of creative writing courses, but I haven't published anything.

In these courses sometimes I take myself too seriously, and the material is serious. I think I'm best suited for taking a warped look at the world. I want to market that view and enjoy writing. I want to see whether my outlook is worthy of publication and whether I can make a living on it. In my darkest moments this is what I tell Maria I want to do.

The independence is appealing; to support myself by writing is intriguing. I've compromised this feeling by opting for the stability of the military.

Jim Ramberger was not promoted to colonel and consequently retired from the U.S. Air Force in February 1978, but not before he got his first submitted piece of writing, a humorous account of going to the racetrack in Panama, published in *Turf and Sport Digest*. After writing but not finding a publisher for a novel of comedy and suspense about an ex-intelligence man and an ex-cop, he took a job as a junior high school mathematics teacher.

His "refuge and passion," however, was chess, which he had been playing and studying for years. In a letter he described the evolution of his approach. "The mist is lifting and occasionally I see brilliant truth that was hidden from me entirely. If you'll pardon the comparison, I liken it to our old friend Spinoza's view of knowledge: I passed through 'opinion' with no trouble and got mired in 'reason' for a long time. Only recently have I been able to catch glimpses of 'intuition,' the final stage which enables one to see the whole fabric."

In the autumn of 1985, hospitalized after a heart attack and struggling to recover, Jim died.

———

While we were in high school, Jim and I worked out a comedy routine which we performed for our peers. As befitted the class clown, he took on the comic role while I played the straight man. And, indeed, I had become serious in high school after clowning around in the classroom for nine years. "Acting out" is the term psychologists use. My adjustment from family to school life was remarkably slow and is painful to remember. I was often unhappy.

On the first day of school my cousin Winnie, who as a second grader would share a room and a teacher with me, accompanied me down the long front walk from the concrete highway to the new brick edifice. By 1939 the eight-grades-in-one-room schoolhouse had become an anachronism in eastern Pennsylvania; the Public Works Administration was replacing it with an expanded, eight-grades-in-four-rooms model. Anyone who lived within a mile of Center Valley School walked to and from school in patrol. The others were bussed back and forth from their farms, except a few of us—outsiders, somewhere in time between an old gentry and the forthcoming suburbanites—whose parents had the time, the dedication, and a second car to pick up and deliver their children.

But the public school is a leveler. On the playground my superiority was evident only in marbles. I could hold my own in the many contests where legs were the only equipment needed. But as soon as a ball and bat became part of play, I was less than competent. And although I could defend myself fairly well, fighting made me feel bad.

My real problem, however, was in the classroom. I was so used to the attention of my elders at home that on the first day of school, whenever Miss Wentz said, "It's your turn," I jumped up to answer. Time and again I sat down in embarrassment as I realized, or was told, that someone else had been designated. Soon I shed my shame and, because I could easily out-talk most of my peers, competed with my teachers to be at the center of the class. And since there were two grades to a room, the teacher had to divide her attention, giving me more opportunity to act out.

Of course, ultimate power lay in the teacher's hands. Kindly Miss Wentz often isolated me in the lonely cloak closet at the rear of the classroom. Miss Hassen, leader of grades three and four, was less forgiving as she dismissed me to the hall and issued me a "D" in deportment, much to my mother's amazement. (Mother was really ambivalent about my antics. On the one hand, I was instructed to behave because unruly conduct reflected on home training and parents. On the other hand, almost anything I did was so amusing that it couldn't be wrong. Dad seemed unaware that I had any problems at school. Aunt Mary, Mother's sister, outright encouraged mischief. The other adults at home, if they knew what was going on, usually did not comment.)

By the fifth grade I had prevailed upon Mother and Dad to let me transfer from Center Valley to the Coopersburg school, a move accompanied by a warning about conduct from my parents. The first day I slipped a slingshot into my lunch pail, thinking my new classmates would be amused and respectful. But my reputation would finally depend on my dealings with Mrs. Johnston, the sixth-grade teacher. I can't recall how quickly we became enemies, but it seemed as though we were locked in combat for years; it was surely a symbiotic relationship.

Mrs. Johnston, the principal would later tell my distraught mother, was a childless, unhappy divorcee who must be tolerated. I was (at least in her eyes) a carefree smart aleck. She would make a statement in class, and I'd contradict her. She would come outside and call, "Recess is over; don't kick that ball again." I'd pass it to a confederate, get penalized, and plead that I hadn't *kicked* the ball and was being treated unfairly. My peers approved, and my cousin John, a mischief-maker like his mother, encouraged me in this classroom warfare. Mrs. Johnston retaliated by keeping me inside during recess. I refused to complete my arithmetic workbook. She had the industrial arts teacher fashion her a paddle, which she applied liberally to me. I smiled. Inside, I sometimes wept.

School was becoming more and more unpleasant for me. Both Mrs. Johnston and I were happy to have sixth grade over with; it had been an awful year. In addition to our running conflict, I lost my two closest friends. One moved to Pittsburgh; the other died. I began to confront my classmates and I felt terribly alone.

Seventh grade proved no happier. Twelve grades were in one building at Coopersburg, and the teachers were privy to each other's problems. My behavior was common knowledge, and I was not highly regarded. That year also brought an influx of pupils from surrounding farm areas who had heretofore attended smaller schools, classmates quite unknown to me. The atmosphere seemed alien and hostile, and I was distressed. So I continued my old tricks.

My nemesis now became Miss Kemmerle, a history teacher who roomed at the same private residence as Mrs. Johnston and, no doubt, shared her opinion of me. She taught well, a quality rare enough at Coopersburg for me to be able to recognize it, yet she sniped at me with venomous accuracy and actually did reduce me to tears on one or two occasions. Mr. Price, on the other hand, quelled whatever energy I might have invested in his courses. He did not dislike me but, rather, reacted to me with insensitivity. He read a geography exam of mine aloud to the class as an example of the "biggest bluff" he had ever seen (which, given the competition, wasn't saying much). He had me stand on a desk in front of the fifty-odd members of the ninth grade and, starting with my scuffed shoes and working up to my uncombed hair, gave a talk on bad grooming. Mr. Reider, the science teacher and sometime basketball coach, regarded me as a "wise guy" he didn't want on his team.

I found a friend in my math teacher, Miss Arnold, perhaps because I was quick at and interested in her subject. And maybe, as the only Jew on the faculty, she recognized another outsider. The precocity that repelled other teachers may even have appealed to her. Then, when I entered ninth grade, Mr. Taris joined our ranks, fresh from the staff of a reform school. I did well in his Latin class, and he appointed me — a freshman — feature editor of the high school newspaper, a challenge I was able to meet. But Mr. Taris left in the middle of the year, Miss Arnold married (and seemed less interested in me), and I pressed my parents to let me transfer to school in Bethlehem.

Throughout my troubles the Coopersburg principal, Mr. Watkins — a stern moralist, an unbending leader in a community where every instinct was to be lax, an old-fashioned man in his brown three-piece suit and rimless glasses, who in retrospect reminds me of Woodrow Wilson — counseled and consoled my Mother while inspiring in me feelings of fear, respect, awe, and admiration in varying proportions. Now my parents told me that they and I would be deserting Mr. Watkins if I left Coopersburg for school in Bethlehem. (Surely he must have felt otherwise!) But I managed to prevail with the promise that this time I would really behave—or return to Coopersburg in ignominy.

Thus my being "at Liberty" was charged with meaning for me. I not only fled Coopersburg; I was captivated by Bethlehem. The friends I made at the country club lived there. And Liberty High School, which I would enter as a tenth grader, was legendary in my mind. My father had been one of its finest students, graduating in 1924. He was large enough to make the scrub football team and had drawn cartoons for the yearbook which my brothers and I often looked through. When he entered the high school, or so he recalled, all students had had to memorize the mottoes above the six side doorways, the words of venerated philosophers. The building was constructed in the classic tradition, with an intimidating entrance. LIBERTY HIGH SCHOOL was engraved on a frieze supported by four Corinthian columns, standing two stories high, through which one passed to enter the marble lobby of a vast auditorium. How could a fourteen- or fifteen-year-old measure up to this impressive architecture? Or to his 6'3" father?

I felt small, almost cowed by the hugeness of the place. It corresponded in size to the nearby football stadium, often jammed to its 16,000-person capacity and always overflowing on those chilly Thanksgiving days when the Bethlehem Red Hurricane battled its blood rival, the Allentown Canaries—my mother's alma mater! After the game Phil Phillippi and his wife Dorothy would come to Coopersburg for dinner. Phil had been a star athlete when Dad was on the scrubs. Now he was the high school athletic director, as well as an accomplished storyteller, and he always brought to dinner the most recent team gossip. He and Dad would reminisce about the golden days as my brothers and I eagerly hung on every word. When I went off to Bethlehem High, it was like entering Valhalla.

I expected to work hard. I faced my teachers as educators, not as competition. The challenge was in the studying, an about-face in my attitude but, given the changed circumstances and that ever-present adolescent striving for identity, not so hard to understand. My mother and the assistant principal had set up a heavy academic load for me, and I meant to carry it. After nine years, I was ready to begin school.

And I did well. In my sophomore year I studied Spanish with Señora Baker, who seemed fussy in her demand that we always speak the language in class; but years later I passed my Ph.D. Spanish exam with no more preparation than my two years with her. Latin II was taught by Mrs. Funk, who fostered competition by seating us according to our most recent grades, held the highest standards of academic performance, lectured on Roman history, and pried into our personal affairs. I rose from a "C" the first quarter to obtain one of the highest grades in a standardized test administered at the end of the year, which surprised Mrs. Funk more than it did me.

Mr. Cook, my laconic homeroom teacher, made demands in Plane Geometry (again, I was so slow at first that I thought I was studying Plain Geometry) which equalled those of Latin class. Miss Harrison taught English in an old-fashioned, iron-handed way, much to my advantage. Our biology teacher, dapper Mr. Jones, though his major interest was youthful female anatomy, was seldom so distracted in class as to neglect daily assignments, the result being that I compiled a thick notebook of drawings and explanations.

Outside the classroom, though my overwhelming desire was gridiron stardom, I satisfied my 120-pound self with hawking programs at the home games and fantasizing about my nonexistent football prowess as I fell asleep each night. In the winter, however, I joined the swimming club, led by super-energetic Coach Martz, and in the spring I made the tennis team, thanks to country club summers and the fact that the city of Bethlehem had so few public courts. Coached by Mr. Kernan, a low-key and humane fellow who was smoking himself to an early death as he drove us to matches in Reading, Allentown, and Easton, I played enough matches to earn a letter and attend the athletic banquet with the football players. I felt comfortable at Bethlehem High.

And I began to pursue my studies somewhat less rigorously. Physics was reputed to be the toughest course in the school, taught by a universally feared man who disciplined his students as relentlessly as he drove his track team and who virtually barred girls from his classroom. My father had taken the very same course and emerged with honors, a burden Mr. Emery immediately laid on me—and I responded by doing as well. But my Algebra 2 teacher, Mr. McLernon, observed in a moment of disgust that I wouldn't make it into one of the state normal schools. Meanwhile, I had become occupied with extracurricular affairs—class committees, a fraternity, and girls.

The high school fraternity lay at the center of my social life. I was thrilled to be asked to join, more than willing to wear the painter's cap with Phi Delta Kappa on the visor, and a red-ribbon bow tie to school during the month-long initiation, and happy to endure the humiliating hazing that made me a full-fledged brother. That the constitution excluded Jews and blacks never entered my serious consideration. This was a gathering of the like-minded: upper middle class in composition (though with an occasional invitation thrown out to an upwardly mobile expatriate of the lower ranks), neither sports nor academic achievement nor even country club membership qualified a boy to join, though money did help make him visible.

Every Monday night we met at the home of one of the members, whose parents were expected to absent themselves. We sang the fraternity song ("Hail to thee, Phi Delta Kappa/Loyal we will be . . . "); conducted a short business meeting to decide where we should have our next hayride, barn party, or dance, and how we would finance it; then turned to the major attraction of the evening, a long poker game during which we drank sodas and smoked cigarettes. At the end of each academic year we spent a week at some lake in the Poconos—seldom would the proprietor be so unwise as to rent us cabins the following June—where we drank beer, played more poker and plenty of adolescent pranks, and laid plans for an overnight visit to one of the vacationing high school sororities. At the time I could imagine no greater experience than being a member of the fraternity.

I entered my senior year with a superior academic record, a feeling of self-confidence, and antisocial behavior no worse than the occasional smoking in the lavatory. It was surely one of the happiest times of my life. I was president of my homeroom, a member of the Class executive council, sports editor of the yearbook, second man on the tennis team, place-holder in the regional swimming meet, Lions Club Boy of the Month, and president of the fraternity. My steady girlfriend, a member of our sister sorority, was a straight-A student who seemed perfect for me. It was a world I never wanted to leave.

There is, I realize, considerable testimony to the effect that the high school experience is awful—destructive to the sensitive, dulling to the creative, boring to the intelligent. I believe, however, that few members of the Bethlehem High School Class of 1952 remember those years as trying ones. Even persons who feel on reflection that they were victims of bad counseling, poor teaching, or plain indifference would add that they did not recognize these faults at the time. Few of us were contemplating what life might have in store for the unready. Indeed, our innocence, our lack of awareness, our "not knowing"—a state of being fostered by the times and encouraged by parents and teachers—may have been the very aspect of our lives which made them happy.

There are many ways this naiveté could be documented. None is more revelatory than our attempts at poetry. Self-expression was a demand seldom placed upon us. The best students could read, remember, and regurgitate—or work problems. Some church youth groups sponsored discussions of matters important to adolescents ("Is petting moral?"). We knew we had feelings about other persons, and that these took on a certain intensity when the snow melted and the flowers bloomed. Thus, when asked by our teachers to write verse, some of us responded with a sort of doggerel based on three major themes: religion (how God cared for us), nature (what spring awoke in us), and romantic love (the unattainable person—or how what was awakened in us must be repressed; yes, petting was immoral). These sincere but saccharine effusions were usually the creations of girls.

Boys were more apt to choose other topics, based on competition or justice. I found it safe to satirize the conventional themes, not showing feelings but hiding them. Cleverness carried its own rewards: teachers could not help but notice it, fellow students found it amusing. I could be serious; we all could. But we did not know how to express our deepest concerns: What was love? How was love related to sex? And, that most disturbing of all questions, What was death? We were informed that religion gave us all the answers. (One of my longer senior papers was a review of Fulton Ousler's *The Greatest Story Ever Told*, which I found "wholesomely inspirational.") Thus, we were implicitly instructed not to think about those deeper concerns, except within conventional boundaries. Cleverness was a relief from such confinement without being a challenge to it.

Furthermore, cleverness—plus rudimentary skills in English, Latin and math—enabled me to excel in standardized tests. And this achievement, abetted by a wide range of extracurricular activities, qualified me for a reputable university—where, again, cleverness would be a basic tool of survival. An original thought, a penetrating insight into one's self or society, these were unnecessary qualities, sometimes better suppressed than voiced. But suppression was not a problem I needed to face. I look backward with a rueful smile. As a high school senior I wrote my sociology paper not on class or ethnic divisions in Bethlehem but on the development of swimming. My year book photo is accompanied by the observation that I "made a splash in all social circles"—on the North Side of town, that is. It was an unexamined and protected existence.

When I considered college my preference was for a coed institution that would allow me to continue my high school experience. Higher education was not the goal of a preponderant number of my classmates, and those fortunate enough to go on often attended Penn State or, if their parents had enough money, a more prestigious university such as Cornell. Otherwise they stayed at home, as my father had, and enrolled at Lehigh or Moravian.

While I looked for a place that would be an extension of Liberty High, my parents had their eyes focused on Princeton. My mother's father had gone to its theological seminary, and she half believed that if I, her eldest son, matriculated at the college I might follow Papa's pious path as a preacher. Dad agreed on Old Nassau, since the prospect of an Ivy League school close to home pleased him, and his building business made it affordable. I was lukewarm to the idea but, ever obedient, applied for admission and tried my hardest on the College Boards, secretly hoping I would be rejected by Princeton but accepted elsewhere. When I was admitted I was both dismayed and proud. But, most of all, I was dutiful. I went.

Once on the campus, I found it difficult to respond to the Princeton spirit. Like my grandfather, I missed the familiarity of home and returned often. I longed for my high school, where I had been an important figure; at Princeton I felt insignificant. Furthermore, the university's many traditions seemed pretentious, its social life too urbane, and its academic standards too imposing. I was unhappy, sure I had made the wrong choice of a college, yet equally certain that I must remain and see it through. Fortunately, my first judgments were not entirely on the mark. And the fellowship of the swimming team, the comradery of the small group of civil engineers I took classes with, and the intimacy of some lasting friendships turned Princeton into a much more comfortable place.

Still, what made the experience most valuable was the *dis*comfort which I felt while traversing unfamiliar academic, social, and even emotional territory. By Princeton's standards I was unsophisticated both in the classroom and outside it. I had chosen engineering as a major because my father advised me it was most useful; the university demanded exposure to the impractical liberal arts. While I often stumbled through this curriculum, I also glimpsed vistas I had never noticed before—and became painfully conscious that my religious faith was slipping away.

I recall vividly a seminar on the Old Testament in which a student raised a question about the truth of the Scriptures that I could not answer. I had been warned about college professors in Sunday School, but I had not been cautioned about my peers. In a very short time nothing of the Coopersburg Moravian Church was left but memories; I felt desolated. But as I lost my religion, I gained new perceptions of literature, art, and history. My identity began to change, ever so slightly.

Still, the codes of social behavior at Princeton never seemed quite natural. I was able to mimic but never to absorb the prevailing manners, hard as I tried. Still, it was important for me to note the relativity of social mores, for that recognition also heightened my awareness to worlds beyond the one from which I was slowly emerging.

During four years at Princeton I was able to adapt and respond enough to survive and even enjoy myself. Prodded to reach for ideas, feelings, and behavior which were previously mysterious or unknown, I was forced to push past some conventions that I previously thought were immovable and timeless. I now feel grateful to Princeton for disrupting my life. While the Theological Seminary had furthered Papa on his pilgrimage, the university helped me embark on something of an odyssey.

Yet it was at Liberty High School that the adventure began. Here I realized I must be a serious student, a response to warnings (based on previous disciplinary problems) from both my parents, neither of whom had encouraged me to be at Liberty. None of us could realize how my experience there would affect me, though it's clear that I already was certain that I would attend college, as my parents had, and that when it came to choosing a university in my senior year, their preference swayed my decision. Of course, it was not their expectation that Princeton would influence me as it did. But then neither was I aware of the small steps from liberty to freedom.

5 | *Work*

Gere Bodey had guided me through his department at Houston's M.D. Anderson Hospital and Tumor Institute, probably the largest cancer research facility in the world, and was now reflecting on his work in infectious diseases, wondering whether despite his clinical success he should have been a medical missionary. His older brother is a minister, his younger a teacher. "We were raised in the Protestant work ethic environment. That certainly had a lot to do with where we all ended up. . . . Very strong encouragement to excel in everything we did. We did excel, particularly in academic activities. . . . It isn't all good. It does tend to make you somewhat obsessive-compulsive. And also somewhat unable to accept success when you achieve it. There's always something over the hill you've got to get."

A few years later I visited Gere again, taking with me another classmate and one of my closest friends, Bill Lennarz, who had recently left the Johns Hopkins Medical School to head the biochemistry department at M.D. Anderson. Bill recalled: "I never worked in high school. Then I went off to college. And I thought, 'My father never got the opportunity, so I'd better do something.'" Doing something included a baccalaureate degree at Penn State, a Ph.D. from Illinois, and a postdoctoral fellowship at Harvard. He described the atrophied career of a graduate student who accepted an inferior position so as to remain in a certain geographical area, a decision Bill never would have made. Rather, he observed, "what helped me immensely [was] going to Hopkins, being around good people, superlative role models."

Gere and Bill, with advanced degrees in areas where research is heavily funded, discovered opportunities denied to otherwise fortunate persons. John St. Clair, for example, studied engineering at Cornell before entering Bethlehem Steel's prestigious "loop course" for management trainees. But he found that being a bachelor had its disadvantages when, passed over for a promotion, his boss informed him that "possibly a married person is a little bit more stable than a single person." Yet his real problem came with the dramatic decline in the steel industry. His long-time job in bar sales disappeared with the department itself, and he opted for early retirement at fifty. Economic circumstances proved more powerful than a personal will to achieve in determining his fate.

But John remains one of the elite — college-trained and well-heeled. At the other end of the occupational spectrum Fran Csencsits struggled along for many years as a mother and housekeeper while simultaneously holding a full-time position in a cafeteria. "You bus dishes, you waitress, you work the dishwasher—when you work that job, you are dead." Still, she is unconvinced that women deserve pay equal to men.

We can guess that most members of the Class of 1952 fit somewhere between Gere Bodey, M.D., and Fran Csencsits. But what sorts of jobs do they hold? How similar is it to the work done by their parents and grandparents? Did my classmates benefit when they sought employment miles away from home, as previous generations of immigrants had done? To answer these questions in a general way, it was necessary to categorize occupations and plot them against Class members and their families (see accompanying tables).

Looking first at male family members over three generations (Table 5), we can see that upward movement has occurred, but the pattern calls for an explanation. Obviously, the farmer/laborer category has shrunk while the professional/technical category has expanded. But the operative category has both swelled (from the first to the second generation) and contracted (from the second generation to the third), while the manager/official/proprietor category has contracted, then swelled. The economy, or more precisely the occupational structure, supplies the explanation. In the first generation, though industrialism was spreading, remnants of individual entrepreneurship persisted. But by the second generation, men who had previously run small businesses found themselves being drawn into factories as operatives. The children of the machine operators climbed into managerial positions as the occupational structure now offered more white collar jobs.

But this so-called *inter*generational occupational mobility, while notable, does not appear so impressive as the *intra*generational occupational mobility of men in the Class of 1952. The ranks of the two highest categories more than trebled from the first to the last job, making it seem as though members of the third generation experienced unusual success. It was helpful to have been born during the Depression, when the birth rate dipped, for that demographic fact translated into less competition for available jobs later on. And certainly the prosperity of post–World War II America was congenial to upward movement. But it is also true that due to the Cold War a large number of men entered the work force through the military, a category that plummets from 31.4 to 4.4 percent. Upward movement is somewhat more apparent than real.

Regarding female family members, it seems that the percentage of women who have worked solely as housewives hardly altered from the second to the third generation. But the kind of work done outside the home has changed, with members of the second generation most likely to be operatives, while the plurality of the third-generation women falls into the professional/technical category, i.e., the female *inter*generational movement mirrors the male. Another way to state this situation would be to observe that in the second generation, working-class wives were more likely to be employed outside the home, while in the third generation it is middle-class wives who are working outside. The women of the third generation who entered the work force in the clerical category (almost 60 percent) generally became housewives, while those now in the professional/technical category began there, i.e., notable *intra*generational occupational mobility does not exist for women.

We have seen in chapter 4 that there was a correlation between the jobs held by parents and the curricula selected by their children in the Class of 1952. Similarly, there is a positive relationship between the courses chosen by a member of the Class and his or her career (Table 6). Half the academic/scientific students reached the top job category, though no more than a fifth of the students in any of the other curricula attained this height. Indeed, if we total categories one, two and nine, these job specifications account for 87 percent of the academic/scientific students, while in both the general and vocational curricula the figure is 48 percent. Within the vocational curricula, however, students from Tech have a profile different from the commercial students; the former are more upwardly mobile.

Although academic/scientific students were more apt to have West-

Table 5. Occupations of Members of the Class of 1952 and Their Families (%)

Class members & relatives:	Professional, technical, & kindred workers	Managers, officials & proprietors	Craftsmen, foreman, & kindred workers	Sales workers	Service workers (except domestic), including military	Operatives & kindred workers	Clerical & kindred workers	Farmers, laborers	Private household workers
Paternal grandfathers	11.2	19.6	18.4	2.8	0.9	16.8	3.7	24.3	1.9
Maternal grandfathers	3.9	14.6	18.4	2.9	6.8	27.2	2.9	23.2	0
Fathers	9.5	13.3	14.2	4.0	6.1	32.7	8.7	9.8	1.7
First job, '52 males	19.2	6.0	7.9	3.0	31.4	13.9	14.6	4.0	0
Last job, '52 males	34.6	20.1	9.4	5.0	4.4	6.9	12.6	4.4	2.5
Last job, spouses '52 females	37.1	17.1	9.3	2.9	5.0	11.4	12.9	2.1	2.1
Mothers	5.2	1.9	0.5	2.9	5.7	23.3	16.7	1.0	42.9
First job, '52 females	17.6	2.1	0	2.1	3.7	11.2	59.9	0	3.2
Last job, '52 females	21.7	3.6	1.4	1.4	2.9	0.7	27.5	0	40.6
Last job, spouses '52 males	23.0	1.1	2.3	1.1	4.6	3.4	18.4	1.1	44.8

Table 6. Occupations of Members of the Class of 1952 by Curriculum (%)

Curriculum:	Professional, technical, & kindred workers	Managers, officials & proprietors	Craftsmen, foreman, & kindred workers	Sales workers	Service workers (except domestic), including military	Operatives & kindred workers	Clerical & kindred workers	Farmers, laborers	Private household workers
All members Class of '52	28.2	13.0	5.6	3.3	4.0	4.0	19.3	2.3	2.3
Members in academic/ scientific	49.5	18.7	0.9	2.8	3.7	0.9	4.7	0	18.7
Members in general	20.7	11.7	9.1	3.9	5.2	6.5	23.4	3.9	15.6
Members in vocational/ commercial	13.6	8.5	7.7	3.4	3.4	4.3	29.9	3.4	25.6

Table 7. Occupations of Members of the Class of 1952 by Religion and Ethnicity (%)

Ethnicity & Religion:	Professional, technical, & kindred workers	Managers, officials & proprietors	Craftsmen, foreman, & kindred workers	Sales workers	Service workers (except domestic), including military	Operatives & kindred workers	Clerical & kindred workers	Farmers, laborers	Private household workers
West European & East or South European	29.2	11.2	5.6	3.4	4.5	2.2	18.0	0	25.8
East or South European	30.6	16.3	6.1	4.1	2.0	2.0	12.2	2.0	24.5
Protestant	31.7	21.5	4.7	1.9	3.7	2.8	21.5	0	21.5
Roman Catholic	30.3	12.5	7.1	5.1	25.0	0	12.5	1.8	26.7

Table 8. Residential Mobility of the Class of 1952 by Occupation (%)

Occupations:	Places of residence:				Residential moves:				
	Lehigh Valley	Pennsylvania	Northeast U.S.	Elsewhere	None	1–2	3–4	5–6	7–8 (and above)
Professional, technical, and kindred workers	48.3	10.6	17.7	23.6	6	20.0	30.0	30.0	12.0
Managers, officials, and proprietors	53.9	15.4	12.9	18.0	0	27.3	36.4	27.3	9.1
Craftsmen, foremen, and kindred workers	81.1	12.5	6.3	0	0	33.3	50.0	16.7	0
Sales workers	87.5	12.5	0	0	0	25.0	25.0	50.0	0
Services workers (except domestic), including military	41.5	8.3	33.3	16.6	0	37.5	37.5	0	25.0
Operatives and kindred workers	81.9	9.1	9.1	0	0	100	0	0	0
Clerical and kindred workers	81.7	9.1	9.0	0	4.2	37.5	41.6	4.2	12.5
Farmers, laborers	100	0	0	0	0	100	0	0	0
Private household workers	75.2	7.1	10.8	7.2	2.9	47.1	38.2	2.9	8.8

ern European backgrounds and more likely to be Protestant than Catholic, neither ethnicity nor religion seems to have made a great deal of difference in occupation (Table 7). However, Protestants are more visible in category two and seven, Catholics in category five.

Finally, we can ask whether the nature of a person's job depends on his or her willingness to relocate. We can safely speculate that grandparents of the Class of 1952, over half of whom were born outside the United States and over 90 percent of whom did not begin life in Bethlehem, or parents of the Class, almost a quarter of whom were foreign born, did change their places of residence in quest of employment. Class members have been less mobile than their forebears. Approximately 60 percent of them live in the Lehigh Valley, married to persons from this same region, and their movement has carried them only from the center of Bethlehem to the city's periphery (Table 8).

Of the 40 percent who have exited the Lehigh Valley, the preponderant number remain in states contiguous to Pennsylvania. These Class members do hold better jobs than their peers who remained. Some of them did not leave in search of employment but simply went away to college and stayed away, reinforcing our recognition of the link between education and work. But there is no clear correlation between a willingness to change residences and the type of job held.

PROFESSIONALS

Before the industrial revolution, which introduced economic class to social ranking, it was possible to attain high status through entry into the professions — medicine and science, the church, law, education. Next to farming, and perhaps the military, the professions represent the most traditional sector of the work force.

Gerald Bodey's father was the minister at the Emmanuel Evangelical Church, where earlier in the century my grandparents had worshiped and my father was instructed as a youth. My Aunt Beulah was still a member of the congregation when I was in high school, but the church belonged to my family's past. And Gere himself had an anachronistic quality. Among the many books he lugged through the halls at Liberty there was always a Bible. That I carried cigarettes was scandalous to him, and he gave me a card which read,

"Thou Shalt Not Smoke because . . . ," followed by Scriptural admonitions. He also asked me to come to Emmanuel to hear a visiting evangelist, an invitation I found hard to refuse because of my family's associations with the church. My presence at the service so fueled his religious ardor that I literally had to escape his clutches to avoid being saved that night.

We both traveled a long distance after that incident, he probably farther than I. But when I learned that as an M.D. he conducted research on the creation of germ-free environments for infection-prone cancer patients, I was unsurprised: it fit perfectly my image of him from high school. And I was very impressed with a bibliography of almost three hundred articles he had authored or co-authored in the field of his research.

I talked with Gere in the M.D. Anderson Hospital and Tumor Institute at the University of Texas System Cancer Center, a sanitized complex of buildings in the midst of the seedy sprawl of Houston. He showed me the sterile environments provided for cancer patients. We drove from his work place to his home in an attractive suburb, where we had dinner with his wife and three children in a room overlooking the swimming pool. He discussed both his work and his family.

GERE: After high school I stayed at home and commuted over to Lafayette College for four years. I graduated, got married that summer, and we moved off to Baltimore, lived there for six years, then went to the Bethesda Cancer Institute for three years. Then we moved out to Seattle for a year, and then came here.

I have a variety of roles. When I first came here I was primarily responsible for running our acute leukemia program. And then I also began an infectious disease section; I've been chief of that ever since. When I came over here from the acute leukemia section, I started a chemotherapy service here to deal with all types of malignancies. And about two or three years ago I became in charge of our whole chemotherapy program in the department.

I travel quite a bit, much too much. I have a kind of unique situation. I'm involved in cancer chemotherapy and also in infectious diseases. A lot of the research I've done has been in the area of new antibiotics. Then, some of my travel is administrative. I go to national meetings to present and hear papers. And I do a fair amount of traveling as a visiting professor at different institutions.

Just recently I was in South Africa at a symposium and several universities. I came back and ten days later I went to Paris. I do a lot of traveling in South America, visiting hospitals and universities. I always try to arrange the trip so I get to see some of the country—colonial towns, the jungle.

I now do some teaching at the University of Texas Medical School and also at Baylor Medical School. I do a lot of teaching at the level of postgraduate, continuing education positions, both local and, literally, throughout the world. As to research, most of the antibiotic work is done under my direction, whether off the scene or on. This has been something I've developed over the years in contact with various drug companies.

I majored in chemistry at college. But a physician doesn't have a lot of interest in the chemical structure of drugs. I would call myself a clinical researcher. There isn't a formal training for that; it's something you just learn in an environment where people are doing that sort of work. I've always had an interest in infectious diseases, and so I focused my attention a good deal on the infectious problems in patients with cancer.

I work considerably more than forty hours a week. I work most weekends, Saturdays and Sundays, usually one of those days here and the other at home. Part of the year I serve as an attending physician on the wards, and when I do that it's a seven-day-a-week job. The pressures of my job are such that they're pushing me away from patient contact into administrative responsibilities. But I keep insisting on spending at least several months of the year with patients.

It's not just the research that compels me, but I could lose my clinical skills. And contact with patients is what medicine is all about. That's what I started out to do, and I still want to keep doing it.

My original intention was to be a medical missionary. When I was in fourth or fifth grade I decided, and I intended to do it until the time I went to Bethesda. I probably would be a missionary today except that I ran into a couple of roadblocks along the way.

There are some days when I wonder whether if maybe I shouldn't have gone out to be a missionary instead of what I'm doing. I suppose anybody at times in their life sits back and wonders whether you're really doing what you set out to do and whether what you're doing is worthwhile. I don't doubt that my work is worthwhile, but I do doubt whether it's really what I want to do. As I've gone along I've ended up having to take on more and more administrative responsibilities. It's not exactly what I prefer to do.

I have maintained my Christian faith over the years. And I think one of the things that has been of some concern to me is whether this is exactly what God intended for me to do. I originally felt very strongly called to be a missionary, and I didn't end up doing that. And I've felt that basically this [job in Houston] is what God intended me to do. If He had wanted me to be a missionary that's what I'd be today. Nevertheless, once in a while there's sort of a lingering doubt that I've reneged on my responsibility somewhere along the line and have taken an easier and more comfortable way of life. I work hard, but I'm not living with any of the restraints on somebody out in the mission field.

When I come back from traveling in South America I always come back wondering whether my work is a terribly useful contribution in that area. When you travel around, particularly when you get out of the big cities, in a country like Peru or even Brazil, you see a lot of people at a very primitive level who have a lot of diseases that are curable if they just had the medical care. I've seen people who are simply starving to death in Peru. And here I am dealing with a situation in which most patients are not going to be cured. Is it appropriate to be putting your resources into that kind of situation when there are so many pressing needs that could be rectified?

When my mother mentioned starving people to me, it never made much impression. When I say something to my children, it has even less impact. When we went to school, we did see poor kids, or kids from different backgrounds. In the neighborhood I live in, my children don't have too much contact. We have some bussing, some black children, some poorer kids. But they don't have anything like the wider exposure we had. They measure themselves by the standards of the neighborhood.

My son with his church group went to one of the poorer areas of Houston. He came back and said, "We really have it pretty good out here." That's one of the tragedies of the way the city has evolved in recent years. We've isolated ourselves. What always comes to my mind when I think about this is the story Jesus told about the rich man and Lazarus, the poor man who died. The rich man was condemned, not because he ever did anything to harm Lazarus but just simply because he ignored him. Our whole way of life is so structured that we could spend the rest of our lives completely ignoring the plight of those who are less fortunate than ourselves. I don't go down to the slum neighborhoods of town, ever.

Our church has some programs. I haven't thought that my contact with these programs has been a compensation for not being in the mission field. But contact with cancer patients has. I don't simply say, "You want to take this medication." I also try to get to know some of the patients and try to help them with the problems they're facing with the disease, to help them be realistic about what to expect.

One thing that has impressed me is that the people who seem to handle it best, that I've run across, are people who have a very deep Christian faith. It's particularly meaningful to me in relating to some of these people. There's a bond there for me. Of course, I try to relate to anybody, no matter what their faith or lack of faith is.

There's a very narrow range one has to walk on in this area. You can become so emotionally involved with patients that it interferes with your medical judgment. You can be so involved that when you lose a patient you can't function. Of course, in this kind of environment every patient ultimately is lost, so that you're constantly faced with failure.

You have to have a certain basic outlook to be able to face this. You can't get too emotionally involved. On the other hand, I reject completely the philosophy that I hear some people espouse that a doctor should never get emotionally involved with his patient. If you don't have any compassion, then you don't belong in the medical profession. Death should mean something to you or you're not human. And it usually does. It certainly does affect me.

I certainly believe in miracles, there's no question about that. Where I have my problem with miracles is why don't more of them happen. I think that a person who has a Christian faith can do a service here, because some people have an unrealistic attitude toward this kind of thing. God doesn't perform miracles for everybody who needs them. I don't know why He does sometimes, and why most of the time He doesn't. But that's the way it really is. I think it's more important to folks rather than to accept some miraculous intervention that they learn to accept what has happened.

I wondered about the origins of Gere's stance on life, his mixture of worldly pragmatism and spiritual predestinarianism.

I have fond memories of my childhood. I had a lot of fun most of the time. I had the freedom to make up my own mind. My parents were obviously enthusiastic about my desire to become a missionary. But they didn't put any pressure on in that way. I was raised in a very strict home, much stricter than the one I maintain. In our church it was sinful to dance. I've never been to a dance; I don't have the foggiest idea how to go about it. My kids know how, in fact, the church has dances. But when it came down to what I wanted to do with my life, my parents were very supportive. My mother worked all those years predominantly to help us kids go to school. If she hadn't I couldn't have gone to medical school.

My mother was a very unselfish person. She gave up what she wanted for some other member of the family. It was a very integral part of her nature. She never resented any of that at all. It was her duty but also, I think, her pleasure. She got a great deal of satisfaction out of the fact that all three of her children grew up to have a better education than she ever had. She went to normal school for two years.

We were raised in the Protestant work ethic environment. That certainly had a lot to do with where we all ended up. No question about it. Very strong motivation. Very strong encouragement to excel in everything we did. We did excel, particularly in academic activities. That environment played a major role in the life-style that I developed.

It isn't all good. It does tend to make you somewhat obsessive-compulsive. And also somewhat unable to accept success when you achieve it. There's always something over the hill that you've got to get. You can't really sit back and say, "Well, I've really got what I wanted. I can enjoy it for a while."

Some people look back on childhood and have certain resentments and so on. They don't feel that their childhood was the way it was supposed to be. I don't feel that way. I'm very grateful that I am what I am. I was quite fortunate being raised in the kind of family I was raised in. Certainly one of the things that I appreciate is what I have now, because I didn't have it then. Evangelical ministers weren't paid well at all. Up till my mother started working, my dad was constantly in debt.

My parents were strict, but they were interested in our well-being. They knew when to stop. Once I got to college they didn't try to impose their wishes on what I did at all. When I decided to get married, they wanted me to wait a few years till I got through at least part of medical school. But when I made the decision that that was what I was going to do, they were very supportive. That was the case with everything.

We raise children differently today. And it's not all good. When we were growing up I don't think we had some of the concerns the kids have today. The way other kids act is sometimes vicious. And there's crime. Life has changed considerably, some of it for the good, some of it terrible.

And I don't think there are simpler answers. There has been a gradual erosion of basic values of all sorts — patriotism. I think this nation's made some terrible mistakes, but I think you can learn to accept that without losing pride in your country. There's been a general decline in morals. Things aren't really black and white, everything's gray, and under these circumstances it's all right to kill your neighbor, rape his wife. It's okay to rob a bank if you're really starving. And things like that. Everything's gray, so there's nothing wrong and there's nothing that's always right. It's easier to compromise—"It's not so wrong to do this today"—then that becomes your norm, now it's not so wrong to take the next step.

I'm sure you had the same experience in college that I did where certain professors seemed to have as their main objective in their course to destroy any kind of values that had been established by your family. This is part of the price we're paying right now. People lost an anchor. They don't know what they believe about *anything*.

Almost eight years after talking with Gere I again flew to Houston, this time to meet Bill Lennarz, one of my closest friends. We had gotten to know one another the spring of our senior year, when the Liberty Hi-Y Club made its annual trip to Washington, D.C. After that we spent a fair amount of time together, usually drinking beer, joking about the state of the rest of the world, and sometimes acting out our boyish fantasies.

Like many of our classmates Bill went to Pennsylvania State University but, unlike any others, he went on to the University of Illinois for a Ph.D. in chemistry and from there to Harvard for post-doctoral work. He then settled into the biochemistry department of the Johns Hopkins Medical School. I had been best man at his wedding, watched him weather a stormy separation, served again as his best man when he remarried, and stayed in close touch with him. When he accepted a job as head of the biochemistry department at the M.D. Anderson Hospital, I decided to visit and take the opportunity to get him into a conversation with Gere Bodey. These two men were the top scientists in our class, and certainly they now rank high in the nation.

Shortly after I arrived in Houston, Bill, his wife, Sheila, and I were in the Tumbleweed, washing our steaks down with beer and tequila and dancing to the country-and-western band. The next morning, on the way to Gere's house, he reflected on how his professional career began.

BILL: I never worked in high school. Then I went off to college. And I thought, "My father never got the opportunity, so I'd better do something." I'm not so sure I ever thought of it that way then, but I'm sure that was there. But I never seriously thought I would be able to get a Ph.D.

The MAGAZINE
of The Houston Post
Feb. 3, 1985

CURING
CANCER

THERE ARE PLENTY OF QUESTIONS.
THESE SCIENTISTS HAVE COME
TO HOUSTON LOOKING FOR ANSWERS

Bill Lennarz and his staff at the M. D. Anderson Hospital and Tumor Institute, as featured in the *Houston Post,* Februrary, 3, 1985.

As I came under the influence of the biochemists—well, there was no market for the field, the recombinant DNA and biotechnology didn't exist yet, so there was no place to go in industry—I saw I had to do a post-doc. They guided me to Harvard. The chairman of the biochemistry group in Illinois sort of considered me one of his boys. At that time you had to have a first and a second minor, which I thought was absurd. So I went to him and said, "I want a sole minor in biochemistry." And he got a dean to approve that, which set a precedent, and I became his fair-haired boy.

During this time we had driven from Bill's townhouse to Gere's residence in the sedate suburb of Meyerland. Gere and his wife, Nancy, who had been a couple of years behind us at Liberty High School, greeted us in the house they had occupied for seventeen years, most of the time they had lived in Houston. Gere pointed out that he left the country far more frequently than he went into downtown Houston. This remark led into a conversation about the international attention his work has received, and soon we were discussing both men's jobs.

GERE: My bibliography now has about six hundred articles. I used to be in cancer chemotherapy and infectious disease; I've pretty much given up the cancer chemotherapy. My writing is on infectious disease.

BILL: My work isn't cancer-related; it's more cell-related. It's not at all patient-directed; it's not disease-directed. The justification for it is simple: if you understand normal cellular behavior and growth, then you'll have better ways to deal with the abnormal. The Anderson made a decision that it wanted a biochemistry department for strong basic sciences, because those people can also act as a support group for people doing more clinical things when they need advice or guidance. The general theme of my department—and this is how I'm recruiting—is going to be normal differentiation and development. You might look on cancer as abnormal differentiation—or lack of differentiation. The people I bring in might be looking at genes or might be looking at proteins, but there's an underlying, common theme.

Most things in the laboratory I can no longer do. I know

the principles involved, but I haven't learned the new generation of instruments. And it would be of no value for me to learn, although it makes me uncomfortable not to know. If I can't operate the instrument, do I really know how to evaluate this person's data? I've got to trust him entirely, because I can't go in and do the experiment myself, I can't check it.

GERE: That's a disturbing aspect of research, because there have been instances where people falsified data, conducted fraudulent studies, and so on. And the general atmosphere is that, by darn, the guy who's in charge is responsible. And yet practically speaking, it's impossible for you to be responsible.

BILL: The problem is that in the cases where there have been frauds, the person on top may not end up being legally involved but certainly it reflects on him.

If you're really "smart-dishonest" you can get away with it totally. There's no way I could know unless I did the experiment. My impression is that it's happening with increasing frequency as the pressure to publish mounts. [Several cases were discussed, as well as the role of bureaucracy in research.]

BILL: The signatures on the many forms are there because you've correctly filled out the form. And many pages—such as those showing the number of ethnic-group members—have nothing to do with science.

GERE: The bureaucrat's motive is protecting his own hide. Some of this has to do with patients' rights, but not much. And with all this bureaucracy—perhaps in basic science it's not so bad, but in clinical science—if you don't follow a certain set pattern in doing your research, you're not going to get funded. Innovation is out the window today. The opportunities for giant leaps forward don't exist. It's very stifling.

BILL: All of that is brought about because there's a limited number of dollars, and a growing number of people trying to get money. After all, we're the review committee—we should blame ourselves.

GERE: It's more complicated than that. After you reach a certain level of success you move on to a different activity, and you're not involved in that stuff anymore. At least that's true of clinical science. In cancer research it's increasingly difficult to get the major researchers to be involved in the review process.

BILL: Well, that's also true in basic science, but I feel an obligation to keep doing it, because that's part of the science.

As Bill drove back to his place, he closed the story on his career. "I had a graduate student who took a job, against my advice, at a university with a dreadful medical school. He was just so tied into family and the location that he couldn't resist the job. He's a good scientist and a good scholar but not a great one. But because he put himself in an environment like that, he's locked himself in. If he had gone to a better place, he would have been better. And that's what helped me *immensely*, going to Hopkins, being around good people, superlative role models."

In their willingness to work hard, in their drive to achieve, both Bill and Gere acknowledged the strong influence of parents as role models at the earliest stage of development. School nurtured and professional associates reinforced the attitudes that underlay their accomplishment. In the winter of 1988 I attended a molecular biology conference with Bill who, as the most senior scientist present, was not only elder statesman but also a role model himself.

I had known Pete Haupert longer than any other member of our class, for we attended together the Sunday School at Central Moravian Church and the Playhouse run for preschoolers by my Aunt Winnie and her friends. His background was more out of the ordinary than Gere's or Bill's. His paternal grandfather was a minister and, for a short time, a college professor. His maternal grandfather was a physician. His father was president of Moravian College in Bethlehem. The burden of great expectations was on Pete, the eldest of four boys, and he bore it through high school by diligently applying himself to his homework, behavior that gained him the accolade (if it was that) of "most studious boy in the class."

When I visited him in Waukesha, Wisconsin, a suburb of Milwaukee where he was commanding the emergency unit of a hospital, he seemed to have changed in important ways. Though as serious as ever, he was candid about his personal life (and openly curious about mine), rid of his provincial religious inhibitions (he served alcohol, for example, and was installing a hot tub in his California-style house), and quite obviously relaxed and happy. His wife, Joan, who had been a class behind us in high school, strongly reinforced these qualities, and both parents appeared to be totally at ease with their four children, who were included in the conversation whenever they entered the living room. The family had only recently returned from six years at a Moravian hospital in eastern Nicaragua, where Pete had been a medical missionary.

PETE: My childhood was somewhat sheltered and somewhat isolated. Some of my early conditioning, such as listening only to good music rather than cheap music and only turning the other cheek and not fighting back, just in retrospect wasn't the kind of advice that I needed. And wasn't good preparation for life.

And so that left me a little bit on the outside of a lot of the gangs. So it's left me with a feeling all my life of needing to work at acceptance. And this is probably something that has motivated and driven me all of my life.

One of the earliest motivations was into basketball, because that was an area in which by dedication I was able to utilize some physical attributes that helped me to excel to a limited degree. And it gave me the self-esteem that I needed and some just really good vibes in high school and all the way into college.

I enjoyed my school work. And it was sometime in the eighth grade where I realized that if I applied myself I could produce significant academic . . . I could get good marks, I guess is what it amounts to. And so here was another area in which I could excel and felt like I probably needed to. So for my own self-esteem and for my parents' pleasure and their positive reinforcement I did continue on the track of being very much grade-oriented and succeeded in being able to mark up the good grades right through school.

At a certain cost, a real significant cost, I think. I got the marks in lieu of an education, in lieu of experience, in lieu of the freedom to choose rather than to perfect an assignment. Or to read a good book, which I didn't do. And so I feel like my education was somewhat shortchanged by this concentration on grades.

It's not that I don't feel educated. I feel reasonably educated, reasonably literate, and reasonably well-read. But I think this came later. It came in spite of my approach to high school and college.

High school was fun. My basketball and track experiences were meaningful. My reticence to stretch my parental restraint I think deprived me of some really good, wholesome times I could have had. College was strange. I didn't realize how strange it was, going to the college that my dad was the president of. But I just hammered on through and got the best grades I could, which were good.

I had a lot of fun playing on the basketball team for two years, but never got my act together in basketball. I think I really had a lot of potential: I had the right physique. I was strong. I was fast and had good reflexes. But there was something about my approach to the game that caused me to peter out, no pun intended. By the end of my second year I realized that I wasn't making it into the main ranks of varsity basketball, as I wanted to.

And I realize now that it was a psychological thing, an inability to let go, an inability to. . . . I'll never forget how painful it was to hear my coach call out to me on the floor, "Hey, Pete, don't get hurt," kind of ironically, commenting on my failure to get involved in the game, my holding back.

I know that I had the basic wherewithal — and this is very important to me; it's amazing how important it is to be able to excel in athletics — because on three occasions I transcended my limitations. But the ultimate fact was that I didn't get it together — and couldn't, despite my most vigorous, conscious efforts. And so I gave it up. The next time I played basketball was on a team in Nicaragua, and it was fun.

After college I went to theological seminary, again at Moravian. I did this for several reasons. One is, I felt it would please my parents. Secondly, I was really programmed to serve the Lord. Actually, my faith got more and more dilute, the more I studied. But mainly, I think I did it because I wanted to go into the mission field. I decided to become a missionary at the age of twelve. You know that, because that is how I was pegged, going through high school.

I decided this on the basis of an evening lecture presented at the summer Christian church Bible camp by a medical missionary, slides and all. I was really impressed. That really looked to be what God had cut out for me, if God cuts things out for people. And I'm beinning to think now, for the second time, that He probably does. Or at least I'm willing to concede that possibility. It makes existential sense for me.

Going to seminary was what Dr. Thaeler [a medical missionary in Nicaragua], whose footsteps I was following in, did. And I guess I was also a little curious about this faith that my parents had given me, wanted to study it a little academically. There were a lot of reasons for going to seminary. And actually it was the best move I made and probably the three most fun years where I really arrived at some academic freedom. Because I kind of reached my adolescence then, academically, and I was able to rebel from all this compulsiveness.

Pete graduated from seminary, married Joan Schnable (Liberty High School, '53) after what he described as "one of the longest courtships in history," took a medical degree at the University of Pennsylvania, interned at a community hospital in Indianapolis, and completed a surgical residency in Milwaukee.

A month after finishing my highly academic surgical program I went up into the boondocks of the upper Michigan peninsula, a little place called Daggett, an old Moravian town of three hundred people, and worked with a physician, John Heidenreich, who ran a clinic. I learned a lot about the practical backwoods wisdom of how to treat patients. In my residency I learned how to treat conditions and how to do operations. What I learned there applied so naturally and so uniformly to the Indians in Nicaragua. If God was designing a preparation, it couldn't have been more appropriate.

Margaret Heidenreich Thaeler, Dr. Heidenreich's sister and wife of Dave Thaeler who had run the Nicaragua hospital, founded the first nursing school in Nicaragua.

We were in Nicaragua for six years of sheer adventure and challenge and pleasure—even the agony produced its own form of pleasure through the challenge. They were extremely busy years, because it was like trying to dig away a mountain with a hand shovel: no way in the world you could get on

Pete and Joan Haupert with their daughter Martita just after their return to the United States. (Photo by JEI.)

top of the situation, so you just wanted to make the best effort possible.

The challenges were many: the challenge of becoming a Nicaraguan, of developing a fluency in the language and an ability to negotiate and develop meaningful relationships with Nicaraguan government officials, including President Samoza and his wife themselves, and at the same time to maintain a credence, a relationship with the people I lived with who represented, in a way, the opposition, was a difficult job. The other challenge was just physically to get an old deteriorating hospital renovated, and to build the necessary additions and get them functioning.

The surgical and medical challenge was trying to meet the medical needs of the people themselves, people who would come in with things I never had seen, things I never had been trained to handle. Because I knew this was going to happen, I assembled a good reference library. The medical students and I would just hustle to the books and design the best operation we could for the problem. What began to happen was that I began doing things that were in their concept miraculous.

It was the relationships with people, the phenomenal intimacy that develops when dealing with hardship in a remote area—with isolated Americans and Europeans, who would come down, and we'd spend evening after evening sitting on our veranda, sipping rum, looking out over the pine trees and hearing the tropical sounds—relationships that we don't find here in our life setting in the States and that we're hungry for. On the one hand, we were in a deprivation situation; on the other hand, it was a very enriching existence.

It was my relationships with the Nicaraguans themselves that produced the very deepest satisfaction. [Pete described at great length his relationship with Eddie Hooker, a black Nicaraguan and "probably the best friend I ever had," his right-hand man in the hospital and his baseball coach.]

I was also given the religious leadership role, a peripheral one, which I carried out with as much sincerity as I could because I was also uncertain enough in my own faith that I didn't want to fool anybody. I enjoyed a spiritual relationship with the people in the churches. They gave me the opportunity to dispense holy communion to our Indian church population on occasion. This, to me, was a deeply meaningful thing.

Our re-entry back into the States has been almost traumatic, because we had so many expectations about how great it would be to be back. And we find now that we actually miss more than we're getting. We're trying now to gradually adapt to life here, to not get caught up in materialism but at the same time to earn as much money at this point as I can so that we can enjoy a meaningful and full life of some limited material comforts, like the hot tub and a pool here at the house, and eventually the freedom to really have the time and money to travel and enjoy people we know all over the world and get to see some of the things that make this world such a neat place.

Pete has remained medical director of the paramedic program at Waukesha Memorial Hospital, arranging his job so that he has ample time for travel—just as he promised himself he would.

––––––

The routes to professional status for women were fewer—or, at least, much more constricted—than for men in the 1950s. Since the mid-nineteenth century the road women most frequently took was through the classroom. Nancy Vaitekunes, whose second-generation parents (Lithuanian and Hungarian) had not finished high school, gained a college degree at Moravian with Pete Haupert—and a teaching credential. As cheerful and energetic as I remember her, Nancy—a single mother—began our conversation by pointing to some family photos.

NANCY: This is my daughter, Jana, who is thirteen; she goes to East Hills [Junior High School] right over here. And that's Robyn, she's nineteen, and she goes to Temple [University]. She's not interested in marriage but in a career, professional or educational, in being somebody. Marriage—take it or leave it.

She doesn't really identify with the women's movement. She's interested in what they do, but she isn't active. She thinks they push a little bit too much. I'm not a member either, although I support some of their goals. Sometimes I listen to some of their leaders, and I don't agree with them. Most of the women I teach with do not relate to the women's movement.

I'm the only woman science teacher at Nitchman [Junior High School], though half the faculty is women. I'm not competing with men at all. I do just as well in my class, and maybe even better. I'm also the oldest science teacher. Most teachers at Nitchman are under thirty-five. I team teach with a man who's twenty-four—he's like a kid to me, like my daughter. The main thing is his life is Saturday night.

You can request a transfer to a high school teaching position. You have to have a stomach for junior high kids, because they can drive you bananas—especially the seventh graders. By ninth grade, they're a little more cool, eighth grade they're half and half. But seventh grade—completely out of it. The bodies are mature, but the minds—forget it.

Ten-year-old, nine-year-old type reasoning. Babies! A little boy will come up and breathe right on you. He'll ask a question, and I'll say, "John, I told you that the other day." And all of a sudden, big tears. I say, "Oh, come on, John, cool it, relax. So you didn't hear it, you missed it. We'll make arrangements." Babies!

They come in September, and by the time they leave we get that baby out of them. Think for yourself. Make your own decisions. If you're wrong, accept that you're wrong, accept your punishment. And don't be shedding waterworks all the time.

You've got to deal with them individually. You've got all kinds of children in class. You've got disturbed children, you've got children that are culturally deprived—and from super backgrounds, out there in West Bethlehem. We've got them all, terrific range.

But there's not a discipline problem at Nitchman. We have a fairly good population. The kids who come from one of the low-class neighborhoods are dispersed. I had a boy from a good family acting up recently—all I had to do was call his dad. He got a spanking, he apologized to me, and he's been good as gold. Generally, we will have the backing of the parents.

It was different when I was a student at Washington [a junior high school, on the far South Side]. We used to get swatted around. Maybe "we" didn't, but we saw actual hitting; a principal or teacher would really let the children have it. I don't believe in bringing back the old discipline, the strict, confining rules that we had, nobody out of their seat. If you were in the hall, you had to go through an act of Congress to explain what you were doing there. And then you had some big football coach grab you and push you around. And now we can look back and say, "They were ignorant."

I reason, and the child himself will have to get it from within. I don't physically punish them. I'm on the phone, right away, and I usually get the father at work. The mothers are no good for punishment. [At that point Nancy's daughter Jana rushed into the room and prevailed on her mother for two dollars for lunch, despite Nancy's "And I've got all this stuff in here."]

When I was at Washington, it wasn't considered a slum

school, but it was the poorest of the schools. Nitchman, Franklin, Broughal, Washington. And yet we had some super teachers, fabulous teachers. So when I went to Liberty, I didn't have too much of a problem, because I had a good English and math background.

At Washington, there wasn't that much to compete with. I was a cheerleader, glee club, yearbook, all that other stuff. Then when you went to high school you were really faced with people that were better than you, and you really had to try hard to get into the organizations, or in a class, for instance, in a Latin class—to sit in the back row! Remember? Mrs. Funk put all the dummies in the first row. I would never do that to my students; that's humiliating. Peter Haupert, number one, in the back—brain!—dad, of course, a college professor; he would know Latin, Greek. And there you were: inferior. I got A's and B's.

My weakness in high school was geometry. Otherwise, I did okay, even in Pop Emery's physics. [William Emery was notoriously tough and insultingly anti-female; few girls would hazard the class. He also seated students by grade.] I wanted to do very well, my best. And I felt slightly stronger competition against students from Franklin or Nitchman. I knew they had better preparation in some areas—let's say their father was an engineer for the Steel and could help them in their chemistry problems or their mother was a nurse and could help them with their biology. My parents were not formally educated, and they couldn't help me at all with my work.

They were curious about what I was doing, and they supported me. My pop still says today, "The one thing I learned from Nancy was never to let the milk set out on the counter." He used to leave the milk in a pitcher for coffee, and it would be there all morning. And I'd say, "My God, Pop, the bacteria." I was taking Biology 2.

But I was inferior—socially. They had sororities, but I wasn't from that group from Nitchman or Franklin. That was always my problem, coming from the South Side into Liberty, then meeting up with the boys and girls who had really gorgeous homes and had fathers who were executives and who had traveled and had very nice clothing. There was a clique, this group, that group. We all hung around together, from Washington or Broughal; we stayed together, and we didn't associate with, let's say, the other girls. My friends were Helen Mavis, Anna Marie Mandic, Maureen Medgie, and there were a couple others. The only friends I had from the North Side were Ann Leh and Audrey Vollman—I worked with her on the yearbook. And Chris Sideris was a good friend; I went on to Moravian College with her.

My kids don't understand about Washington and Broughal—how could they? My parents still live on Fourth Street, and my kids simply accept that. They're not even aware of the economic class. I wouldn't have Jana go to Broughal. My outlook has changed, and the schools have changed. The Puerto Ricans and the colored are there. Northeast [Junior High School] may even be worse, because of Pembroke Village [a low-rent housing project]. Those are the people who stone the police or the firemen when they come in. They're bad!

I think my girls would recognize that Puerto Ricans are different, because they see it in their own classes: how the Puerto Ricans cause trouble, fights at school, setting fires, use of drugs. But I go to Holy Infancy Church—with the Puerto Ricans. That's their church.

I asked Nancy, who had been divorced for five years, whether she had adapted well to it.

If you asked me whether I prefer married or single, I'd say I prefer single life. I am independent. I enjoy it. I like my job. I have a fairly nice apartment. I do things I like: theater, tennis. I don't go out to singles bars. Never have I felt I needed a male companion to go out. I travel a lot to see my friends—Reading, Kutztown, Philly, New York. I didn't get around much when I was married.

And my daughters have a lot of independence. Jana takes care of herself if I go away for just a day. Robyn has had a car since she's sixteen, and she's never had to sit home with Jana. I'm more like a friend than a parent to them. I never talked about birth control or sex with my mother, or drugs. God forbid! My daughter takes birth control pills; my daughter has smoked pot. Now if I were to tell my mother that, I would have found myself laid out somewhere. I am liberal. And I thought I'd never be. I'm still old-fashioned for myself, my own morals. But for my daughter, I can't impose my upbringing on her. Yes, I created her independence—my Frankenstein monster in the laboratory [laughs with pleasure].

I had wanted her to go to Moravian—I was very happy there—or perhaps Lehigh. But she definitely wanted to get away from home and be out on her own. I'm proud to have a child that is, at nineteen, mature, an independent thinker, a doer. People that know her compliment me. The other one is too early to tell, but she also appears to be heading for independence.

When I returned to Bethlehem several years later to resume my conversations with classmates, I was unable to reach Nancy at home and, therefore, called her school. "She passed away a few years ago," I was told. Her parents were unable to talk about her death, but from her daughters—the older in Philadelphia, the younger in Los Angeles—I learned she had been in remission from cancer when I talked with her in 1976. Finally, it caught up with her.

The other conventional route into the professions for females was through nursing, a "caring" occupation, like teaching, and thus tailored for women. Alma Shurts traveled this road, and along the way was drawn to psychiatry. Her husband's long career in police work had guided him in a similar direction, and their son was majoring in psychology in college.

ALMA: I did my nurses' training at St. Luke's, but you can't do psychiatric study there. I had worked at State Hospital [which handles the area's mental patients]. The last job I was doing was working for Northampton County Mental Health and Mental Retardation. It's all out-patient work. I was helping to run a clinic for discharged patients. Schizophrenics, neurotics, the whole gamut. I was doing a little bit of counseling, making home visits. And there were counselors or psychologists or psychiatrists who were picking them up in therapy.

When I started working, nurses were geared to be the underdog to the doctor: "Do what they say," "don't question them." This is how you were taught twenty-some years ago. So we had to go along with the idea that you never told patients anything about the pills they were taking, and if they asked, you said, "This is to make your cheeks pink." They had a right to know, it was their bodies, but we didn't tell.

Now it's changing. Nurses have a right to question. We couldn't do anything on our own. You couldn't even tell a person you were giving them aspirin. Now you can tell, and doctors are seeing the role of a nurse differently. The education of nurses has changed tremendously; no one goes to a diploma school anymore, but gets a college degree instead. Now they get master's degrees and doctorates, and as they're moving up they're becoming nurse-practitioners. They still can't diagnose, but they can treat well people. So they are now working, in conjunction with doctors many times, in their own offices. Doctors resisted this, and many of them still do.

Psychiatry's altogether different. I was treated as an equal, and many psychiatrists and psychologists would come to me and ask me questions—how would I do this or that? Of course, psychiatrists have a lot of needs to be fulfilled and a lot of problems of their own. We all do, regardless of what kind of work we're in. Some psychiatrists are in this field because they were too insecure to do surgery or actual medical work.

My husband has always been in law enforcement. Sometimes our work comes together under a mental health act in Pennsylvania. So I might be at the hearing, and he might be bringing a person in. Both of us dealt with juveniles for a while, too. We also dealt with the school system—special education for the emotionally disturbed, and so forth.

I wondered whether schools were receptive to such intervention or, rather, regarded deviant behavior as a matter simply requiring more discipline.

Unfortunately, that's how schools have looked at things for years. Educators have to change a little bit in their thinking. For a while, I've said that it would be great to set up crisis centers in schools, and I'm sure there are a lot of people who would be behind me. But you'd have to be very careful of who you put in those crisis centers. Kids won't come if they knew it had anything to do with the school or with school people. There would have to be kind of a free-lance agency.

I don't see education changing much, but that's the beginning: the educators seeing things differently. Why are we teaching some kids in school subjects we know they are never going to use? And not teach real-life situations? That's why we get so many dropouts. Who teaches you how to be a mother and father? The school really ought to be helping kids.

Maybe teachers see themselves up here in this superior role to these inferiors, and if they'd come down—well, that's the trouble with life. Somebody's on this level, and they're on that level. I've seen families like that! Mother's going in her circle, and son's doing this, and father's over here. And they never get together in any way. And that's kind of sad.

I learned a lot about these matters through my job at the state hospital, and then I picked up a tremendous amount working for Mental Health, plus I took every kind of workshop and seminar I possibly could. You have to open yourself up if you want to be successful in your work—and I was able to relate.

Alma has recently retired from psychiatric nursing, but her son Brett has carried on the family tradition by taking a Ph.D. in psychology.

Management and Labor

John St. Clair left home for an education, traveling a few hundred miles to Cornell University, then returned to Bethlehem Steel to join its "loop course," presumably preparation for the highest rank of management. In high school John was known to be pleasant, accommodating, and so candid that some persons took his remarks for rudeness when, in fact, he could at most have been accused of naiveté. Such a demeanor in the world of adolescents almost seemed to demand that John be taken advantage of; usually there was someone to oblige. When I first talked with him about his work, he wondered whether he was again the butt of a bad joke.

JOHN: The way to get ahead in business is to marry the Company's daughter. I think I was the only member of our

class to go into the Loop. It's not easy to get into: in 1956
they hired only nineteen men. Maybe it had something to do
with my father being in the Company. I probably keep in
touch with more than half the Loop class. Most of them
have gotten farther than me.

It might sound like sour grapes, but it holds me back to
be a bachelor. I've read articles about how few single people
get ahead in the great corporations. Executives probably feel
that bachelors in their thirties or forties have wider interests
than the Steel Company. And the Company wants you to marry
it—if you haven't married a woman. Well, I'm not tied down.
I can take off to go skiing, so forth. A married man has kids,
and his other outlet is work. That shouldn't say that a bachelor can't be devoted to the Company.

When I was recently passed over for promotion—somebody was brought in from the outside to take the spot my
boss vacated—I went to see the vice president of sales. When
I asked him whether being single had anything to do with it,
he said, "No, what you do with your personal life is your
own business. But possibly a married person is a little bit
more stable than a single person." What a bunch of bullshit.
I know both single and married people who are whoring
around. I feel discriminated against.

If there are two people my age in the same job bracket,
both getting excellent ratings, but one has a great wife who
is an asset in entertaining and other things, has a nice family—obviously the Company is going to choose that guy.

Well, maybe I'll get promoted tomorrow. In fact, the shock
of being turned down was probably the best thing that happened to me. I'm working harder than ever. I'm a great believer in whatever happens to you is always for the good or
some good comes out of it later on. In essence, what the vice
president told me is that if I don't get promoted before I'm
forty-six, the chances are very slim afterwards.

I fully intend to get married sometime. I'm waiting for the
ideal woman, though I know she doesn't exist. But knowing
and feeling aren't the same. I'm looking. I'm horny as hell all
the time. But it's no hang-up, really. There's no pressure except from the church biddies who keep finding the perfect
girl for me. I get angry about that.

John St. Clair (far left) with colleagues. (Courtesy of John St. Clair.)

That's the sad part about the organized church these days —
a lot of people are into everybody else's business. The big thing
is openness. Fellowship groups, marriage groups — tell your
problems and have other people solve them. It's great with people you can trust, who aren't going to say anything — but it gets
around. This is a small town.

In November 1983, John and I got together again, having had little
contact since our previous conversation.

Well, things have changed in seven years. The steel industry as a whole is in financial trouble because of imports,

competition from mini-mills, high labor costs, government policies. And the big mills didn't keep up to date. Now Bethlehem Steel is going to become smaller and do what it's best at, like structural steel.

I was in bar sales for eighteen years. We started losing money because of the competition of mini-mills. Last Christmas the corporation decided to make a business unit out of bar production, with the total management in one unit—then go back to the unions and negotiate a contract. All the Lackawanna [Buffalo] plant was closed except the bar mills, and the operation was shifted to Johnstown, including the commercial or sales end. This is Bethlehem's first attempt to run things this way, and if it doesn't work the Johnstown unit will be sold.

I didn't want to move out of Bethlehem. The Company found me another job here—in marketing. I'm in a small unit, tool steel, and I've got to develop a market. I'm more or less left alone to do this; and marketing is a new concept at Bethlehem Steel. For me it's a lateral move. I don't want to go any farther; I'm content. Several of my loop course buddies have been very successful. One is a vice president. Several are district managers. But for me, moving up doesn't matter anymore. That's not where life is. I'm trying to become financially independent so I can tell the Company to shove it. I just want to stay long enough to get a pension.

Bethlehem Steel has gotten rid of everybody fifty-five and older. Those people made out very well by investing their lump sum payoffs in the market or small businesses. The Company has to keep me—I'm an expert. The Company's philosophy has changed. The chairman is from the outside—Price, Waterhouse—a numbers man. The Company had to do that. Now the city of Bethlehem can't depend on Steel so much, and United Way contributions are down. And I had to change my way of thinking to survive. Bethlehem Steel is no longer the Godfather. And I'm not intimidated anymore. I was before.

There's no optimism at all around the office. Everyone's walking the halls, shaking their heads. Damned if I'm going to live that way. They're thinking, "Is it me that's next going to be laid off?" In our department, most chose not to go to Johnstown, and most were laid off. They kept us college grads who went through the Loop course. The Company hasn't been handling this change right; it doesn't know how to handle people. It never had to handle people before! How much should employees be told? The Company was caught. It wanted to upgrade the quality of work and shaft people at the same time. The people who are laid off have about a year to look for a new job or get called back.

Actually, I have a much better attitude toward Bethlehem Steel. It's just another company, and we've got to work together to keep it afloat. And the vice president, when I was put in my new position, kind of gave me a pat on the back. Which was long in coming.

My activities outside the job have changed. I'm a Rotarian! What I'm involved in is their overseas exchange program. Housing students who come here and sending students overseas. And I bought a house — for a tax shelter. I go overseas to Norway and Denmark every year. I have a few friends around here, including a family I am sort of a substitute father to — I met them through one of the children in Explorer Scouts. I'm having a lot more fun. But I don't think I'll ever get married.

At the age of fifty John was offered and accepted early retirement from Bethlehem Steel. He immediately became the tennis coach at Liberty High School. No one in Bethlehem expected that high-level management would suffer much from the decline of the steel industry simply because its members would find ways to protect themselves. For workers the story appeared to be different.

———

I stopped by Gus Romero's house on a chilly Saturday morning in November 1983. Davy Salgado was soon there, and several of Gus's and Davy's children wandered in and out of the kitchen as we talked. I didn't see Gus's ninety-one-year-old granny (Davy's mother), who was somewhere nearby, but it was apparent that the growing family (Davy now has grandchildren) remains a tightly knit unit. In fact, Gus told a story of a job opportunity he once had, fifty miles away;

his wife refused to move. Both men clearly had close relationships with their children.

GUS: My son graduates from Lincoln Tech in February. That's an electronics school in Allentown. He's thirteeth in his class of sixty-five. But he can't find work anywhere. We even hired an employment agency. My son John works where I work, at the post office, and he's planning to go back to school in January. My daughter just graduated from Freedom High School. She's undecided on what she wants to do. She may go to the community college for a couple of years.

DAVY: The door opened up for me about three months ago—not jobwise but moneywise. I've gotten kind of loose. And Paul, my son, bought my mother's old house down in the coke works, the house Gus and I grew up in. Then he got a grant of six thousand dollars from the city to fix it up. He remodeled his whole house while he was laid off. Now he's back at Steel. Only Gary's having trouble getting work, though he's talented. But the other kids—and Gus's—have push.

Some of my kids and Gus's John have divorced and remarried. This divorce—I hope our generation isn't to blame.

GUS: Women have greater freedom now. They're in the job market competing. So if you have a woman who's self-reliant, she won't take no flak anymore, like our wives did.

DAVY: That's true. We have girls coming into the plant— payloaders, welders, machine operators. I have about twenty-two of them in my department. Eighty to ninety percent of them are good workers. When they get that money in their pocket and they know they can compete with men on an equal basis—and then you have a marriage—if it isn't fifty-fifty or better you're going to have problems. We've seen it. It's just like Gus said.

GUS: You can get a no-fault divorce for two hundred dollars.

DAVY: I don't know why they make it so easy. Just think how good it can be with two incomes.

GUS: My wife works part time. Nowadays you have to. When Reagan came in, then you couldn't get a grant or even a loan from the government for your kids in school.

Gus Romero and Davy Salgado in Gus's kitchen. (Photo by JEI.)

DAVY: Gus's kids go to school and mine get in training programs. We do it differently.

GUS: The days when you could say to you kids, "Well, you can always get a job in the Steel Company," that's gone.

DAVY: That's gone, Joe. A lot of people have been laid off.

GUS: They're moving away.

DAVY: Kids that have ten to twelve years in the plant, if they don't have trades like mine do, forget it. Or if you don't go to college, forget it. That day of getting something with a high school diploma is just about over.

GUS: Even college doesn't help that much. We have people with teaching degrees working as clerks in the post office.

DAVY: Steel has offered people ways to retire. But I can't. I have twelve years to sixty-two, otherwise I'd get $542 a month. That's nothing. Since 1958 it's been shaky at Steel. We got guys with twenty, thirty years behind them, working labor. They're waiting to get sent back to better jobs, but they won't be.

To appreciate the full irony of the respective fates of managers and workers, the relationship of the two must be traced from its beginnings.

Charles M. Schwab was the first leader of the Bethlehem Steel Company, and he handpicked his successor, Eugene G. Grace, who became president in 1913 and chairman of the board in 1945, where he remained until 1957. Schwab established and Grace reinforced a policy of paternalism, not only within the hierarchical and inbred ranks of management but also for the labor force. In 1918, with the blessing of the National War Labor Board, Bethlehem implemented a company union, or Employee Representation Plan (ERP), ostensibly an effort to open communication between labor and management and grant collective bargaining.

Bethlehem, like other steel companies, was adamantly opposed to trade unionism — the Amalgamated Association of Iron and Tin Workers hardly had a foot in Bethlehem's door — and saw company unionism as the alternative. And it worked, since practically no labor problems even reached the management level but, instead, were resolved by foremen and supervisors in the departments where grievances arose. In 1924, through publication of *The Bethlehem Review*, the Company regularly praised the operation of the ERP and, of course, condemned other forms of worker representation.

Furthermore, in 1924, Bethlehem created an Employees' Saving and Stock Ownership Plan, which would give labor a personal stake in Company prosperity. There was also a Pension Plan (1923) and an Employee Relief Plan (1926) providing disability benefits. There was even a program to help workers with their housing. Bethlehem's efforts to develop loyalty were typical of the business philosophy of the 1920s. And when the Depression came, the Company developed an Emergency Employment Program and systems of part-time employment and work sharing.

But by this time, the federal government had become more active in economic affairs than ever before, and section 7(a) of the National Industrial Recovery Act of 1933 called for collective bargaining. Bethlehem claimed to offer as much through its ERP. In 1935, the National Labor Relations Act (Wagner Act) gave an even bigger boost to the industrial organization of labor, essentially underwriting the formation of the Steel Workers Organizing Committee (SWOC), which had little support at any of Bethlehem's plants. In 1936 the Company instituted a plan of paid vacations for its employees.

And the Company became actively anti-union. Praising the accomplishments of ERP, President Grace warned that "anything that disturbs our present condition will imperil the interests of all," and promised the workers "that we will use our resources to the best of our ability to protect you and your families from interference, intimidation and coercion from any source." When SWOC successfully organized U.S. Steel in 1937, Bethlehem and four other "little steel" companies granted the same wages and working hours. Soon afterward, Jones and Laughlin negotiated with SWOC and the Wagner Act was declared constitutional. Ten strikers and sympathizers were killed at Republic. But worker protests at Bethlehem's Cambria works in Johnstown were quelled; the Company was standing firm.

A tough, uncompromising anti-union stance may be the breeding ground of a tough, uncompromising union. Certainly it is clear that unions in America resemble the industries which they have organized. SWOC, which in 1942 became the United Steel Workers of America, was headed by Philip Murray, a former lieutenant of John L. Lewis of the United Mineworkers who was almost as adamantly outspoken as his ex-boss. This union was put together from the top; it was and is highly certified; its leaders have always come from its own management and not the local level; and its voice has frequently been autocratic. The United Steel Workers of America was not unlike the Bethlehem Steel Company.

The Company fought hard against its growing rival. In 1939 it was ordered by the National Labor Relations Board to cease interference with the self-organization of its workers—and to abolish the ERP which thwarted the will of the workers! (In the 1970s, oral historians found many Bethlehem workers who by the late 1930s, at least, considered the ERP unresponsive to their needs. Pro-union men were outright contemptuous of it.) SWOC began an intense organizing campaign. Meanwhile, because of defense contracts in 1940, the Company was showing terrific profits. When wages did not follow profits, SWOC called a strike—very short but successful—at Bethlehem's Lackawanna plant in February 1941. In another short strike in March, SWOC scored a victory at the main (Bethlehem) plant. Later in 1941, the NLRB conducted an election throughout Bethlehem's mills and SWOC won it handily; soon all of the "little steel" companies were organized.

Negotiations, however, stretched into World War II, an era when company profits were high, national defense was an issue, and labor's rights under the Wagner Act were guarded by the National War Labor Board. The United Steel Workers Organizing Committee, which now replaced SWOC, not only got a good contract but established the precedent for a pattern: from 1940 on, steel profits were high enough to grant steelworkers top wages and employment conditions. It looked as if it could continue forever.

It did last a long time. The United States emerged from World War II the most prosperous nation on the globe. In 1950 it produced almost half of the world's raw steel. Without undue modesty, the chairman of U.S. Steel announced: "Americans, of course, don't like to take second place in any league, so they expect their steel industry to be bigger and more productive than the steel industry of any other nation on earth. It is." In 1982 another chairman of U.S. Steel confessed: "We now realize that American industry has no manifest destiny to be always first, always right, always best."

But the postwar boom was deceptive for a long time. Domestic steel was being used to construct the infrastructure of the nation: buildings, bridges, roads (at a time when the federal budget for highways was second only to defense spending). Not to mention automobiles and beverage cans. Steel was shipped overseas to rebuild Europe and Japan. Now the infrastructure is in place, other products have superseded steel (more concrete in bridges, plastic in cars, aluminum in cans), and the rebuilt nations are competitors. As early as the 1950s the growth in demand for steel was sluggish; in 1959 for the first time in the twentieth century, steel imports exceeded exports. Seemingly unaware of these developments, the steel companies not only expanded capacity but did it at a time when the technology of steelmaking was on the verge of being revolutionized. What obsolescence means is that whereas in the 1950s the Japanese required thirty-six man-hours to produce a ton of cold rolled steel and the U.S. required twelve man-hours, in the 1980s the U.S. requires 25 percent more man-hours per ton than Japan.

Thus, labor's demands in the 1950s could be met through technological superiority. And the United Steel Workers of America made demands: there were strikes in 1946, 1948, 1952, 1955, 1956 and 1959. The last one, long and bitter, neither side willing to concede, was ended in its sixteenth day as President Eisenhower invoked the Taft-Hartley Act. The union won its battle against changes in work rules, but neither side won the war.

It was not high wages, however, nor foreign imports, nor government intervention (though the consolidations proposed by steel companies probably should have been allowed), nor the creation of the mini-mills which melt steel scrap in electric furnaces to produce special products for regional markets (and are usually non-union) that was the dominant feature of steel's decline. Rather, it was the inability of management to forecast changing market conditions (a mature economy spends in the service sector, on such goods as computers and, therefore, requires less steel) and to use investment dollars for modernization instead of distributing funds among declining plants in the unrealistic hope that a boom in demand would utilize all existing capacity. Just before his death in 1960, Eugene G. Grace pronounced the dogma: "I have no doubt that the story will be one of increasing per capita use of steel in spite of the development of competing materials. I have no qualms about excess capacity. The United States will never catch up to its material needs and aspirations."

Grace's attitude was reflected in management wages. In the fateful year of 1959, *Business Week* listed seven Bethlehem Steel executives among the ten highest-paid in the nation. Still, it was not until 1977 that the Company showed up in the red, and profitability was apparently restored during the next two years. Before retiring as chairman of the board in 1980, Lewis Foy hosted 250 managers and their wives to a company-paid trip to Boca Raton, Florida—fishing, golfing, and drinking in the opulent manner for which the Company was famous. But Foy's successor, Donald Trautlein, delivered such a grim message about Bethlehem's future that one attendee referred to the closing banquet as the Last Supper.

Bethlehem had already begun to cut its capacity in response to losing much of its West Coast market to Japanese imports, and by

1984 its production of raw steel stood somewhere between 17.5 and 18 million tons, down from 25 to 26 million tons in the early 1970s. Not only the small Los Angeles mill but the large Lackawanna plant was closed, while the Johnstown and Steelton operations were reduced to electric furnaces (and the small electric-furnace shop in Seattle was up for sale).

Burns Harbor, Indiana, the only fully integrated steelmaking plant to be constructed in the U.S. in the 1960s (in response to the government's blocking Bethlehem's merger with Youngstown Sheet and Tube) is operating at capacity but, except for installation of a continuous casting machine (now deprived of steel slabs from the defunct Lackawanna operation), no new expenditures are planned.

Sparrows Point [Baltimore], the largest of Bethlehem's plants, has been partially modernized. The continuous casters being installed at Burns Harbor and Sparrows Point have been financed by outside investors who get depreciation and investment tax credits that would not benefit Bethlehem, which lacks large profits that need to be sheltered; consequently, the Company can make mill improvements worth $540 million without using its own cash. Financial creativity is becoming an important element in steel's survival. The mill in Bethlehem, whose principal products are structural shapes and bars, installed a basic oxygen furnace but is cutting back from four to two blast furnaces. Bethlehem, like other companies, is moving away from the integrated supermarket of steel production into marketing products where it has an edge.

While the growth of mini-mills that already provide 25 to 30 percent of the steel sold in the U.S. cannot be arrested, foreign imports that contribute about 22 percent of steel shipments can be fought. Bethlehem's Chairman Trautlein has led the battle for import quotas, and the United Steel Workers of America have backed him on this issue. President Reagan, who wears the image of free trade but wanted support from industrial areas in the election year of 1984, delicately straddled the matter by calling upon fair trade laws and "voluntary restraint agreements" with steel exporting countries. Import quotas are in place until 1989. But protectionism has its own dangers, as critics of this policy have pointed out. Nor did the president's proposal provide that profits from protectionist measures be reinvested in steel (rather than non-steel) areas, as proposed by a bill pending in the House of Representatives. Everyone knows the problems faced by the steel industry run deeper than those of foreign trade.

In the second quarter of 1984 Bethlehem Steel showed its first profit since the fourth quarter of 1981. Dividends have continued to stockholders. And labor is resentful as suffering goes on. Membership in the United Steel Workers, which rose from 660,000 in 1942 to 1.4 million in 1979, has dropped dramatically to 750,000. A study of laid-off steelworkers in Chicago over five years shows their income to have been cut almost in half. Bethlehem Steel as of Christmas 1983 had cut its employment costs by $1 billion — and its work force from 90,000 to 60,000 employees.

_____

I remembered Judy Newell from high school as lively, bright, and attractive. She was unchanged when I visited her, along with her husband, Walt, and three children, at their home in Lakewood, Ohio, a suburb of Cleveland.

I had last seen her when she left high school to enter Penn State, where she was the first woman to graduate with a major in labor relations, a fitting tribute to her father, C. B. Newell, who until his untimely death had been the director of the United Steelworkers of America for the Middle Atlantic region.

After college, she moved to Pittsburgh, married, and cut her career short to have a family. With two pre-schoolers in the house, she weathered a move to Cleveland where she knew no one. Walt, after working all day, attended law school at night. They had little money.

But she had already known strict economy, if not poverty, during her childhood in Kentucky, and she reminisced about those days and about her father, who worked as a movie projectionist, drove an ice cream truck, and even went into the coal industry.

JUDY: I remember my mother and my father talking about these jobs. Every job he had he tried to organize. He must have felt there was some kind of injustice with the way they were working. He started his organizing in steel at Armco in Kentucky. I can recall him talking about very nasty strikes, picket lines where he had gone. He was in jail. He came to Bethlehem right before the end of the war. He may have been a staff representative there earlier, but that's when he was appointed director.

We moved to Allentown from the hills of Kentucky. At that

time labor unions in Allentown, Bethlehem, and Easton were really a dirty name. We were scorned, and living along Route 22 was just too much of an adjustment. So we moved to Taylorsburg, out into the Poconos, back into the hills. My brother and I went to a one-room school.

Then we moved onto New Street in Bethlehem for three years, then out to Freemansburg. I was at Moravian Prep for two years, and I wanted to stay there. But my parents wouldn't allow it. They said I was becoming a snob.

When I was in school in Bethlehem, I still considered myself a hillbilly. It was me against the world, I guess. They were all the same to me. They were all Pennsylvania Dutch to me. They all had that Pennsylvania accent. Of course, I had a hillbilly twang to them.

I can't tell you what year it was—I must have been in high school, maybe college. I can remember driving in the car with my dad in Bethlehem, and that day or the night before there had been an editorial in the [Bethlehem] *Globe-Times* on the labor union and C. B. Newell. And it was glowing. [Unbeknownst to Judy, my Uncle Dale wrote it.] I was so proud. We were reminiscing that day about what it was like when he came to Pennsylvania and how the unions were thought of then.

People made me aware of a class distinction between Bethlehem Steel people and me in high school. When I was finally asked to join a sorority, it was kind of late to be asked to join. I was flabbergasted that I was asked; my mother was too. I wasn't too aware of sororities, and I wasn't so interested in joining. It was my mother who wanted me to widen my circle of friends. Not necessarily with children of management people. But through high school there were certain kids that I would have liked to loaf around with, and I simply could not.

A lot of teachers at the high school recognized the name "Newell"—and, if anything, that was in my favor. They were all for that. I can remember going into an American history teacher's room, and he said, "Oh, are you C. B. Newell's daughter?" A's. No sweat in that class.

This was true in high school—I don't know about the boys, it was with me and maybe with the other girls—I could pick out maybe one girl that I considered a really close friend. I might have a lot of friends, but I might have only one person that I considered a really best friend that I could talk to, tell them everything.

And it seemed to me like the guys, they didn't have any close friends, they didn't pick on one person being special.

WALT: Because the guys didn't have to confide in anybody. It's a different situation. I don't have to confide. There's nobody I have to talk to for anything.

JUDY: I don't mean *have* to; it's just something that you do.

WALT: I know what you're saying. You call up and say, you can tell one girl who's your best friend everything. I don't think that man's nature is that I have to call somebody and tell him everything. There's a different nature between a man and a woman.

JUDY: I had one or two close friends in high school. But my mother was the person I always confided in. And also my father. I was very close to them. My children don't do that with me, but I think it was unusual for me to do it with my parents. I think it was their nature, their personality, their way of handling situations and any problems that I brought to them. I think they were quite unique. I wish I knew how they did it, that made me feel so free and confident in them.

I could come in from a date, go up and sit on their bed, and go as far as telling them about a guy wanting to make out and I didn't want him to. And they—heaven only knows how they managed to not laugh at me when I was talking to them, but they did it. And they told me what they thought. My father was the one who told me it was all right to let a boy kiss me good night.

I don't feel hurt that my kids don't do that with me. Maybe they feel they could, but they don't. I don't think many kids do. Maybe I'm the odd one. But it sure was nice to be able to do.

My daughter thinks nothing of calling her boyfriends. I would have turned green before I called a boy. I think it's nice to have that freedom. In that sense, I think women's lib is great. That they can understand each other that well.

But this is probably blasphemy to the women's libbers. I

would feel if there's both a man and a woman applying for the same job and they were both equally capable of doing it, I think the man should have it. He is most likely the bread-winner; he needs it more than she does.

Judy could hardly have anticipated what was next in store for her. As she wrote several years after our conversation: "My own life has changed so drastically since I saw you. I'm sure it's a good thing we can't know our future because I would have said 'I can't do that!'" In 1980, Walt had brain surgery to remove a cyst which almost killed him. The operation has left him with impaired memory and unable to drive due to the loss of right peripheral vision.

His law firm let him go, so Judy is working full time as a secretary at the high school. The two older children graduated from college magna cum laude, though one of them had to amend his plans for medical school, and the third has just begun his academic work. But the impact of Walt's condition is evident five years later. "It is truly stunning to have your life changed so overnight—almost like the death of a loved one [I thought of the untimely death of Judy's father] only this pain lingers on. . . . We have learned to cope and there are some days—or parts of days—when things seem almost normal. . . . When I look back on my remarks in the interview, I marvel at how much I have changed."

———

Fran Csencsits finished her education at Liberty, married her junior high school sweetheart, moved into a house adjoining his parents' home, and had two children, who were sixteen and ten when I first visited her. She had not expected to be a working mother nor had I pictured her in that role, since my memory of her was as a majorette with the Liberty High School band.

FRAN: I grew up down in the Heights, where the oxygen furnace is now. Whenever we told anybody we were from the Heights, we thought the other side—South Terrace [a housing project]—was bad. We're still on South Side because of my husband, his not ever having a steady job. My mortgage is paid off now, and I don't intend to ever move from here. My girlfriend keeps telling me this is my security blanket, this house.

My husband just decided to go in business for himself
three years ago. So we're just where we started at again, you
know? We never had a great deal of money before, and now
we have less. With two growing kids, especially a boy, you
can imagine what that is.

Maybe if he makes a lot of money ten years from now.
But I'll be fifty-three by then. To me it's half of my life wasted
already. I've always struggled. He was making good money
before he went on his own. That was the longest he worked
at one place, almost seven years. We avoid arguments—we
just don't bring up the subject.

I work up at [Bethlehem Steel] Research three hours. I
thought of going full time again, but then I did that all those
years. After our son was born. Then when I had Donna I
worked full time. My mother and my mother-in-law watched
the kids. We bought this house partly because my mother-in-
law lived next door. I guess it worked out. Then from here I
could walk to work.

I don't feel I can put in eight hours anymore. I've just had
it. My house was very neglected when I worked full time.
And he didn't like to hear me complaining that I was always
tired. But the money was nice. So I really have gotten independent—I would say in the last five or six years—for myself
I just don't cater to him as much as I used to, because I think going into this business has driven us apart. And it's too bad,
but that's the way it is.

Frank and I have been—not that we were able to date or
anything—but I was in ninth grade at Washington Junior
High when I'd meet him after football games or we'd go to
the school dances together. And like it's just been him and
I—and maybe that's the reason I'm getting, I don't know, disgusted or whatever you want to call it. It's just so much of
one person, and now after all these years—I don't know what
it is.

I see quite a few of the girls that lived around in our section of the Heights where I was brought up. Rosey John,
Skip John's wife—she's satisfied with her life. He makes a
good living for them, and she has three or four nice children.
Elsie Spishak, she comes up to Research for lunch. Her and I
used to be at the West Building together, shortly after we

both got out of school. She married an older fellow. I understand she has a good life. Do I sound like I'm envious? I try not to sound like that ever.

When you're in the home you have a lot of time to think about what could have been, what you should have done. Everybody's so different. They say money is the evil of all things, right? But I still say that's half of your battle. It's nice to have it. And especially if you started out and didn't have to struggle all the years that you do. Like if we always had the money, and if I didn't always feel like I had to contribute, maybe I would feel different, too.

I'm a big mouth, a lot of people tell me. If I don't like things or I don't agree with people—that's another change that I think that I've found in myself—I've always said what I've thought or what I didn't like, but in the last five years or so I *really* say what I think. I do this at work. I feel if it's the truth and that person gets mad, well, that's too bad. Because I don't really care. I'd want someone to tell me.

This is a lot with Frank and I. When we first got married we were both thick, really thick. Italian blood, German blood. Nobody was giving in. Over the years I found—I thought I gave in a lot. We'd sit down and talk—he thought he gave in. How do you win? I hope I'm teaching my kids the right thing—from how we were living. I just don't want them to end up the way Frank and I were, or are, you know—crabbing all the time, or finding fault with one another.

But see, a lot of that is the way Frank was brought up. Because his dad, he only worked construction. And there was never any money there. And I still say, the kids do follow a lot like the parents. Now my dad always struggled and worked, and when he didn't work he went up on the farm and worked. Whereas my in-laws expected everybody to hand things to them.

My dad, he was so strict. And do you know, I find myself doing the same things to my kids that he used to do to me. And yet at the time he used to do things I resented it—I stayed in the house for a week, or if I didn't do this right I got punishment. I don't want to, but I do it.

But I show, and my kids show, a lot more affection to each other than my mother and dad did with us. If we walked out

the door to school or anywhere, we never kissed my mom
and dad. Even when my mother was in the hospital—isn't
that terrible that you'd feel ashamed to kiss your own mother?
But we never did that in our house. We were never an affectionate family. Now my kids, whenever they leave this house,
they always kiss me goodbye. I feel I've done a lot better with
my kids.

I'm not saying it's my mother's fault or my father's fault.
Well, my father is one of those hard Germans—he wouldn't
show affection, if you were on your deathbed he wouldn't
show affection to you.

Frank isn't as involved with the kids. Mike wouldn't give
him a kiss on the way out of the house. Donna always gives
him a kiss good night. He loves his kids. But he just didn't
spend the time with them. There's a lot of things you would
think father and son could talk about, but they don't go to
him for anything. It's always me they come to. First of all, he
doesn't have any patience. He has less patience than I have,
and I don't have too much.

And—he would deny this, I know he would—if the kids
wanted to talk to him about something at supper, or if he
just walked in the door he never had time when they wanted
to tell him something. He'd say, "Not now, later," or, "Not
now, I'm reading the paper," or, "I'm reading the paper; talk
to me later." Well, they don't want to talk to him about it
later. So now they don't say much to him.

And maybe that's my fault too—well, not my *fault*. I've
just always taken time out, no matter how many times it really
got me mad that I had to stand there and listen to all this
stupidness.

I have two girlfriends that I'm kind of close to. But they're
both completely opposites. The three of us never get together.
I talk with one on the phone a lot of times. But the other
girlfriend, we do things together; that's Elsie Spishak. The
other one is Rosie Fertal, Rosie DeDonato, her brother was
police chief until the new administration took over. I like
Rosey because she gets me to look at things in a different
way, like, "It's not all that black." Which is what you need a
lot of times. If I'll complain to her about something, she'll
say, "Well, my kids do it too." Or maybe it's Frank. After I

get off the phone with her I feel a lot better. I look at it, try to see it his way. Rosie and I have really gotten close.

The job I have now, it's only three hours. It gripes me anyone says, my husband for one, "I could stand on my head for three hours." For three hours we are constantly running. You bus dishes, you waitress, you work the dishwasher—when you work that job, you are dead. How many men will pass us and say, "I wouldn't work this job if they gave me ten dollars an hour." It's constant go, go, go. Those are the men we like, right? They sympathize with us, they know we're really working hard.

But I find when we get talking up there, talking about home, he's not the only one that says that. But the thing of it is, you don't just work three hours—that's in addition to everything I've done here. Then there are men that think it's just great that their wives will get a three-hour job in addition to taking care of the house. I guess it's a good thing we're not all alike.

Anyway, I would never quit this job. The hours are nice; like I said, I get my housework done in the morning. If I do too much in the morning before I go up there, I don't know what to do with myself, I get so tired.

I like the job. I like being around people all the time. That I enjoy. We have a nice gang. We're kind of our own bosses up there. We all know what to do, we don't have to be told what to do. We have a real nice guy for a boss, sometimes too easygoing, we feel.

That woman should get paid as much as men, that they shouldn't be discriminated against, I think that just holds true in certain jobs. I'm not for the woman being in the home all the time. Nor am I for the woman who wants to do the man's job, not do it near as well and get the same pay. Any job that I ever wanted or tried to get, well, I wouldn't want a laborer's job. For the woman that wants it, I guess it's okay. My job is constantly going, but it isn't a dirty job. It's often just cleaning up and stuff. And office work is nice, I like that. I did that at Steel. Yes, men are the ones in power. I think that's the way it should be, don't you?

A few years after my conversation with Fran she wrote that her husband had moved out, she was looking for a full-time job, and after finding one she would file for divorce: "Sad ending for some stories, but for mine, a happy one." When I visited her in 1984 (with news of distant relatives of hers I had called on in Hungary), her son Mike had married, and her daughter Donna, star of Liberty High School's victorious girls' basketball team, was alone at home with her mother. Fran seemed absolutely content.

SERVICES

Since World War II the sector of the American economy which has grown fastest is services — people taking care of people. This role had already been assigned to women through teaching, nursing, and even acting as secretaries to needy male managers — all of which presumably prepared a female to be a good wife and mother. Nicky Klinkoff found her way into the job market after she had done her domestic duties; her route was unconventional. She and her husband, a steelworker and band leader (an enterprise he conducted with Katy Trivanovich's husband), ran an entertainment agency. And Nicky got on the lecture circuit.

NICKY: I've had four knee operations, two on each. The last time in the hospital I realized how many were hung up on soap operas. Anytime in the afternoon, the televisions are on. My roommate was hung up on "The Young and the Restless," and they had this love affair between Jill and Mr. Chancellor going on. She went up for surgery. And the first thing she said to me was, "What happened between Jill and Mr. Chancellor?"

So I started researching it. I spent three years writing to everybody and anybody about the early days of radio. I've got letters from Stella Dallas — I'm supposed to do an interview with her. And I started reading books about the early days of radio and black-and-white TV and then went into the color of today.

There are fourteen soap operas on during the day, and "Mary Hartman" at night. Actually, if you're watching "Mary Hartman" — a lot of people say, "It's the silliest thing I've ever seen" — but if you read between the lines, it's today. It's really today. There's supposed to be some startling things happening with "Mary Hartman" this year. I was at a fan club party in New York last week for twelve of the stars. And I talked

Nicky Klinkoff as featured in the print media watching TV. (Published by permission of *The Morning Call*. Phil Boyle, photographer.)

to Paul Dennis, who's the author of *Daytime TV* magazine, and he says, "Startling developments."

I started a while ago learning about the stars, about the programs, about the contracts. I started putting everything together. Then the girl over at the library asked me to do a lecture there one night—and that started the whole thing. The response then—I couldn't believe it. And a lot of people won't admit that they watch them until you get them together in a group. It's a private thing—you can cry with them, laugh with them, you can get mad. But when you get a group of anywhere from thirty to a hundred together, they watch this program or hate that character. They won't even give me a chance to finish the lecture.

Mostly they want to know what's going to happen. They're curious about the lives of the actors, especially the ones that play the so-called "bitch characters." Like Morgan Fairchild on "The Search for Tomorrow." When you meet her she is so completely opposite of the part she plays. They want to know what it's like on a set—I was on the set for "The Edge of

Night" last Friday. What it's like to put it together—a program is done in one day. And the actors want to know what the fans think. Like "The Edge of Night"—they have a couple of bitchy parts. And the people hate them, as characters. This is why a lot of the studios have to have guards. CBS. It looks like Jack Benny's vault when you to to CBS. Security guards all over the place. People can't be told that an actor is playing a character part.

The response to my lectures has been fantastic. I try to keep my lecture to an hour. They often have me there for two hours. Cedar Crest College had me there for three hours. Dr. John Lyon at the University of Maryland is doing a study of how soap operas affect people's life styles. He's asked me to send him anything I come up with in my lectures.

You know who really gets involved in these things? The ones in nursing homes, where the families have left them. They take on the families as their own. And they talk about them just as if they were their own family.

When I saw Nicky several years later, things had not changed.

I still do my soap opera lectures. I didn't get to see *Tootsie*—I got too much going now. Monday nights I sing with the church choirs; Tuesday during the day I go to NCAC women's college; Tuesday night I sing with the Choral Society; I just finished my arthritis course; Thursday mornings I swim; Fridays every two weeks I play cards. I figure Charlene's going to college next year—I am not sitting home.

I haven't been to too many parties lately, because I'm on the women's clubs lecture circuit. Now you got your nighttime soaps, you got "Dynasty," "Falcon Crest"—you got them all. Most women's groups like me as a change from travel lectures. And you'd be surprised how many men watch.

Soap operas are manifestly escapist. But the merchandizing of dreams and fantasies is not limited to these melodramas, as Dick Johnson's career clearly shows. He was characterized in the *Cauldron* as "a fellow with the middle name of 'Fun,'" who disliked gloomy people. This is the trait he capitalized on, with the full support of his wife,

Lorraine. They grew up together on either side of a double house on the West Side of Bethlehem, but some years after they married they built a home in the woods near Coopersburg, where they live with their two children and Lorraine's mother.

DICK: I basically didn't like school in that I didn't like to study. So that I didn't really want to go to college. For the first three years out of high school, I just worked in a grocery store and waited for the day that Uncle Sam would take me, which he didn't, and I finally volunteered to get it over with.

And then after I got out of the service—I spent a year in Germany—I was working in advertising and sales promotion for Durkee Foods. It was a big job. They had just moved from New York at the time, and they were hiring. Boy, I think of being at the right place at the right time. I went to fill out an application—they had an opening in their advertising and sales promotion department. Having had no background whatsoever in it, I got the job. I don't know why; I can't tell you why. And I worked there for five years.

And then I had reached a point, I had reached a plateau without a college degree, I had reached my limitations with the company. So that I looked for another job. It took me six months to train my college replacement! I say that with a little bitterness. I really wanted to stay. I loved it.

I was doing consumer contests, and I was answering letters from irate housewives that opened the can of pepper and all the pepper went in the stew and that kind of nonsense. It was an interesting job, and I'd worked up salesmen contests and this type of thing, set up sales meetings. So it was kind of an interesting job.

And I left there and I went to Stanco Electronics in Easton. It was another completely different field as a sales correspondent. And yet I was the liaison between the plant and the customer. The customer being people like Western Electric, this type of people—it was a transformer kind of thing. I *hated* the subject. I hated blueprints; I hated everything I did. Every day I hated it. I hated to go to work.

So, Lorraine was pregnant at the time, and I went into the

unemployment office and they at that time said the only thing they had was something at Hess Brothers. I said, "I certainly don't want to work at Hess's. I don't want to be involved in retail." But they suggested that I go for the interview anyway, which I did, and they of course offered me a job right there, that day, and I said I'd have to think about it. I slept on it and the next day I called and accepted the job, and it's probably the smartest thing I could have done. I've been there ever since and I've progressed rather rapidly.

LORRAINE: That's one place that doesn't necessarily go on a college background. One of the few places.

DICK: Right. I think it does more so now than it did. At that time the store was run by Max Hess. If he liked you, you stood a good chance of progressing. He, I guess, maybe liked me. I think everything is a personality thing. Everything is personalities. Personality is being at the right spot at the right time and all that. I had a lot of personal contacts with him. He was an eccentric merchandiser who was a showman.

LORRAINE: A comical man.

DICK: Yeah. You never knew what he was going to do from one day to another. That didn't bother me and that's why he liked me, I think. I respected who he was and the fact that he owned the store and was signing the paycheck, but I was not afraid to talk to him, and I think that's what he liked, because most people were kind of afraid of him. Those were the people that he would like to squelch, so to speak.

I started in the store in a training program; I trained for fifteen days and I was made a buyer. This is without any retail background. I bought men's hats. It was the smallest department in the store, but it was a good one to train in because you got all the basics of what a buyer would do: look for quality material, style; knowing what your customer wants; knowing the area that you're buying to sell in. And this kind of thing. Keeping up with the trends.

LORRAINE: Being ahead of the trends.

DICK: Being ahead of them, in our case. From there I bought men's accessories, which was a much, much larger department, which incorporated all the men's jewelry, small leather goods, belts, gifts, and all this kind of thing. A good department that I liked.

I opened the first men's fragrance bar in the area, and I

Richard and Lorraine Johnson at home. (Photo by JEI.)

think that's where I started to get involved in cosmetics and fashion. I put in fake mustaches and beards and all that kind of thing. The first time I ever did any kind of modeling was with my fake mustaches and beards.

We did a publicity stunt with the Allentown police. It was back at that time when they weren't allowed to have hair on their face, and we did a whole thing where I glued them up, and then I was even into styling them and trimming them and everything. I'd never done anything like this before either. That's why I say I think you get thrown into situations.

So from there I got involved with cosmetics. I was made cosmetics buyer, and I bought cosmetics for, I think, maybe three years, and then I got into women's ready-to-wear. This is basically when I started to travel for the store.

I was involved in women's ready-to-wear as assistant merchandise manager, and I did that for about a year and a half. That's when I started to travel with the fashion director in the store, for television, for fashion shows. More or less traveling with her, not really getting involved in it, but just being there.

When she left the store, I was made fashion director. It must have been about four years ago, and I was fashion director for about two years. I had made about twenty buying trips to Europe in that time. I was fashion director for two years, doing all the television bit—I mean you talk about becoming extroverted!

The first time I did a fashion show, a live one, I thought I was going to die. I thought I was just never going to survive the whole thing. I discovered during the show that I was getting off on the people; they were psyching me up. First of all, I didn't know anything about a dress—what is a dress? It has a hole and you put your neck in and you wear it, and there I'm gonna stand up before five hundred women and describe thirty fashions, and then do it with some kind of a story behind it, and some kind of meaning. I did it.

We do our shows for charity groups, so these were not professional people, maybe wealthy Main Line Philadelphians, very critical audiences. I shouldn't say this, but the first time I did a show, they loved me, and that was the feeling I had, they loved me. So it was fun to do. It also was a rat

race, because we did shows *every* night of the week, every
night. Not always in Philadelphia. I did a black tie thing
with Gina Lollabrigida at the Holiday Inn in Allentown. *That*
was an experience, I want to tell you.

Then the fashion director that left the store came back.
And I was asked how I would feel about going back to cosmetics again, because they were having problems in the area.
This time I said, yes, that I would go back, but only if I also
could be the merchandise manager and buyer and run my
own show in cosmetics, which I did, and this is about a year
and a half now, doing that. It was a promotion. Financially,
the job I'm doing now is much, much greater than the glori-
ous job of fashion director. This is certainly much more challenging mentally because of the people and the fact that you're
controlling millions and millions of dollars and how to spend
it wisely.

The companies create the demand by their own advertising
in fashion magazines. My job is to be on top of what they're
creating and make sure that we have it, when they're creating
that demand. And also to promote it wisely. Cosmetics has
got to be romanced because you're selling dreams, really,
first. Most of those things, take a ten-dollar jar of night
cream, probably is worth about fifty-nine cents. However, the
dream that you're selling, a woman will pay any amount of
money for a dream to look better.

I'm not sure that women fantasize more than men. I would
say that women *admit* to more. I remember my experience
selling men's hats. I discovered then that men are probably a
lot vainer than most women. Really. Even after having sold
dresses and this type of thing, a woman is a much easier customer, not nearly quite as vain as a man. I think it's in the
male personality.

And I think it's just maybe in the last five years or so that
we're bringing it out; we don't hide and use our wife's hair
spray, we buy our own. We use bronzers for face color and
admit to it, where we used to sneak around and do these
things. I think most men are now very conscious of fashion
changes and like to change their wardrobes with seasons rather
than keeping one thing from one year to another; they want
new things.

I think even the women that are really into the women's movement are still very conscious of how they look. Every woman wants to stay young forever, as does every man.

LORRAINE: It's getting to be an equalizer, too, that the men are doing as much in cosmetics as women.

DICK: Not "as much." It's gotten to be even greater. In California, I don't know how much you're into. There are complete make-up lines on the coast and in New York City for men. They're wearing lashes and mascaras and shadows. I think the movement is saying that, "Why can't a guy look great, why can't he take anything to accent his face like a woman can?"

You take men's fragrances. Maybe ten years ago we opened our first men's fragrance bar and it was like putting in a men's cosmetics line today would be.

LORRAINE: The hardest part was naming it!

DICK: We called it "The Men's Bar"—you have to really keep it masculine because most guys have this big hang-up about this. They were very reluctant; "What are you going to do to me?" and that kind of thing. Men have changed a lot in ten years.

LORRAINE: You also have to have someone who's able to get a man to do something that he normally—you know, is just going to sneak up to the counter.

DICK: I had a girl at my men's bar who was so flamboyant—she was very pretty, not sexy, very pretty, long blond hair—that had a personality that never quit. Never quit. She'd just jump out at you—you just couldn't help but talk to this girl, even if you were afraid to buy something, you had to talk to her. And that's what you needed to get the guy over his nervousness. She would say, "Try this, just try it, *smell* it," or something like that. It had to be this kind of girl. You couldn't have some little mousy—I cringe when I think of those kind of sales clerks, they're so mousy and hide behind the counter.

LORRAINE: He says it's like show business.

DICK: I think you're dealing in show business. If you're introverted, you've got to get out of it. I love the phrase, "Have a nice day." Say, for example, our store made every person say that. Some people could say, "Have a great day," and mean it, and some would say, "Have a great day," and they can't pull it off. I don't think you can make people—it's a personality trait. It's charisma. I would approve of hiring only the first kind of person, but I don't know that it could be done. You wouldn't end up with enough people! There's not that many people around like that.

LORRAINE: He hires a motivator from New York to talk to employees.

DICK: He tries to do this. He comes in twice a year, and he's really great. It's all the flag-waving. It psyches you up. Some people can't even be psyched up. You must get very frustrated with some students that just don't react. It's like when I did fashion shows. Sometimes I thought I was really great and all these faces looked back at me, looking at you, just waiting for you to say a wrong word.

LORRAINE: Then every now and then he'd say, "Are you out there?"

DICK: I would say, "Is there something wrong?" I would try to put them down. But an audience like that is so oblivious that you put them down and they didn't even know it. How a group of five or eight hundred people can all respond the same way—it's kind of incredible. And then you can get an audience that's so turned on—and I'm sure that anybody who's in any kind of show business must react this way. They must react to their audiences and an audience turns you on; it makes you better.

When I visited the Johnsons again, Dick had just been given a major promotion. Lorraine was doing public relations work for him; their daughter Kim was also employed at Hess's; and their son Todd—recently out of college with a psychology degree—referred to mealtime discussions as "the Hess's round table."

DICK: I had been an assistant vice president for almost seven years. Now I'm a full vice president. What that means I'm not really sure. We're really expanding; we're talking about a major acquisition of twelve or fifteen stores in Virginia or Maryland. And now we're owned by Crown America, so this is more of a corporate matter. This vice president thing will involve me in decisions on expansion; it has nothing to do with my major function which is merchandizing cosmetics for all twenty-nine stores.

I have 275 girls working for me. They all have problems. I think I could teach a psychology course. Often the problems are with their store managers, and the girls bring their problems to me. A month ago I celebrated my twentieth anniversary with the store, and the girls surprised me with a roasting at the Hotel Hershey. I took it as a tribute—the girls came from stores in Maryland, Pennsylvania, and New York.

LORRAINE: No other division in the store would do that. They're "his girls." They remembered things from twenty years back.

DICK: I think that I still—and maybe it comes from the old school—that retailing is a people business. And I still feel that that relationship with the people that work for you is very important. I think they do perform because—I'm not easy: I tell them I hate them, and I also tell them I love them. You can tell them you hate them and be demanding, as long as you also tell them you love them. And include them. Sometimes I make my stories a little more glamorous just to make the whole thing exciting in their eyes.

I suggested that, should I wait yet another seven years to talk to Dick, he might be president of Hess Brothers.

DICK: I doubt it. Number one, because I don't want to be. I also believe that you get to a point in a career or anything you're doing, and you can go here—and suddenly you've gone too far. I don't believe that I could handle it, mentally or physically. And I really don't want to. I'm very, very happy at the point that I'm at.

Where Dick is "at," literally, is in a house half a mile up the road from my parents, on a property adjoining my brother Tom's place. He settled where I was expected to be, and would have been, had I followed the example of my Illick ancestors.

Three Illigs—Andreas, Christopher, and Rudolph—came to Pennsylvania between 1729 and 1739, having left the lower Rhineland of today's Germany and Switzerland. Probably they and their progeny worked hard, but most of their descendents did not move far, geographically or occupationally. My grandfather, Joseph Illick, operated a grist mill on the fringe of Bethlehem and in 1902 moved into the city to become the proprietor of a flour and feed business. Later he bought, renovated, and sold properties on the North Side of town. Judging by his wife's unceasing activity in the kitchen, she had been nurtured in the same hard-working tradition he had.

On my mother's side of the family, the Flexer branch was also of German ancestry and also industrious. The reason my great-grandfather's coal and feed company collapsed was overextension of credit, not lack of energy. His son, my Papa, bypassed business for the ministry. The other branch of my maternal tree, Griffiths and Joneses, were penniless Welsh immigrants whose talent was iron-mongering. If in my mother's family there was less acquaintanceship with commercial enterprise, it cannot be said that hard work was considered undignified. Nana was simply incapable of it, and Papa had to handle some of her tasks as well as his own while they raised a family. When I knew him, he arose before 5:00 A.M. every morning to read his Bible and write articles for the fundamentalist Protestant quarterly he edited.

True, my mother worked as a librarian only until she started a family, but she was not still for a moment around the house. Dad taught briefly at Lehigh before finishing his M.A. and leaving for McClintock-Marshall Steel Company in Pottstown, thirty miles away. When he returned to work at Bethlehem Steel he resumed his teaching at Lehigh part time and began to move into the remodeling business. For relaxation he laid up the dry walls that gave Stone Fences one of its names.

I seemed destined to follow in my father's footsteps. I was restless in the classroom but enjoyed working in the school cafeteria, proud to be earning a free meal (twenty-five cents) for an hour's work in the fifth grade. I felt the same way a couple of years later when I began caddying at twice the pay I got at the cafeteria. At fourteen, I now and again would spend a Saturday mowing lawns at my dad's apartments, more than willing to work for the dollar a day. Though I had played Tom Sawyer on the stage in sixth grade, I did not in reality share Tom's pleasure in escaping labor. Rather, I wanted to be noticed at work because it seemed manly.

Working to me was different from thinking about a career. I did not see my father as an explicit role model; for a long time I did not know what job he held. I wasn't looking forward to any special vocation. And despite my occasional commitment to toil, I can recall summer days when I would wonder how any adult could bear to be indoors working when the world was saying "play." But I did get the message that a choice would have to be made some day. So I told my mother I thought I would be a gym teacher. This so alarmed her that she relayed my decision to our family dentist, whose office we were approaching when I revealed my choice. He ridiculed my selection of life's work more devastatingly than she could have.

I realized that my profession must be dignified, so I chose doctor. My mother, ever watchful, brought this up with a local orthopedist who happened by our house one evening. He replied that I'd have to master Latin — and be willing to travel to wherever the best job was. One of his medical school pals went all the way to Seattle! In the Illick family, New Jersey was plenty far enough.

I was not without dreams of going somewhere. The Liberty Bell, a swaying interurban trolley dating from the early years of the century, was my romantic connection with the outside world. It passed within half a mile of our house on its journey from Allentown to Sellersville where, it was said, you could transfer to another trolley going all the way to Philadelphia. When I heard its horn in the distance, especially on summer nights from the sleeping porch, I had visions of faraway excitement. My mother, too, felt I ought to experience a wider world, so she enrolled me for two weeks at Camp Miller, a Lutheran boys' get-together in the Poconos. Everyone seemed to be enjoying it. I was miserable, and a letter each day from my mother made me only the more homesick. I was torn between dreams of adventure and the reality of separation and anxiety — just as I was torn between an image of myself as a manly worker and the desire to remain forever an irresponsible child.

My father as well as my mother participated in tying me to home; it seemed quite natural to him, a man who had never lived outside the Lehigh Valley. Thus, when I graduated from high school and wanted to accompany three friends to the Oregon lumber mills for the summer, Dad discouraged me from going. A decade later, when I took a job in Kalamazoo, he often referred to it as Oshkosh; when I left for San Francisco, he thought it was Los Angeles. If it wasn't home, the name didn't matter.

Surely one reason I considered becoming a minister (but not, I hasten to add, a missionary) was that it seemed exalted enough, yet

Joe Illick at work with his father. (Photo courtesy of J. E. Illick, Jr.)

safe. Mother encouraged my leanings toward the clergy. Dad wasn't saying a word, though I noticed he always had a secular job available for me. At fifteen, I was apprenticed to a carpenter, shingling a house. Soon I was helping to stake out lots, dig foundations, pour concrete, excavate sewer lines, lay block walls, put up siding, nail down roofers, hammer in flooring, paint closets and sash, grade and sow lawns.

But my most enduring lessons were along more human lines. Dad's workers consisted of several families in addition to our own (my brothers Flex and Tom and cousin John also eventually joined the gang), plus a few odds and ends—mainly odds, such as Tommy the painter, who described his religious visions at length and in detail to a rudely skeptical audience. The senior inside carpenter and his two sons were alcoholic and ornery, ready to fight. The oldest outside carpenter, also a drinker, was an irredeemable slob who left a trail of chewing tobacco on his work and sometimes even vomited as he hammered yet never slowed down, all the time showing his contempt for the younger craftsmen who couldn't keep up with him. They, in turn, mercilessly picked on an illiterate handyman who was the bastard nephew of one of them.

Half the conversation among the workers was about how they cheated on their wives—or would, if they had the opportunity. There was irony in the fact that we were building homes. I missed the irony but unconsciously, at least, noticed that Dad (who may not have heard the choicest tales, since the men were at their busiest when the boss was around) absorbed the stories and witnessed the evidence of drunkenness, adultery, and mean-spiritedness without losing his composure. And certainly without changing his own sober, faithful, loving way. He was discreet, however: not once did he reveal to mother what went on at the job. I learned that men compartmentalized their experience and protected women from parts of it.

Any one of my father's construction gang could have earned more money at Bethlehem Steel; each seemed instinctively to prize his freedom from the factory. But I was curious, not to say greedy, and as soon as I reached the minimum age of eighteen, I took a job as a laborer in the mills.

On the construction site our largest machine was a ready-mix concrete truck. Now I was among the giants. My assignment was the erection floor (talk about images of male power!), where two mobile overhead cranes, running on tracks three stories above me, raised and lowered massive parts onto and off of the machines whose operatives repaired them. The potential for accident—a careless chainman who did not properly secure his load, a craneman who carried his cargo too low and struck a standing object, a stress failure in the chain—somehow increased the thrill of working there.

I signed up for the middle shift, 4:00 P.M. to midnight, which not only allowed me to continue working for my father during the day but, because the pace at the plant slowed as we moved into the evening, gave me the opportunity to slip off into other shops and observe the beauty of steel-making: the fiery open hearths reflected in the Lehigh River, the ceaseless activity of the bar and sheet mills, and the newly poured ingots glowing in the night. I felt as though I was part of the biceps of the nation, flexed and strong. (When I think that young men in postindustrial America today must take jobs in electronics or data processing, I pity them.)

Of course, I was only passing through. I knew that I would not be permanently working with my hands in the machine shop or at any other blue-collar job. It was the managerial class that I expected to join with my college degree. There was no shortage of jobs for engineers in 1956, when I graduated from Princeton. That spring I visited Pittsburgh, Cleveland, and Cincinnati; toured steel mills, oil refineries, and soap factories; talked with hiring personnel, production managers, assistants to vice presidents, and at one place a psychologist who told me, as a result of a day's testing, that I'd be happier in a classroom than an industrial plant or office. That only sanctioned what I already sensed. (My choice was also confirmed in a report commissioned by the U.S. Department of Health, Education and Welfare in 1972, where it was noted that 93 percent of urban university professors would choose similar work again, the highest percentage of all groups polled. At 21 percent, unskilled steelworkers were close to the bottom.) That I could contemplate a change of course from manager to professor says less about my wisdom than it does about the privilege of choice afforded some people, such as me, in modern society.

As an undergraduate I had slowly and reluctantly begun to realize that my engineering skills were weak while my enjoyment of liberal arts electives was strong. Still, when I thought about making a living I viewed my interest in art history or English literature as frivolous. And I worried about myself as I came to realize that while my college classmates were primed and eager to move into the world of business, I felt uneasy in every job interview I had. The extended family and rural setting of my youth were almost pre-industrial, not brought up to date by the working experiences of my adolescence, and I felt inadequate among the aspiring Princetonians whose outlook was so much more modern than mine.

Yet I had moved too far from home to be able to return to the family construction business without suffering the shame of retreat. Even the managerial training program at Bethlehem Steel seemed too familiar. And in both situations I would remain an engineer. I turned to graduate school as a way out of this dilemma. It appeared to be an independent step — and one that would fulfill my yearnings for the liberal arts. Yet it did not have the finality of a decision about a career. In fact, it was not really a decision at all, since the industrial options would remain open. And, to my satisfaction, I found I could teach civil engineering at the University of Pennsylvania while pursuing my goal of an M.A. in history, after which I would have the option of becoming a secondary school teacher.

Yet graduate school was a strange place for me to be. Its atmosphere was not active and manly, as I had thought work ought to be, but reflective and even feminine, insofar as during my youth I thought that reading was activity for girls. Books had been a last resort for me, and I turned to them only when driven by a teacher or my mother. Now I had to reconcile myself to living with them — and I found the adjustment surprisingly easy. Indeed, reading seemed a very small price to pay for settling among congenial people in graduate school. The library provided a haven from a world I did not want to enter.

And, as a relief from studying, there was teaching. At Princeton the undergraduates referred to the Gothic graduate school edifice as "the goon castle," and we never doubted that the intense and unfashionably dressed creatures who emerged from it to direct our classrooms belonged to another and inferior order of being. Consequently, I was unsurprised to encounter among some Penn graduate students the flip side of that coin: undergraduates were stupid philistines whose function was to provide work for scholars who would rather be doing research than teaching.

Experience proved that students at the University of Pennsylvania were mainly pleasant and bright, not terribly interested in history but willing to give it a try, most of them strangers (as I was, and for a long time continued to be) to a world of ideas rather than things. I regarded them as peers in an experience most of us were not well prepared for.

At ease in the atmosphere of library and classroom at the University of Pennsylvania, I pushed on for a Ph.D., landing in the job market of higher education. Upward progress led to lateral movement as well. A large, public urban university seemed the best of possible worlds, and I could not resist an offer from San Francisco State despite my parents' obvious displeasure with my taking a job three-thousand miles from home. I rested uneasily on what was, for my previously stationary family, the cutting edge of mobility. Summers I taught on the East Coast, while the rest of the year I lived in California. How else could I apply both lessons that I, like so many American children, had learned: stay close to your family and act upon the opportunity that draws you away.

The books I have written are about Pennsylvania. When I managed several large historians' conventions and even when I served as president of the teachers' union I realized my style of operation closely resembled my father's conduct of the building business. I have thus remained close to my family in several ways, and I have worked as hard as my forebears. Most of my labor as a university professor has, happily, been in the classroom—sixty semesters (plus summer schools) since I began in 1956, or six thousand students, all of whom I once knew by name. A few have become my closest friends. The classroom itself is reminiscent of the family experience—and in that sense I haven't traveled so far after all.

6 | *Marriage*

"There's a great gap between men and women," mused Forrest Kalmbacher as he described his ex-wife's interest in the piano and weaving compared to his own absorption with athletics and beer drinking with his buddies. "She was shocked when I said, 'It's not working out.'"

"I think he kept himself so busy for almost twenty years that he never stopped to think where he was going or what he was doing," Sandra Styles recalled over dinner one evening. "All of a sudden he realized he wasn't getting any farther. There was no talking to him. All of a sudden he was talking to *her*, and *I* didn't make any sense." Later she reflected that, unlike her ex-husband, she had a great capacity for contentment and happiness. But she also confessed that for decades she had not taken control of her own life, and she wondered whether she had wanted to.

Is the "great gap" to be understood in anthropological terms: the male hunter and protector bewildered by the female gatherer and homemaker and vice versa? And to what extent does this "great gap" exist? For I saw many classmates who gave every appearance of enjoying felicitous unions. Yet one of the most content, who is in constant contact with other women through the chorus she directs, expressed astonishment at "how many people that are married are not happy [and] they won't admit it."

If observers of modern marriage agree upon anything, it is that the institution—once forged and maintained for economic reasons, frequently in response to parental wishes—is now formed from love, and emotional harmony is expected to sustain it. And, as we all know, feelings are not reliably consistent. Furthermore, life expectancy has risen so dramatically since the turn of the century (from fifty to seventy-five years) that partners are faced with the prospect of being together for much longer than previously. If familiarity breeds contempt, divorce now accomplishes what death used to.

Nor are feelings likely to be the same for both sexes. Feminists argue convincingly that since women are the primary caretakers of both boys and girls, the psychological consequences will be different for either gender. *He* must achieve his maleness by repressing his attachment to his mother, building defenses against the pleasure she gives and, in the process, perhaps becoming angry and aggressive toward the gentler sex. *She* may remain attached to her mother, becoming a nurturer and love-giver to both sexes, but a person whose inner life is more complicated than her male counterpart's. "Can these two persons be anything other than 'intimate strangers'?" ask feminists such as Lillian Rubin, who certainly believes the "great gap" exists.

I did not expect my married classmates to acknowledge or discuss joyless relationships, if indeed such relationships existed, and only a few ventured into such a private area. But I realized that those persons who had experienced the agony of divorce and had already articulated the causes of pain might willingly speak about the circumstances and their feelings.

Among the few married persons whose conversations appear in this chapter, I included a classmate who could say why her union was strong and what she cherished in her mate. As noted in chapter 2, couples predominate in the Class of 1952. Almost 96 percent of us married, 3 percent have been widowed, and 80 percent of us remain attached to our first partners. Pennsylvania is one of the very lowest divorce-rate states for reasons, to the best of my knowledge, never conclusively explained. Perhaps the personal accounts in this book will give some clue.

Other clues come from the figures. A classmate of Southern European background is most likely to have remained married to his or her original spouse. There is probably a religious dimension to this fact, since Southern Europeans are the most predominantly Catholic of the ethnic groups, and only 60 percent as many Catholics as Protestants in the Class of 1952 divorced. (Persons claiming no religious affiliation represent by far the greatest percentage of divorces, more than triple the Class figure, but they account for only a small number of Class members.)

Former academic/scientific students were more apt to divorce than students from other curricula, but on the other hand persons holding the best jobs have not been more divorce-prone than Class members in general. However, since the figures are so sparse in some job categories, we may not be able to read anything significant from them.

———

Sandra Styles always seemed happy and active, singing and doing. Her constant companion was Scott Muller. They appeared to share interests such as music, not to mention class, ethnic, and religious backgrounds. They married in 1953 and divorced twenty years later. When Sandra and I had dinner not long after her divorce, she looked as if she had aged little since graduation. But her feelings had changed dramatically.

SANDRA: Women as well as men think of regaining their youth at mid-life, I can tell you that from personal experience. Especially when you're married as young as I was, you think of what might have happened if you had taken a few years first and done a few things. There were some things I wanted *for me* after a certain time, when the children were a little older. And there were things that Scott was reluctant to let me have. It was a matter of personal development. He felt threatened, to the point where he began looking for companionship in somebody else.

For most of the nineteen years we were married he was out in the evenings, he couldn't sit still, he was doing some sort of club work, four or five nights a week, and then he was selling insurance—that gave him an out in the evenings—any kind of an excuse to get out of the house so he didn't have to sit home with me and the children. And why, I don't know, because I think he enjoyed both of us. We couldn't talk about it. I used to tell him I didn't like it, and he would say, "Stop complaining. It's my job." He became very defensive about it. So I lived with it a long time.

And then, all of a sudden, it wasn't a club or a job or an excuse like that anymore—it was a woman. And I don't think he could reconcile that in his own mind. He became very indiscreet. He would tell me everything, stuff I didn't want to know. I think he kept himself so busy for almost twenty years that he never stopped to think where he was going or what he was doing. He just plowed on to get ahead, and all of a sudden he realized he wasn't getting any father. He blamed a lot of his troubles on me. When he felt cornered it was always somebody else's fault.

It was only the last year that he was *so* dissatisfied, and then there was no talking to him. All of a sudden he was talking to her, and I didn't make sense to him. All of those things I felt were important to me were not important to him anymore—our relationship to each other, most important, but also the children. He refused to go to a marriage counselor, arguing that a counselor would take sides. I think he felt guilty. Then one day he called me at work and said he was never coming home. I guess it's hard to face somebody like that, especially after being together for so long.

He lived with her while getting the divorce. He left in June and married her the following January.

I accused myself: "What did I do to drive him out?" It took me a long time to recover. The first two months the children did not think I was going to come out of it. I was very depressed. For two weeks I cried constantly. But I forced myself to go to work; it was the only diversion I had. At home, around the children, that would depress me. I'd think: "Here they are, without a father." And he didn't come back to see them very often. The children felt guilty, too; they also thought they had driven him out of the house. He had demanded a great deal of them and didn't give much response in the way of love or encouragement. He wasn't home enough to do it. I know he loves his children.

He was an only child. I started dating him when I was fifteen. We dated about three and a half years before we got married. We thought everything would work out. We had a family right away, which wasn't something we had planned, but we accepted it. Once we had one child, we decided we'd have another within two years. Both of us thought that to be an only child was not a good thing.

After Scott moved out, he would not pay for the education of the two older boys. I was not left very well off. As soon as he left, Scott wanted me to sell the house so he could have his share of the money—and I had four children in it! I did finally have to sell the house.

They feel bad about their father because he has no ground for conversation with them anymore. He offers them nothing. I can talk with them, and they appreciate it. My daughter, who's fourteen, is the only one of the four who is responsive to Scott. She'll go and visit him.

I've been very frank with the children about our separation. I've tried to tell them what I thought. I've also tried to tell them that I may not be right, that I have my own feelings and they're one-sided.

My reaction to our separation was: "All right, if you don't want me, if you don't want to be with me anymore, then I don't want to have anything to do with you, I don't want to see you." It was very, very difficult for me to communicate. I had to stop right there and build a new life. It was painful. I felt so rejected. After all we had been through together, he threw it away. I wasn't willing to throw it away. I thought there was something there to be saved. I loved him dearly, but now I don't even like him.

Before the divorce, I had already been working for several years, though I was very family-oriented. That was the way I was raised. My father always helped my mother out, and he didn't stay out late at night. Scott never helped in the house. He really disliked being stuck with the children on those few occasions when I would go out.

When the children got a little older, I decided I would like to get out and do something. I started to work when Paul, the youngest, was in kindergarten—though I still had the full range of household duties. Scott encouraged me to go out and earn money, ostensibly for the children's education. But it somehow got spent—on things that I didn't think important. For example, the children got their clothes from Robert Hall, but he would go to an expensive men's shop. I didn't need many clothes; often my mother would buy me something. She was too good to us.

When I went to work I found out I had a brain in my head. I had never really accomplished anything before. Anybody can raise children. It's an important thing—and, unlike Scott, I could never have left them. But I'm happy with them.

I have a capacity for happiness that surprises even me. I can be content. I feel so bad that Scott is not content, he's very unhappy—and he's going to be more unhappy. He's never tried to find out who he was and to like himself. Maybe he was afraid to look at himself inside. I've never been afraid to do that. Especially when you sit around for fifteen years raising children—you become like that. I think maybe my marriage would have broken up sooner if I hadn't been so content. Now I wonder whether I didn't waste a lot of time. But there's no way to go back.

Now I feel sometimes as though I'm twenty-two—I never *was* twenty-two—but I feel like I'm enjoying it more than a twenty-two-year-old could. Now I could get a motorcycle. I bought myself a little Baracuda with a racing stripe down the side, and I drive it at seventy miles per hour. I love it. I probably have some hidden desire for adventure. I wouldn't have done these things when I was married if he wouldn't let me.

He made all the money decisions. I was surprised that I could manage household finances alone. I was deathly afraid of that. I knew I had a brain—but I didn't know how far I could go, what I could do. And I'm still finding out. I don't agree with the women's movement—burning bras and all that. Women should have equal pay for equal work. I still believe in a certain amount of femininity. What makes me most bitter about women coming out and working is that men resent it. They still don't believe that a woman can work intellectually side by side with them. There are a lot of jobs women can do as well as men.

If I married again, he would *have to* respect my independence. I'm not in a hurry to marry again. I think I'd prefer a married life, but I don't want to do it while my children are still home. That might create fuss that I don't care to go through. I don't take anybody home that I don't think my children will like. And if I find that my children don't like a man, I won't date him anymore. Because I'm not satisfied either.

If I didn't like someone, I wouldn't sleep with him. But some parts of life are very necessary for me. Sex is one of the greatest nerve tonics; it's medication for me. I won't give it up because I'm not married. At the same time, I don't feel I'm obligated to raise children and keep myself chaste. I'm very discreet. I have relations only with one man at a time. I can only have an emotional feeling for one man at a time.

My parents have terrible feelings about my going out. I'm supposed to stay home with my children, never date. My mother asks where I've been, whether I've spent the night. It would only hurt her to know. I've told her not to ask, and she doesn't.

My mother told me about the time I was divorced that they no longer had any sexual relations, that my father wasn't interested anymore.

I had never held the opinion that marriages were all bliss. My family believed you had to accept certain things and that's all there was to it, you can't have what you want all the time. They didn't have the opportunity to do the things they wanted to do. This was a principle they impressed upon me. But I've found out I can do as much as I really want to do.

I've always been able to be very objective about myself and about those around me. I put up with anything from the people that I love. And did at home, when I was a child. My father had a strong temper, would fly off the handle—he was Irish and German—but he would never hold any grudges. He believed, "A child should be seen and not heard." He put me in a place, and I accepted it. As I did in my marriage.

When I was young, I was conscious of being ostracized from some events. My father did not have the kind of job that some fathers had. He was only a machinist. He wasn't a big boss. So consequently we were not eligible to belong to the Saucon Valley Country Club. I didn't belong to the dancing class that sponsored the Christmas dances at the country clubs. And when Scott asked to take me to one of those dances, it had to be approved. I wasn't approved. Yet so many of my friends belonged at Saucon Valley, because they had money. I felt ostracized.

I belonged to the second-best sorority in high school. I always could stand outside that system and judge it, or at least ask, "What does it mean?" I always felt, if people don't want me, forget it. Money and position were not important to me. But I married someone who valued both. My feelings for him made his values not matter. That couldn't happen to me today. If I married again, the man would have to be warm and sensitive. He would have to like art and music. He would have to be able to respond to me.

Now I'm looking for a real relationship. I had a marriage but not a relationship. Marriage is for raising children and for two people who want to get along economically. I'm still looking for love, I guess. In the last few years I've been very surprised to have the attention that I've had. From friends and from people I work with. I was a little suspicious, but I've come to believe that people can love others in a deep and platonic way.

I thought, when I was divorced, that my boss was going to go out of his mind, that he couldn't stand to see me in such pain. He would call me into his office at lunch time and say, "Talk to me! Talk to me!" because he knew I had only the children at home. It was difficult for him to look at what was happening. He's married, his children are the same ages as my four. I think he looked inside his own marriage at that time and could see what I felt because he could appreciate what he had.

But at first I was very suspect of my boss's attention to me. I thought, "What in the world does this man want?" I didn't want to talk to him. He was able to say, "Be friends. You've got to open up." Now we have a great friendship, and we work so well together.

He was very helpful in making me confident about myself. He told me I was intelligent and attractive and able to get where I wanted to go. He's the man who helped me put myself together again. At the same time he promoted me from the accounting department to his executive secretary. When I told him I couldn't do it, he said "Oh yes, you can, and you will." And I did. He had faith in me.

Everybody's marriage is different. And nobody knows what it's like except those two people. And even they don't know, or they'd be able to reconcile problems. Or know what the problems were.

It wasn't until I was thirty-eight years old that I was put in a position where I had any control over my situation. Now I have. I don't know whether I wanted it before then.

Seven years elapsed before I saw Sandra again. As we lunched together, she recalled our first meeting.

I had just found out that there were so many things I could do all by myself—and now I've found I have a few limitations. At the time I was very unhappy because I was not attached to anyone and was lonely underneath. I have been living the last four years with a man that has been marvelous to me, and we're great friends, and we enjoy each other.

I had to write my mother a letter and tell her all about what I was doing—that bothered me no end. She doesn't approve of those situations. But when you're older you *know* whether you're going to fit together; it didn't take long before we did know. I never wanted material possessions. All I wanted was to be treated like a person, a companion—and that's what he is to me.

Very privately he can show his feelings. He is very tender. At age fifty-nine there isn't much sex, I can assure you. I don't care. He's very affectionate with me. But out with people, it's different. He can't say "I love you," but he shows it to me.

You remember when we last talked, I was working at Apex? The officers of the company, not my boss, hired another girl in the department. She was given a lot of the jobs I did; I didn't mind sharing because I was very busy. But they gave her the *glory* jobs and left me with the typing. I went on vacation in February 1982, and the day I got back I was told that I didn't have a job any more. My salary had risen to the point where I was making almost $18,000. They had hired her at a lower salary and found she could do the job. Then they took me out with all the managers and treated me to an expensive luncheon and gave me a $250 leather briefcase which I'll never use because I'll never have a job that goes with it. I think they had a guilty conscience after letting me go.

I worked as a temporary for almost a year. I had a five-month job with Dow-Jones but got laid off when two departments were consolidated; I had no seniority. Since then I've been looking for another job; I run out of severance pay the end of this month. I'm really happy with Sam, but I'm worried about being dependent on him. Right now I earn what I spend on the household by doing the chores.

When Sandra and I finished our lunch, we walked up East Fourth Street to the offices of Bethlehem Steel, where we chatted with a mutual friend. We then drove to her parents' house, visited some more, and I left, full of respect for a woman who had taken her life in tow. But I was uncertain what to do with a story she had related to me on our walk. "Just before I got married," Sandra recalled, "I dreamed I wed my father, and I couldn't tell whether my mother was about to laugh or cry. When I told her about it the following day, she said, 'That's a stupid dream.' I reassured her that it was only one of those goofy things that sometimes happen."

Lucy Hendricks lives a few miles outside Bethlehem, where I visited her one wet autumn morning. She told me, "I think I was typical of the '52 Class of Liberty High School: get married, raise a family, raise those kids to go to college." Her two older children were already attending small liberal arts institutions, and the two younger were very likely to follow in their footsteps. Then Lucy added, "I considered myself at the time of graduation typical. I hope I'm different now."

LUCY: We've lived in this area eight years. We bought the house and this piece of property. So all this open field we own around here. That was the closest to the country I could get. I love the country. I don't like neighbors. I like being by myself, raising my kids the way I think is right. Of course, you can do that all your life and they grow up and leave home and go out and meet up with these other kooks.

I have a very good feeling about my kids, I really do. I've had people say to me, "Lucy, what did you do right that I've done wrong?" And all I can say is love. I think love goes a long way in relationships. I've never hit my kids. Oh, when they were little I'd wamp 'em on the backs, but I do not believe in violence anytime. And I think trying to understand that they have a problem, loving them in that respect, goes a lot farther than screaming and yelling. And now that they're older and they come back and talk these things over with me, I've happy about it.

We grew up in a very happy home, where there was not a lot of money but a lot of love. And there was always time for us kids. Nothing in this world was ever more important to my mother or my father than us kids. I wore hand-me-down clothes. My grandfather made a lot of my toys—he was a great carpenter. My grandmother was a great seamstress—she made a lot of my doll clothes. But we grew up in that type of a home, where you went to church on Sunday, and there were a lot of things you didn't do on Sunday that I allow my kids to do today, believe me! But there was always that love.

My marriage is not the greatest in the world; I'm very open about that. Our marriage leaves a lot to be desired, a whole lot to be desired. But then Frank came from a different type of family than I did, and he sees family life differently. He was from New Jersey. He went to Moravian, that's where I met him—my downfall. I think the biggest differences have mostly been children, money, and sex, in that order—as most people would tell you that. Why pretend? We do not have a great marriage. But it's this thing I have about family life.

As an alternative I do not consider divorce, separation. Because Frank and I are two adults. The problems we have we made ourselves. The kids didn't make them; we created them. And I don't think they should have to pay the price for this relationship between Frank and I. Therefore, as two adults I think we can discuss these things not in front of the children. Whatever differences we have I think we should be able to keep apart from the kids but both love them in our own way and give to them what I feel they deserve in life. Right or wrong, that's the way I feel about it.

I've done most of the child-raising. He didn't come from a home where they believed in religion. He to this day wouldn't be a member of a church if my dad hadn't insisted when we got married that he joined the Reformed church. But he never goes to church. He never fights me on these issues, never. But something has come out right, regardless of how bad our marriage has been, because there's two of them that are in college now that are doing very well. Mark is a tremendous football player. And his grades are rotten, but he wants to go to Colgate. Frank's trying to pull strings to get him in there.

I've always said this: as bad as the marriage is, I've never regretted the last twenty-five years of my life. I sat back the other day and was thinking a lot of women my age, in their forties, say, "Oh, I've missed a lot in life." I haven't missed a thing. I am completely contented and happy.

The only organization I belong to is the Women's Club. And even that takes second place. Because if the kids have something coming up, or Frank's out of town and I don't want to leave them alone, I don't go to that either. I don't want to go out and work. When the kids come in in the afternoon, they want to talk.

I'm very unaffected by my neighbors. They have lovely homes, new cars, a lot of material things that we don't have and probably never will. But then again, what their kids don't have is that mother in the home, that somebody caring about them. The mother's at work all day. Now this man over here, three years ago, his wife up and left him one morning and—unbelievably—the two older children knew she was leaving that morning. They never told the father!

Getting back to my marriage. Frank goes out a lot, and I know there have been other women in his life, as a matter of fact. But that doesn't bother me. Because I feel if he's out looking it's because it's something lacking in the home, and he's entitled to it. As long as he's a good father, a good provider, and my kids don't suffer—that sounds far out, I don't know.

It only works one way. I'm the only one that feels that way about the whole thing. He doesn't feel that way about it. If I went out of the house—forget the whole business.

You can't have everything in life. If you had everything, what would it be, anyway? You've got to take the bitter with the sweet, the good with the bad. And I'm willing to accept that.

All my life all I really ever wanted to be was a mother. Now that sounds weird, I know. But when I was a kid, my brother was always in sports and my sister was the biggest tomboy, she hated dolls. But me, I had a house going every day, and all these dolls. I couldn't wait till the day when I got married. Back in high school a girl in our graduating class got pregnant in our senior year. Do you know that in my senior year I could not figure out how she got pregnant when she was not married?

I'm sure you'll talk to a lot of people who, over these years, have felt they've missed a lot, especially if they're career-oriented. I was never career-oriented; I was home-oriented. I am very sure the women's movement is doing good in many fields, for the working woman, the single woman, the woman out in a career. But for me, I don't need it. And I know I'm typical of the women who are anti-women's liberation: forty and over, middle-aged, upper-middle-income-bracket-type people. These are the people that are anti—that's me. They're trying to get me rights I feel I already have. There are no rights that I feel I don't have that I want. I feel liberated, free to speak my mind, anyway.

I was a Nixon backer, I really was. I know the man had problems. I don't deny that. The only thing I credit him with and always will is that he ended the war in Vietnam, and none of my sons had to go fight in that war. For this I will always be eternally grateful to the man. For whatever else he did, I knew he was wrong. I was sweating it then. My oldest boy was coming of age, and I had another not far behind him. And war is one thing I am terribly opposed to.

Between our first conversation and our second seven years later, Lucy and I had talked on the phone and corresponded. Our major topic was the transcript of our first get-together. "I can't believe I said those things—it must have been a bad day." I was happy to give her another chance. Perhaps as a further precautionary measure, she had invited her closest friend, Gretchen, to join us for coffee later in the morning.

Life gets better. I was one of these people who always felt when my children grew up I'd have a hard time adjusting to them leaving home. I still have one at home, so how it will be then, I don't know. But my son Jeff thinks I will adjust to it magnificently, because I really have a very positive outlook. Like when I went to the seashore this summer. I never before this would have dreamed of going away and leaving a family at home. But this was *my time*. I've earned it; as my son would say, "You've earned it." And I love it.

The marriage hasn't changed at all. But you learn to accept—*I* do. You marry probably for all the wrong reasons, which I'm finding out every one of my friends have done. You stay in a marriage because of the children. And then you hit the point where I am in life, and you stay there for security reasons. It's simple, really.

And I found out with my children, when they went away to college thinking, "My parents don't have such a great marriage; they're the only ones like that." Then they found out that their friends had the same problems my kids had at home.

As we talked on, with Lucy explaining again why she wouldn't divorce, how she had freedom anyway, as well as the friendship of her children, Gretchen arrived. "This girl is better than a sister to me," Lucy happily observed. It was almost immediately clear that she knew everything about Lucy and vice versa. Gretchen was about to leave her husband to marry the older brother of one of our classmates.

GRETCHEN: Lucy I can be myself with. I would never tell Charles how I feel about anything. He hears, but he never listens. Lucy listens. We were always friends. But now that the children are grown up we can go places—and talk.

LUCY: Basically, we're married to the same sort of men.

GRETCHEN: O gosh, I know what her husband's going to say before she tells me.

LUCY: Our husbands are very possessive.

GRETCHEN: He knows I am going to leave him for someone else. We don't talk about it. He seems to feel if it's not discussed, it will go away.

LUCY: He would buy you the world with a fence around it, and he does sometimes.

GRETCHEN: You don't buy people. He tries to buy people, not only me but the children, other people. He's power hungry.

LUCY: Frank has no friends. His problem comes from his

home. Frank's mother was not a loving person. She did not know how to love. She is a cold person. He grew up in a home where there was not a lot of love to go around.

GRETCHEN: Charles' mother is also very cold and doesn't show any affection. I've never seen her touch her husband. There are no affectionate words. My home wasn't warm either. I guess I was loved. But I never talked to my mother; I never told her anything. I was never quite good enough, compared to my sister who did get attention. It wonders me. But I've never had trouble expressing love to my children or to men.

Out of curiosity, I raised the subject of politics, thinking that since there are connections between the household and a person's view of national affairs, it would be interesting to hear Lucy's opinions.

LUCY: I approved of the invasion of Granada, for this reason: I am tired of being walked on, as a nation, by third-world countries. There were students of ours down there — were we going to run the risk of another Iran? I feel very bad about the Marines whose lives were lost [in Beirut], believe me, I do. But this is a free country; they were not drafted; they enlisted willingly. They knew what they were getting into when they enlisted in the Marines. They were being paid for a job to do.

I see President Reagan as a very caring, loving man who is looking out for mankind. But I also see him as a man who, like I — I'm just absolutely sick and tired of these other countries walking all over us as a nation. The happiest day of my life was the day Jimmy Carter got on that airplane and left Washington for Georgia.

I am not a violent person. I detest violence. I never hit my kids. I don't believe in bullyism — I *hate* bullies, as a matter of fact. But there's something about being a strong country that I have a thing about.

I had not known Elsie Nagy in high school, yet she obviously made a special effort to get together with me in response to my request for an interview. When she later described herself as a compliant person, I felt as if I had inadvertently given her no choice but to meet me. On meeting, she immediately remarked that I probably didn't remember her from high school, that she had been much heavier then, observations I recalled later when she told me she worried about her nine-year-old daughter Nancy's poor self-image. "Nancy chatters all the time, just like me," a judgment she seemed determined to prove.

At the close of the evening Elsie recalled how much she liked junior high school, how high school was a less enjoyable experience partly because she worked the middle shift at the Laros Silk Mills and was always tired, that she did not have the money to go to college. Now she was back at work, but happier with it.

ELSIE: This is the beginning of my third year with the Bethlehem School District. After my husband and I were divorced, I had to find a job, and I wanted to take a job that I would be able to enjoy as much as possible. I work as a teacher's aide. The pay is terrible, but it has the hours I want and the days off I want—I love the kids, I really do. In fact, my daughter Nancy's going over there. I take her along with me because it's much more convenient. I don't like this business of her coming home and being alone.

Women our age are going back and doing work of this kind, for the same reason that I did. You go back to work in this way because you can still be with your children. Contrary to what people say, things *are* much different today than they were when we were growing up. There are a lot more things that kids can get involved in. And they say, "Oh, if you teach them right they're not going to get involved." Well, maybe that's true to some extent, but I still feel better knowing that I can be there when Nancy needs me. She's an only child too, which makes it a lot more difficult. I wish I had more children.

I think that men's outlook when we were younger was that raising kids was a woman's job, and I think people are realizing more and more how much men can help the children because they really need that strong father image. This is the problem I have with my own, because she's with me so much.

Her father was just here this afternoon. That's why all this stuff is out; they were building. We get along fairly well together; we almost get along better than we did when we were married. We were married twenty years ago, and that's a long time!

Nancy came along very late in our life. We were married eleven years before she was born. There's no backing away from it: this has been one of the problems. And he was not mature enough to handle the situation, and it's really been a big problem for us. I'd *never*, never tell her that her birth affected our marriage, even though it made such a terrible difference; but it did. But I could no longer let it be. I couldn't split myself up. I was almost ready for a nervous breakdown; it was just really bad. That was my own fault.

Bob wanted to be free. That's what I was trying to say about restrictions in our childhood and the way we were brought up. I think he's a person that really should have never married. He likes to be with men that . . . he builds and flies model airplanes, this is his hobby and has been since he was a child, and I never made any objections to it. After Nancy was born it was too much trouble, and he didn't want us to come. I always worked before I had Nancy, and weekends he would go to shows, like out in Harrisburg and so on, and I was never included in any of that.

He didn't want family ties. He didn't want the responsibility. He wanted to be free of me. I don't think he wanted to be free of Nancy. He wanted to be free of me. He just wanted to get away from me. He didn't want to be with me any longer. It's the truth. And it doesn't hurt me anymore. It's just something that you have to face. I guess the thing is I made a poor choice from the beginning. I should have seen it coming. I wasn't important enough to him.

For me it's been very difficult because I'm a very home-type person. I think this is a very old-fashioned community. I know how my mother feels about my divorce. She thinks divorce is a terrible thing. I can't talk to her about it.

I've always been tied very close to the church. I go to the United Church of Christ. The minister that we have in our church, he doesn't know how to reach people. He was not at all helpful when I was considering a divorce. I could have been dead, and I don't think he would have cared. I don't hold it against anybody in our faith or anything like that, but I really had no one to turn to, really no one. I really surprised myself. I never knew that I had that much strength.

I'm trying very hard not to smother Nancy. I want her to get out and to do things. She's on the Y swimming team, and she's done very well, and I'm very proud of her. I want her to keep up with her swimming because she's not an exceptional student. In fact, she has a real poor image of herself, and I don't know where this has come from. They say you do that to your children, you make them feel insecure and so forth, and I'm trying very hard because as soon as they're eleven years old the pattern of their life is pretty well set. And Nancy's nine. She was six when my husband and I separated.

I think the hard part for me is going to be to find a balance for this child, trying not to overprotect her, and let her develop on her own. This is the hard thing—you want your children to be perfect. And I guess that's the word. And you want them to have everything that you haven't had. You want them to be attractive; you want them to be successful; you want everything for them.

There's another thing. Even as old as my mother is, she says, "Why don't you relax and enjoy yourself more? Don't try so hard." But I think it's your nature—there isn't really much you can do about that. I mean, you can talk to yourself and say, "Why don't you laugh more, why don't you find things to be funny about? So the room is messy all the time, don't get upset about it, what are you doing anyway?" Seeing *this*[gestures] in my living room and not really being upset about it is terrific for me, because there was a time I couldn't have it.

I had Nancy tested at school. They do psychological testing, and I had this done in second grade when she was really having so many problems, and the psychologist said that she was so wound up emotionally that she just couldn't do her work, she just couldn't do it. Every year, when she begins school again, she goes through the same adjustment period. I'm really concerned about it. I don't know whether this child really has a learning disability—they don't seem to think so. It's an emotional thing.

When she doesn't come in anymore, then it's time to worry. But last night she came in to kiss me, and she banged me right in the mouth with her teeth because it was dark, and I was angry. Then she started to cry, and she said to me, "Oh, Mommy, why do I do such dumb things?" She said to me, "People don't like me because I do dumb things." And I said to her, "I think you'd better tell me about it." So then she crawled on top of my bed, and she said, "I'm cold," and I said, "Well, you can get in beside me"—and the cats were on the bed!

So she crawled in and said to me, "Mom, I'm just a dummy." And I said, "No, you're not a dummy." And then she said to me, "Why do I do dumb things? I walk into things and kids call me dummy." And she said, "I don't know my work, and kids call me dummy." And I said, "Oh, Nancy, you're not really a dummy at all. You know what you have to think? You have to start having more confidence in yourself. Say, 'I can do it. I know I can do it, I'm *not* a dummy. My mom says I'm a *super* kid!'" I keep telling her this stuff. I hope it helps. I do. Because I think she's a super kid.

You know, you try so hard. When I was having so much trouble with him coming to see her so often, I thought maybe it would be better if I'd leave, solve everything and find a new place to live and start again somewhere else. And then I thought, I don't think I'm really brave enough to do that. These people that belong to women's lib and all that, I think they're very strong women, I don't think I could do that, you know, cut out. Those women always seem so brash, this is the thing that annoys me about them. All the people I've seen give lectures on television. I don't know, I have bad feelings about them, that's all I can tell you about it. I don't know why, I just feel uncomfortable.

I don't think the women in the movement hate men. Not at all. I don't know, it's just some of the things that they say that I don't really go along with. I'll tell you what I feel about abortion though. I'm against anybody legislating any-thing to tell me what I should do about myself. I think that really is invading your privacy, I really do.

I listen to the Phil Donahue show once in awhile, and some of the things these people say about themselves, I couldn't imagine standing up in front of the television audience and telling my inner thoughts like that. I just couldn't do that.

And yet they say that this is what liberation is all about. To me, that's just talking too much. Everybody should have their own private thoughts about some things.

I returned to Elsie's house on a November afternoon seven years later. The night before, she and her daughter Nancy had taken in a friend of Nancy's who had, apparently, good reason to fear her father's violent temper. Elsie, who now worked for an agency that employed the mentally handicapped, expressed a worry about the legality of sheltering someone else's sixteen-year-old daughter, but she was not at all uncertain about it being the human thing to do. And she complimented Nancy on having the presence of mind to take this young woman to the guidance counselor at Liberty High School.

ELSIE: Nancy has a tendency to pick up lame ducks. She has a tendency to gravitate toward those persons who have problems.
NANCY: Dennis is the only boyfriend I've had who doesn't have problems. He's a healthy, normal human being. I've been going with Dennis for a year and four months. He graduated last year, and he'll be going into the service—the Navy—February 7. He's really happy about it. He scored the highest in the aptitude test of anybody this year.

The phone rang and drew Nancy out of the room. I recalled to Elsie that seven years ago she was worried about bringing Nancy up, but that she seemed to have done a superior job.

ELSIE: Sometimes I wonder. We're not as close as I really wish we were. We get along pretty well. Scholastically, she's not doing well at all, and I know she's capable of doing more. Her guidance counselor said that lots of kids have trouble adjusting to high school, especially now that they begin in ninth grade.

I added that Elsie also seemed a lot more confident and relaxed than she had seven years ago.

Yes, I'm happy with the life that I lead. It's kind of a lonely existence for me, because I don't have a husband or a com-

panion. And I don't date. I was dating; in fact, I was engaged. But things just did not work out. It was for the best.
Since that time, I've not gotten involved with anyone else.

I have some very good friends. We do things every weekend.
So I always have something to look forward to. But the responsibilities of having a house, a car, and taking care of all the bills
and worrying about Nancy—it was very burdensome for me for
a while. But I kind of worked through that—and I think you do.
You go through different stages in your divorce, and there are
lots of things you have to get over and have to live with.

But I went to a divorce recovery group at the Presbyterian
church a couple of years ago, and in fact I was one of the
leaders of one of the groups. We had a guy from California
come in and teach some of the classes. You listen to some
people's stories and it's all you can do to keep from crying.
What was greatest about the groups was that we all found
out we didn't have it so bad.

It was always considered bad manners to tell about your personal life to anybody else. That was all to be kept within the
household. To a degree, I think that people talk too much about
their private lives. There are many things that are private and
should be kept in the home. I'm not all for Phil Donahue shows
and everything; I think some of them are very enlightening, and
yet I think there are others that exploit people. To me it would
hurt to bare my soul before twenty million people. There are
some things that are best discussed in smaller groups or more
intimately with somebody who really cares about you.

I've passed the point of looking backward. I look forward
to what is. I want to move to a warmer climate. The only
equity I have is this house. When I get old enough to retire,
or even before, I'd like to move to Florida or Arizona. I'd
take my mother. She's the only family I have, besides Nancy,
of course, and she has her own life.

A year later Nancy had a baby who was allowed to accompany her
to school. She and Dennis married. Elsie has not moved yet.

My memory of Shirleyann Finn focused on a smile and a song. And
I was not deceived. I visited her in midsummer, suffering from a

cold and the uneasy feeling that in these earliest conversations I wasn't reaching my classmates. I left her house, my cough unabated but my energy restored, wondering if I could do justice to the dynamism of our reunion.

As she talked about herself and her work with Sweet Adelines, a singing group she directs, some of her children and friends passed through the house. (To her son I was "the brother of Flexer Illick, at church, the one who looks like Abe Lincoln.") There were introductions but not interruptions; we drank beer and chatted as though we had been friends always. A few months later, when I returned to see her husband, Chick, and some of her children, I again felt as though the decades had hardly passed. Yet, judging from the matters we discussed, time had made a difference.

SHIRLEYANN: It's really amazing, I've talked to so many girls just in the past year. I've always allowed people so close to me, never any further, because I'm not open as far as my personal life. I feel that's mine. Chick's and my life together, that's ours. I don't think it's anybody's business. But when you begin to open up to people, which I've begun to do in the past two years, they really begin to open up to you. Because people don't want to admit that something's bothering them, unless you'll admit to them first that something's bothering you.

Yet women, particularly our age, all of a sudden—now, not me in particular, because I've always been involved in Sweet Adelines for the past twelve years, which has been my salvation. I have a sister, whose kids are not as old as ours, but in about five years she's going to find herself with *nothing*! She's spent so much time with her kids that she doesn't really know her husband as well as she knows her kids. And soon they're going to be gone, and those two—they'll probably split up. Many girls . . . unbelievable, unbelievable to me how many people that are married are not happy, that they won't admit it.

I'm very close to many of the girls that are in my chorus. I can tell. I've been directing for at least seven years, but when you're standing up in front of those girls and something's bothering them—I can tell. I can tell a look on a face that's different from a week before just because I'm not used to see-

Shirleyann Finn with husband, Chick, and children, Susan and Bill. (Photo by JEI.)

ing that face. And if I give them the opening, nine times out of ten they'll just bare their souls. Not just girls in my chorus, either, girls I'm — oh, God, a girl I met through a mutual friend in Virginia, who was so miserable, and she's so young, to be so miserable. Miserable married. So why hang on? You only go this way once. There's so many people that are — how did we get into this? How did we get into this subject?

Things have changed. I think it has a lot to do with this women's lib thing. I like to be a woman. I like when a guy opens a door for me or fixes me a drink. I've never been competitive with men. I've never worked. I went right from high school into nursing school and I got married. I've work-ed part time upon occasion, but I've never had to keep my-self. So that I can't imagine what it must be like in the busi-ness world, doing the same amount of work that a man is doing, and you're not getting paid for it. I probably work as hard here as any man does, but I never thought of it as far as money is concerned.

I think women are killing themselves with this movement. I don't think it was meant to be that way. But now I hear men say, "Oh, I won't open the door for her, she's a women's libber." Things get out of perspective before they get back into perspective.

Guys at our age are content. Now Chick, he's made his mark in the world. He doesn't even care to make more of a mark. He's done his job; he's raised his family; he's going to send them all through school.

Women—they're just beginning to come into their own. Because they can. One girl said to me, "I'm a mother and a wife, and I do this and that and the other thing. But something's missing. Where am I?" She's not distinct as a person. I think that's all women have wanted for years and have never even realized it.

Like here. I don't work. I do a lot of things, and I know a lot of girls that work that probably couldn't do the things I do. First, they don't have the time. Second, maybe they don't have the desire. But I'm not Mrs. Charles Quigg all the time. I'm me. And this is what a lot of women miss out on.

And this is why I love Sweet Adelines, because this is what we do to girls: we make them people. It's such a good feeling, where I see a little girl come in, and her hair's a wreck, and her clothes are a wreck, and she just doesn't take care of herself. After a couple of months, all of a sudden you see this beautiful woman coming out of—you know, she takes care about what she wears to chorus because everybody else looks sharp, and she fixes her hair, and she wears makeup. And this is why I go though all this baloney of Sweet Adelines, because it is such a service—though it's just barbershop singing.

The age level has gone down. All three of my daughters joined, which really floored me. It's really great. This weekend we sang in Scranton. All of us went, us girls, and Chick came to hear. Bill, who's my seventeen-year-old son, came because his girlfriend, who lives right down the street, sings with us. So we were all participating in my hobby, which was really—oh, I'm telling you, it just wiped me out to think these kids want to hang around the chorus with their mother!

But they do. We sing four-part harmony. In October my quartet goes to Cincinnati to compete in the international competition. Last year we were twelfth, the year before we were seventh. Last year we had a *bad* year. But this year we replaced a tenor and hope to be back in the top ten. Quite an honor, quite a thrill. Because we're doing what we really like to do. Girls don't realize what a beautiful hobby it is until they get involved.

This is why Sweet Adelines is so fantastic. Because when I'm a Sweet Adeline, nothing else . . . well, when we sing, there's just four of us and there's thousands of people watching you sing, and it's up to you. And God, nothing turns me on like walking on that stage and having that whole place packed. It's just *un*believable, the thrill you get.

Shirleyann then mused for a moment about how, when she was in nursing school, she would return home at every opportunity. She also talked about how difficult life had been when her husband was transferred to upstate New York, where there was no family connection. What she learned from the experience was how to make friends. Then, upon their return to Bethlehem, the issue became one of how attached children should be to family.

I met Chick because he was [her brother] Tommy's best friend. He had one brother who moved from Bethlehem and has never been back. Chick was so enthralled with the big family life—our family. And that this was one of the reasons he wanted to get back here. He thought it was wrong for our children not to have a family-oriented life. It's very important to Chick—family structure—and his *old* friends. He just loves to have old friends when he goes to the store and sees all these guys that he knew back when.

So we've raised our children mainly in Bethlehem. Bill is our only son, and he's the apple of Chick's eye. When he leaves us this fall, ohh! It's good for Bill, but I'm not so sure if Chick can handle it. He's *so* close to him.

Our Debbie, who went away to Indiana University [in Pennsylvania] this past year, had never been away from home. She'd never visit anybody overnight; she was never away. She was so miserable for two weeks before she left, and I knew this was on her mind. I was a basket case when we left [her there]. She cried her heart out. But she said the minute we left, she was fine. It made me feel so good to know that she could handle that.

Our oldest [Kaye Anne] is a nurse at St. Luke's. When it was time for her to go to college—and, of course, being our oldest daughter, it was just a couple of years ago when the drug scene was really bad. She was a young graduate, like seventeen, and being the oldest for some reason was very gullible, and it scared me, to send her off somewhere to school. Where I'm sorry now that I talked her out of going away. I think that's so important.

I trust them [the children], which I hope someday I'm not sorry for. Our job is done. They know what's right, and they know what's wrong. And I don't expect any less from them than I was capable of.

I think the problem with a lot of kids is that their parents don't take a stand. Right is right, and it was right when we were kids, and it's going to be right when their kids are kids. And wrong is wrong. Although I don't judge people, which maybe I did ten years ago, I do feel that I'm right in telling my children what I think—and what I expect of them.

I have had one experience, and that's with Chick. And it's lasted a hell of a long time. It couldn't have been all that bad. And I would love for them to at least have that much. Not accept something that in my own mind can't be as good. I don't want my girls to accept anything I don't think they deserve. And to me they're pretty nice kids and deserve a lot more than living with a guy. And then what do you have? You get pregnant, who's got the baby? You do. It's a lot different when you're talking about your son and when you're talking about your daughter.

The longer I went with Chick, the earlier I had to come home. But I feel if you let them think that you trust their judgment, that means a lot. I know it did to me because I didn't get it. However, what happens . . . I'll write you a letter and tell you whether I was right or wrong.

It was seven years before I saw Shirleyann again, and lots had happened to her family. Yet she remained very much the same person I had visited before—cheerful, self-assured, optimistic.

I take care of my two grandchildren every day because Kaye works as a nurse. Life is more fun, but it's more hectic.

I spent a lot of time with the chorus. My quartet has won an international championship since I last saw you; Susan, my daughter, is my choreographer.

My older sister died quite unexpectedly. She was only forty-eight, and we were very close. My other sister just got a divorce after nineteen years of marriage. I understand, I don't agree, but I don't judge it. I don't think there was anything wrong with our generation, do you? What is there in life that you don't have that you have a burning desire for? How many women—now I'm not bragging—have achieved international success as my sister and I have with the quartet? And I have really neat kids and they know, especially my son Bill, how much I enjoy them.

"Silence is golden." So read the lead sentence of Priscilla Tremper's biography in the high school year book. I recall her as shy and studious, the latter quality being the pay-off—she was able to go to Vassar College. When I established contact with her more than twenty years later and discovered that she was an active member of the National Organization for Women, I wondered why. She responded immediately that it was the novelty of Vassar that opened her eyes: "Without the *absence* of the male hierarchy and power structure, one just does *not* see how unnecessary it all is!"

When she attended the Democratic National Convention (as an alternate delegate) in San Francisco during the summer of 1984, I was able to speak at length with her.

PRISCILLA: I think a lot of us that are active in the women's movement are starting to look back, not at our mothers but our grandmothers, to see what they did and who they were. My grandmother was a widow, her husband died when my mother was two years old, and she came back to live with her family in a working-class neighborhood near the docks and the banks of the Hudson River. And she went to work in a cigar factory. She was called the "forelady," that was the term that was used. She had a position of authority: she was the supervisor. And she sort of extended that into the family.

My grandmother was a strong influence on my life. Even my mother looked to her for guidance. Then, in the summer of 1938, my father got the scholarship to go to Germany; he was in the process of getting his Ph.D. at Cornell. So my mother and I moved to Kingston [N.Y.] and lived with my grandmother that summer.

But our home was Bethlehem, because my father taught at Lehigh. I went to Moravian Seminary for three years, and that was an all-girls prep school. There were only four of us in the class [another Lehigh faculty member's daughter and two girls from the most prominent families in town]. Then in fourth grade I transferred out into public school. It was very hard for me to get used to boys.

Priscilla was an only child, living on the South Side so her father could walk to Lehigh. The boys in her back alley were fellows *I* knew as roughnecks. In 1946 the Trempers moved to a markedly more genteel neighborhood in northeast Bethlehem. I observed to her that she did well in high school, went on to a very fine university, and on the face of it did not seem to have anything operating against her. But I added that she might have felt very differently.

I did. I think my father's having taught at Lehigh, which was an all-men's college, had a fair amount to do with it. Because he was always into "the boys this" and "the boys that." And I was different. If I had been a boy he would have included me in things that were going on at Lehigh more. My mother and I could go to football games. But I couldn't use the swimming pool. My father never really helped me to use the library until I was in college. He was not interested in my academic or social development.

You see, I had had a brother who died. He died when he was a baby, before he was one, before I was born. And that always came back. It was, I think, an underlying thread between him and me, between him and my mother. He died of pneumonia; they blamed themselves. My mother and father never knew—I uncovered this when I was doing family history research—that in my mother's family, her father had had something on the order of five brothers who were born and died before they were two years old. I think that that syndrome was just something genetic. And I think there was

Priscilla Tremper taking a break from the Democratic National Convention in San Francisco. (Photo by JEI.)

just nothing my parents could have ever done to save this child.

My father kept insisting, "If only my son hadn't died." He never said it outright, but it always came through. I think I've become aware of this only very recently. When my father died things were very difficult, because my mother died first, and he lived two years after that. And he and I never got along that well. He tried to order me around all the time. He was very domineering. And he did have a drinking problem. He smoked quite a lot, and the smoke bothered me, but he would just pooh-pooh it.

As a faculty member at Lehigh my father was entitled to

send any of his sons to Lehigh, free of tuition. There was no provision in 1952 for the daughters of faculty to have any tuition-free education. At that time he was getting barely five thousand dollars a year; there was no way of getting what I considered a decent education. He, my own father, programmed me on a track that I should to go West Chester State Teachers College—or some equal place—and become a teacher. I had belonged to the Future Teachers Club at Liberty, but I never found it particularly exciting, and I never really wanted to teach. It was just that that was the thing women were supposed to do; that was more or less the best thing you could aspire to for a career.

I got interested in Vassar when I had to do a project on a college for some class at Liberty, and I asked for the catalogue and the materials. So I ended up putting down on my College Entrance Boards application that I wanted them to send my test results to three colleges: West Chester State, Vassar, and Wilson. Then I applied for scholarships. I got no scholarship from Wilson, which I thought is where I would end up going. I got half-tuition scholarship from Vassar College. And I got a small one from West Chester. So I was in the position financially that I could just as well go to Vassar as West Chester.

It took me a long time, arguing with my father, that it wasn't going to be more expensive for me to go to Vassar. My mother was all on my side, but she didn't help too openly. She just kind of encouraged me. I accepted the scholarship, and we figured we could do one year, anyway, and we'd see how it went.

I went, and I really enjoyed it. I just loved the college and everything about it. It was a complete eye-opener to me to meet people like that and have the high caliber of faculty they had. We had a lot of women in their fifties and sixties who had been through the women's suffrage movement [a sixty-five-year-old woman in 1955 would have been thirty when the Nineteenth Amendment passed]. I didn't know it at the time.

I think there was a lot of sisterhood at Vassar, because we never had sororities or any kind of clubs that let in only a certain group or a certain kind of people. The college fought that successfully, the Alumnae Association has a strong feeling that it's wrong, and we never allowed sororities or anything like that to get established on the Vassar campus. Dorms are very important; there's a lot of "house" feeling.

After Vassar, I took a job in San Jose with General Electric. In the winter of my senior year, three friends and I decided we'd go to California after graduation. I was hired to be the mathematician for a group of engineers who were designing nuclear reactors. You could count the women working there on one hand that were not secretaries. There were two of us that were engineering assistants; there was one female engineer in the entire plant and office, known to everybody because it was just so unusual.

My main reason for being in California was not my career, it was to see California and the West and have a good time. My father thought I should stay in the East; in fact, they both really wanted me to live at home, but my mother saw clearly that I was not going to be happy living at home. She understood me better, but it wasn't out in the open because she didn't want to alienate my father. She tried to be conciliatory all the time. She thought it was nice I got the opportunity.

In California I met my future husband, Doug, who was an intern at UC Medical Center in San Francisco. [His father had also been at Lehigh]. We were in Hawaii for two years in the Navy. During those two years, being a Navy wife, you learn to get along on your own.

Then we came to Madison in the fall of 1959, where Doug was going to take his Ph.D in biology. That's where I read *The Feminine Mystique*. It was a well-organized, documented presentation of how American women of my generation and the previous one, my mother's, had been led to believe that if they just married and were good wives and mothers they would be rewarded. And how, in fact, American society had used them, and was paying them back with no social security and widowhood that was likely to mean very frugal living and no money. And they were doing a lot of work for which they were not getting paid and were encouraged to do so—volunteer work. I was doing a lot of volunteer work in Madison.

The book just made everything very clear to me; it brought everything together, you might say. Here I was, somebody

who had a good college education, had worked hard to get
it, been on scholarship for four years. I figured I had the
equivalent of a Yale degree or a Harvard degree. And I had
had a good job; I think I had been told by the Vassar vocational bureau that I had the second-highest-paying job of
anybody in my class.

Then I got married; then I had two children, and I was
right back down at the bottom of the heap again. And there
was always an excuse why they couldn't hire you or why they
couldn't pay you well. I wanted to work part time, earn
money—and a lot of the graduate school wives helped me get
part-time jobs—but I felt it was because I was a woman that
I couldn't do better.

I went to a League of Women Voters meeting on Wisconsin state government. I was impressed with the League and
their meetings related to government. I learned a lot, because
in college I never took any political science or history. I also
volunteered to help publish a newsletter about what was going on in Eagle Heights [graduate school housing at the University of Wisconsin] that affected our lives, and I became
one of the editors of that. So between 1959 and 1964 in Madison I learned everything that you could want to learn about
lobbying, how to elect an alderman—our district had the
only woman alderman—how to pressure your local elected
official, how the government works at the national, state, and
local level. And the League was engaged during that time in
two referendum campaigns. I became a member of the board
in 1963.

It was a short step from the League of Women Voters and
living in Eagle Heights with all these well educated women to
NOW. We were very angry, and we were ready for Betty Frie-
dan's book. And the political climate was still not all that
open to women, although Madison was years ahead of anywhere else in the country.

I'm married to a physician who believes in birth control
and abortion and a woman's right to make that decision.
One night Alan Guttmacher came to the University of Wisconsin; Doug thought very highly of him and thought I should
go and hear him. That's where I got my education on birth
control. I could see what a horrendous situation we were get-

ting into with the world population increasing. Poverty is directly related to the birth rate. Anyone who tries to say it isn't is just fooling themselves. Especially Ronald Reagan.

NOW is full of ex-Catholics and practicing Catholics who disagree, vehemently disagree, with the official church position on abortion rights.

NOW supports the family. But there's a division of opinion on what "the family" means. When Ronald Reagan says "family" or the press says "family," there's an image of a married couple with children. That is very much resented by a large segment of the active NOW members because the active NOW members tend to be divorced; and a high proportion of the national board are lesbians. They get real defensive about the traditional definition of the American family.

And they do not relate to my problems. And I find this hard to accept. I really resent that the national board's constant, constant pressure for all of us to support gay and lesbian rights, when, in fact, they have not had the interest in pursuing the problems we as married women face in the tax structure. Because my husband earns over fifty thousand a year, I'm in a tax bracket that's about 44 percent. That means if I earn $5,000, I pay almost half of that to the government every year. That's not fair.

I can't get elected to the national board of NOW. It's practically impossible the way the structure is organized at this time. And I think it needs to be changed. And I think that's one of the serious problems we have in the organization is that the people on the board cannot recognize what's happening.

It's difficult not to quit. I have withdrawn several times from leadership roles. When I went to business school that was true, but I came back. Because I really need it in a lot of ways. But it's frustrating to see some of these women in NOW who are supposed to bring an issue from the national level back into the community. They cannot do it. They don't understand how to make long-range plans and carry them out. I do.

Anybody who has gone to a college like Vassar, Wellesley, Mt. Holyoke or a good, public-funded institution knows how to do that. Just somebody that has a degree from a good institution. But most of these women have gone to small colleges, if they've gone to colleges, and they've never had to really fight out in the real world and learn to organize in society.

They don't deal well with men either. And the Boston media is pretty much a male institution. So they just make nasty comments about how male-dominated the *Boston Globe* is, or the television stations. And they write nasty letters to the editors and the news directors and call them up in a fit of pique. And that is the extent of their efforts to carry out the policy that NOW adopts.

Priscilla was, needless to say, jubilant at the nomination of Geraldine Ferraro—and, I presume, deeply disappointed by her defeat. But it is the future direction of NOW that really occupies her thoughts.

———

The yearbook captured Billy Maioriello as well as it did anyone: "Sixty-five inches of boundless energy on the soccer and tennis teams . . . and his gymnastics leave the girls gasping." He was my doubles partner on the high school tennis team, so I knew a lot about his energy, and he never failed to talk about his girls—in fact, he was the only person I knew in high school who was equipped with condoms.

When I finally located his home on the sparsely settled outskirts of Bethlehem twenty-four years later, where (I discovered) he fancies himself a country squire, my entrance was at first blocked by an Asian woman who told me he was sleeping. I gave my name and was eventually admitted. Then Billy introduced her to me in his inimitable way: "This is Kim—she's a princess from Korea. Her people, they stole all the money and came over here. Her brothers went back but she stayed here because, she says, she likes us white American people. She's yellow; I'm Italian brown. A lot of people say there's no difference between colored people and Italians."

As in high school, I was uncertain how much of what Billly said I should take seriously. Then I realized that he was never bothered by this issue. He didn't care.

BILLY: I have a boat down at Ocean City, a forty-foot yacht. What is the secret of youth? Get a nice young girl, teach her everything she doesn't know—because if she already knows, she's worldly—then you got to keep moving on, you need variety. But this one here, she's treating me so good.

I went to East Stroudsburg State and met some young girl up there—and within six years I had five kids. I've been divorced almost twenty years—well, seventeen. I get along beautifully with my ex-wife. She did a helluva job with the kids. About '61 [actually, 1964], I brought her down to Bethlehem to try to work things out again, and while she was down here I got her pregnant.

I was the black sheep of the family, always up to bad things, very promiscuous, a male whore. Not any more. Since I met Kim I settled down. We're going to get married shortly. [Laughs.] Get married and ruin a beautiful friendship? I told her if she would get married and have children with me—I want to have a couple kids like this [pulls eyes up on outside to make them slant]—but she doesn't want to have any.

She understands me. If I want to go out, she lets me go. Don't worry about nothing. If she wants to go out, fine! See you tomorrow, see you Friday. "Hey, you have a good time?" That's all. We don't rap on each other. As long as she treats me right, that's all I'm interested in. I don't care about that jealousy thing—that's horse shit.

I don't go for that—what do they call it?—communes. I might dig on that for awhile, but I don't think I'd want that. Because I like people of my caliber. I don't want to get tight with some zeros. I don't think I could take a lot of those people.

At Five Points, the best-known intersection on the South Side, Billy had recently purchased a bar called the Velvet Underground and renamed it Broadway Bill's.

I'm putting a computerized, synchronized light show in there. This thing is so great that I'm going to start another corporation to sell these all over the country. First one I'm going to sell this to is either Elvis Presley or Elton John or Frank Sinatra, one of them dudes. It's unbelievable. I'm having disco in there. You have to see this! My carpenter is an electronics genius. There's nothing he can't do! [He described an elaborate light and music show for dancers, explaining the

Bill Maioriello relaxing on his boat at the New Jersey shore.
(Courtesy of William Maioriello.)

novelty of the scene and how much he will market it all over
the country.] They'll never stop these kids from dancing. And
there's no end to electronics and what you can do with it.
Pictures and names, designs and patterns. There's no end to
it. I got fourteen grand in this stage already. I'm going to
advertise the largest light show in the world.

At Broadway Bill's, no disco until 9:30 at night. Open up
at 11:30, serve sandwiches. Going to have super sharp wait-
resses in there—low cut, you see their tits bulging out, short
dresses. All barmaids, women—women, women, women.

Right now, I'm in the same line of work as your brothers—I buy old houses and convert them. And I still do industrial cleaning—the Clean Window Pane Corporation. I
used to do both cleaning and maintenance, but I got out
of maintenance—too many headaches. I had it tough for a

while. My brother's father (I call him) never gave me a penny; I haven't talked to him for eighteen years. I spend much more time working than playing.

After Broadway Bill's, I'm going to buy more places—down at the shore areas. Then all over—Florida, Chicago, New York. In all of them, I'll put these stages in. But I've always loved the [Jersey] shore, I love the ocean, boats, water. Like right now I'd like to head south, down to Fort Lauderdale, then come up in May. This is my goal. I'll let my kids take over the work. Next year I'm going to absolutely do this on my boat—it's got two bathrooms, sleeps eight comfortably. But this summer—August was super here—I didn't get down to my boat one day in August. I had rented six apartments, and I had to have them ready!

I've never been to a high school reunion. I want to accomplish something before I show my face. I think I'm ready now. I would have been very happy as a physical education teacher—I love gymnastics, stuff like that. But then I got interested in bucks, in money, and due to circumstances—five children and a teacher's salary—I decided to work for myself.

I used to run. If I didn't go out every night—I used to go out and hit all the clubs. I thought I was missing something if I didn't go out. I want to live; I don't want to die. I've excited my energy in different paths now. I want to accomplish something now. I want to develop this hotel; I want to get super satisfaction out of saying, "This was a zero, and I made something out of it." Just like this mountain here. I'd like to develop this whole mountain. You look at it in the beginning, there's nothing, just trees. And after awhile, there's still trees but there's people. I get super satisfaction out of that—making something out of nothing.

Broadway Bill's has closed, but its ex-proprietor may have the chance to undertake some development work on the mountain as Route I-78 from New York now slashes through the countryside in clear view of his home.

I knew Forrest Kalmbacher through high school, yet my recollection of him is indistinct—one of many fellows whom I greeted but never spent time with. Nor did I see much of him after graduation, though he went to nearby Lafayette and, when he married, settled near my parents. He and his wife Barbara separated after twenty years together.

I visited him at his real estate office, located on the North Side. I was unprepared for the energy he exuded as he virtually ran around his desk while talking to me. I could imagine him on a basketball court.

FORREST: There's a great gap between men and women. The fellows who are interested in the women things, like Historic Bethlehem or the Moravian Book Shop—we disassociate ourselves from those men. We hang out with our own type. I hang out with a salesman from Gemco and a service manager at A-Z Tires. We go to a ballgame, have some drinks, go to Florida.

I should be more friends with these architects and the engineers, because then we could be strong, talk about city development. Where would you become friends with a woman, except church and the Y? I don't go to church. Bars are different. Then we don't talk real estate; we talk whatever they're interested in.

You [Joe] have experiences in front of classes—you can talk to women. I went through a divorce. I was married for over twenty years. We never had a squabble—maybe we should have. Our interests . . . Barbara's a fine person, she did very well at singing. I was invited to travel abroad with her choir, but I wasn't interested. Now she's married to someone like her, and she'll do great, singing and working at church. Gardening—she's the best gardener in the world; I didn't care if it was asparagus or a carrot.

I was playing basketball three nights a week until I was forty-one or forty-two. I got good after thirty. I took a clinic from Tom Gola. I went down to Kentucky to Adolph Rupp's camp. I was thirty-five. Everybody else was twenty-two. I was dunking the ball at thirty-eight. When I was a kid I was running around in circles, wheezing, in and out of St. Luke's with asthma. I played with the next generation. Now I jog. I want to be a good tennis player and take up sailing. I will

take the best lessons there are. I don't like to go into something and be a hacker.

The music people would come; I'd shoot baskets. I paved
the back yard and put in baskets. Guys from all over town in
our back yard—drinking beer, shooting ball. She didn't even
come out and say hello. It wasn't her thing. She couldn't stand
my best friends; she called them shallow. She said little to
them, and they never asked about her.

My life makes sense now. I didn't know where I was ten
years ago. You go to college, you get married, you raise your
kids, one-two-three—but then they're gone! They're gone!
They love you just as much, and they call you all the time,
and they're always in jams. This is great. But then—you, too,
you're important also. So it's fun. I really enjoy life. I'm looking forward to Christmas; I'm looking forward to a trip next
summer.

I'm very bigoted about women. Women that I enjoy I'm
very good with—in fact, I enjoy their company more than
anybody. But that's one percent. If they're really sincere. For
instance, if a woman is really interested in one of these jobs
I'm doing, and she's really keeping herself sharp, taking care
of her assets to the epitome, if she can keep physically strong,
maybe she wants to jog. Maybe it's the masculine thing I like
in them. I don't know. The doilies, and the candles, and the
services—I can't.

Barbara is competent, more competent than I am, and
accomplished. She's efficient, she's able. But she never came
in here. And never got into physical shape—and she's a
beauty. She's been in beauty pageants, but she didn't bring
it out! She didn't push her potential. She's a beautiful
woman; you'd never know it. I like knockouts. That's not
in her book.

Important to her was a good solo the next day, or her little choir, God bless her, make tears come to the audience's
eyes. She used to look like one of the kids. But they don't
stay that way. When the natural is gone, they can do things—
I don't know what they do—but. . . .

She was shocked when I said, "It's not working out." She
was devastated. But she snapped out of it real fast. I watched
carefully for six months—I stayed there. I did, of course,

have another girl—Stacy—that was 50 percent of why. But I wouldn't have had someone else if we had been doing stuff. But we didn't. Stacy and I went to Las Vegas, and here and there, and the whole bit. We're still together.

We have fun. We have our friends, we have our athletics, we have our work. She has a twelve-year-old boy whose interest in athletics I've encouraged. She's much younger, but that's not the point. People are going to find somebody similar. They say, "Two pluses, two minuses repel." I don't believe that. I think they attract, I really do. When two people are different it might look good; it's not! You do all these things, you're a carpenter, she's a singer—but you both have to hammer that nail sometime. We have blow-ups that . . . I never even heard of an argument. My family, the Kalmbachers, never had arguments, we never did fight. We had disagreements. And I certainly didn't in my marriage. Now we have terrible blow-ups. I don't know over what. And somehow we make up. That's a new experience for me. We have highs and lows.

We're interested to know what's going on, what we're going to be doing next. We went out drinking last night, and we will tonight. Then I'll go out with my boys, my buddies. I did that when I was married but I felt guilty, because Barbara had something Saturday—eight and nine things she'd list for me. I don't mind a list, but the storm windows, or the grass, or whatever I'm doing. If I had that list now I'd take it and shove it. But I would do those things anyway; I know no one else is going to. But Stacy will be up there with a hammer, doing it. I appreciate that. She's one of the boys, I guess. Sure. But that's what happens, and I was proud of her for that.

You remember when I ran the Butztown Tavern? The fun we had—the bartenders were just like part of the family. What did I need a tavern for? I was into the stock market, I had an excavating company. Those were lazy things—I was the boss, they were easy to do. When you're thirty you can do it all. I went into the Butztown Tavern for excitement, music, women—I wasn't looking for other women; I simply enjoyed their being there. I had a gas station over on South Side—why? What was I trying to prove? Now I don't care.

And I don't know what changed. Maybe I know I can do it. Nobody around me was impressed. What has happened?

Of course, everybody seems so happy on the outside. My doctor, lawyer friends, when you get them alone, they are miserable. Then they have to get drunk—and they're different people. They want to go to the shore, go to the Copa in New York and see the women undress. It's sad, sad. They should sit down with their wives and say, "Want to have some fun?" And there's nothing wrong with fun.

Did you see *Educating Rita*? Boy, is that good, touching. There was nothing spontaneous in my marriage, but I didn't know it. But I was doing it on my own—basketball, going out every Wednesday and Friday with the boys. Then I met Stacy and started doing the same things with her, then with my buddies and their girlfriends.

I can talk about anything with my friends. But we don't pry. And we don't know about rifts in each others' personal lives. When I was divorced, I didn't have anybody here. We went on like Day One. They let a man alone. Women come on—and they like to find the fault. We're not talking fault. Guys are so much better among guys.

Tonight we'll start at what used to be Joe Rich's [former Liberty High School football star] place, and we'll talk football for a while. Then we'll go over to the Fairgrounds Hotel, where the kids dress up. Then tomorrow night Stacy and I will go to dinner somewhere. Then Sunday we'll go to the mountains and take a hike—then we'll have good sex and good food on Sunday night.

As soon as her kid gets out of school, our goal is to go to Florida. I bought the condo, and she bought the furniture. Marriage? I don't know. We've been together seven years. Not being married is tough on her family, tough on her. She wants to get married. I don't know what I want. It's kind of on the line.

The life is kind of a utopia. It's pretty good. You go day by day. Is this immoral, having so much fun? Is anybody else having so much fun?

What are we going to do when we slow down? I'll be bugs. I could be in trouble. I don't read. I'm not very deep. Talk about my friends being shallow. I never taped anybody or took their picture [as I was doing]. I just do what I do best, that's all. At Lafayette I just took the required business courses and had fun—we did it all.

Forrest and Stacy were married not long after we talked. They still have plans for Florida.

———

Mike Randal and I spent a great deal of time together during our first year at Liberty. We had known each other for several years, and our family backgrounds were similar. With him I discussed what I now recognize as the troubling issues of adolescence, although he had a way of making them humorous as well. They were *his* issues, while his parents, intent on his success, determined much else that went on in his life. Their efforts paid off in the public realm, and Mike established himself as a journalist in Washington, D.C. He continues to struggle with his private life.

MIKE: I certainly envy some of my friends their amorous adventures. I myself would find it tiring trying to live two lives. Furthermore, I just don't think I could do it. There's too much rigid Presbyterian morality shit locked up in my psyche. And the only way I can even temporarily rid myself of it is to drown it in booze. And booze, of course, takes its toll on The Member. To make matters worse, I seem to have severed the psychological connection between upstairs and downstairs. Or the slow disintegration of the marriage did.

In the latter days of that decline, my erstwhile wife developed the gruesome habit of raging uncontrollably whenever The Member failed to satisfy. And naturally, each time around it became less and less interested. The half-a-dozen sexual encounters I have had in the last year and a half have been similarly disappointing. Most of the women involved have been understanding and patient, my thirty-two-year-old musician friend, particularly so. But I'm tired of asking each new bedmate: "Can I wake you up at 3:00 A.M.?" Apparently, at that hour, the connection is restored, no doubt due to the fact that the brain is too sleepy to keep it severed. Sandy's reaction used to be, "Will you stop poking me in the back?"

A mate I met in Chicago a year and a half ago had a more

pleasant reaction. Suffering from some vaginal infection at the time, she opted to lather me with Johnson's Baby Oil until I lathered her and her bed sheets. We have been writing each other ever since. She's dating a lute player, I a flute player. The flute player and I spent a couple days last August on the Jersey Shore. I confessed to her that I had been consuming about two quarts of scotch a week, to which she responded, "No wonder you're having problems, you've pickled yourself."

So I went on light beer and we almost made it in the shower. But to no avail. I've tried to distance myself from her a bit in recent months, not because of sexual problems (she's super patient) but because things were getting too hot and heavy intellectually and she couldn't understand why the hell I wasn't getting a divorce to make room for her. She's also only thirty-two and she wants kids and that gave me nightmares. Pressure from her, pressure from Sandy who keeps floating in and out of the house, usually pissed off about something I've said or done, today, yesterday, last year, in 1963, during the Middle Ages — so now I'm trying to distance myself from both, and I've been on two light beers a day for two weeks and, what with the half mile every morning at the Y, I'm feeling better than ever.

So now I have to figure out what's wrong with my connections, and to that end have had an initial session with a local Jungian analyst who promises to reprogram me for seventy-five dollars a week. Told him the price is prohibitive, now hoping for some biweekly program. I like the way these analysts think. People are basically whole and healthy, but they get turned in the wrong directions in the course of life — by the parents, their wives, their careers, etc. The thing is they're not aware they've been turned in these directions, believing perhaps that what has transpired in their lives is only normal progression from one thing to another; college to marriage, job to job, etc. In any event, whatever sessions I do arrange for ought to provide some intellectual challenges, or at least food for thought.

These guys are big on dreams. One old recurring dream, familiar I'm sure to many, has me entering spring of my senior year at Amherst, not having read a single textbook or having attended a single class. I used to think that was some sort of inadequacy dream. The Jungian interpretation says that subconsciously I may have not wanted to graduate, that I was only persisting because others wanted me to. Of course, this then opens up a whole can of worms.

Decisions were always made for me as I was growing up. Not that I minded what these decisions were. I happily went to Amherst, then on to law school, etc. Perhaps I should have stood up and said I wanted to go to music school.

I only raised my fist in anger once during my entire childhood. My father, ever in control, tried to show me how to change a lightbulb, which I was perfectly capable of doing myself. I punched him in the right arm. He didn't even feel it, didn't even know I had hit him!

The household in which I grew up, you somehow weren't encouraged to go against the standard wisdom of the time. Interested in women with a serious bent like my mother's I paid scant heed to those chicks that were easily bedable and went after the egghead hard-to-bed types instead. My mother, of course, scorned my father because he organized and ran her life and wasn't much of a thinker, though he made lots of money and provided her with a pretty good material life. And the coldness they felt toward each other because of that and other things, somehow gets translated into the distance I keep between me and my smart girlfriends, who in protest against my seeming coldness begin to feel like my mother. "You're turning me into your mother!" Sandy would scream. Perhaps she was right. Whew!

Strangely enough, I like this kind of shit. I am even tempted to ask this analyst if I can tape the session and turn it all into a novel.

Mike recently remarried and now works as an editor. His novel on domestic relations has yet to appear.

Love was assumed rather than mentioned in my own family. I took for granted that my parents, grandparents, aunts and uncles, brothers and cousins all cared about me, and I never considered whether I had to qualify myself for the attention of one or the other. Love seemed then to be an intangible quality that would not submit to analysis. Still, I knew that I was to love my parents more than other adults and value my brothers before other children. Loving and exclusivity were linked in my mind.

When, as a first-grader, I informed my mother that I had a girl-friend, she laughed good-naturedly. As the years passed I began concealing the objects of my desire, first, because I thought I was supposed to do my loving at home, and later because the content of my longing became more recognizably sexual—and interest in sexual matters seemed necessary to conceal. Perhaps that's why I attached gender to numbers and to letters of the alphabet.

But as a child I was monumentally innocent about sexual activity. My curiosity, which I assume must have been intense at an unconsious level, was not encouraged and certainly not to be discussed. At the age of twelve I was given by my parents a book on human reproduction. By that time, however, I had been educated through playground banter and dirty jokes. I do recall, some years earlier, having heard the word "fuck" used in a context that made it seem mysterious and bad. My father confirmed my judgment, for he responded to my search for a definition with uncharacteristic irritation, informing me that I would not understand and warning me never to use the term.

Meanwhile, strange things were happening to girls' bodies, not to mention my own. Their new bulges often excited an embarrasing one on my part. In seventh grade someone passed around a lurid essay entitled, "The Wedding Night," with a description of sexual intercourse that was for me mysterious, alluring, and even somewhat frightening. The following year, on a dare, I sat in the assembly bleachers behind a girl acknowledged to be willing and during the movies reached over her shoulders and touched her breasts. But what I felt more than the soft flesh—most—was great guilt. It was preferable to read Micky Spillane and masturbate. But in either case, sex was hidden, naughty, exotic, scary.

If Coopersburg had a sort of peasant, earthy quality to it, Bethlehem was bourgeois. In junior high school I began going to dancing class and to parties where the fairer sex was touched discreetly. My taste in jokes became less crude, more within the realm of my experience. ("What is dancing?" "A navel engagement without the loss of semen.") Hayrides were events where middle-class boys and girls joked with one another, although we had heard enough stories from older friends to know in what direction that wagon was moving. By tenth grade I had kissed a girl, not one of the dancing-class set, full on the mouth, lips closed. And that's where my relations with the opposite sex remained for a long time—at an ethereal level where love, such as it was, had nothing to do with genital sexuality.

The adolescent mores of postwar, middle-class America governed my behavior and, it appeared, that of my friends. "Going steady" was the natural state of relationships, but it meant no more than that a partner was always available for social events, which were ordinarily followed by an hour or so of kissing—we called it necking, which meant touching only above the shoulders—usually in a car which might contain one or two other couples. The boys then dropped off their dates, talked about them for awhile, and went home.

The girl I escorted to most social affairs as a sophomore was passionate, Presbyterian, and lower-middle-class, someone about whom my mother and father showed no enthusiasm. Early in my junior year I began seeing an equally ardent Catholic, whose parents allowed us to neck on the living room sofa until our togetherness seemed too serious, at which time they judged my Protestantism an obstacle to continued courting.

At the end of my junior year I found a wonderfully suitable partner. Shirley Anthony, named after a movie star of the thirties (along with twelve other Shirleys in the Class of 1952) but known to all as Toni, was a straight-A student who played the leading roles in dramatic productions, belonged to the best sorority, and could beat all the other girls (and probably many of the boys, though *that* wasn't done) in tennis. She was pretty, curvaceous (though rumored to be untouchable—a trait acceptable to my moralistic side), a Catholic who derided confession and ate meat on Friday (appealing to my upright Protestantism). I was surprised that she enjoyed my company.

As seniors we attended all school and club events together. Untempted, and therefore never plagued by the potential consequences of sexual intimacy, we forged a bond from shared social experience, friends in common, similar senses of humor, and matching views of propriety. We were voted typical American girl and boy in the senior class ballot. By graduation time we were talking of being true to one another forever.

Our colleges were separated by hundreds of miles; we wrote to each other daily. But in my room at all-male Princeton I was anxious about her dating at coed Penn State. I would phone her on a Saturday night, gauging my call to catch her just before she went out, hoping she would feel guilty. There was a strain on both of us. At the end of her freshman year Toni transferred to a women's college only sixty miles from Princeton.

During the next three years we were together virtually every weekend, totally happy. Yet as our wedding date approached, I began to experience uneasiness, even a sense of being trapped—feelings I did not know how to handle except by suppressing them. When Toni sensed something was wrong, I denied that anything had changed. She was ready to be free of her family, even to the point of agreeing to a Protestant wedding, and to begin a life with me. I was still tied to my parents, yet at a deeper level yearned to be free of familial responsibilities altogether.

When we did marry, our inexperience and tentativeness, our unrealistic expectations after years of virtuous courting, and the experience of being together constantly created tensions which were only slowly resolved. But by the time our first child came along in 1959, we were closer than ever. We truly enjoyed being parents together. And we slipped easily into the roles of husband-provider and wife-homemaker. Although both of us wanted a larger family, it was I who began to worry when Toni did not conceive again as planned.

Meanwhile, I accepted a teaching job in the Lehigh Valley after a successful year as professor at a college in Michigan. Yet somehow the independence nurtured by living far from Coopersburg for the first time in my life, combined with the failure to produce more progeny, deeply depressed me. Here I was, back home, but I felt an unhappiness bordering on desperation. My salvation, as I then saw it, was dramatic geographical change. I jumped at the chance to teach at San Francisco State.

For years we lived in San Francisco from September to June, migrating to the East Coast in summer and frequently at Christmas. We lived on the periphery of extended family, welcoming Toni's parents and mine for West Coast visits, celebrating holidays with her nearby sister or cousin, dropping in regularly on my aunt and uncle and their California children. We adopted Katie, bought a house, conceived Clara as our son Joey was about to flee the nest for a musical career in Europe, and took great pleasure in entertaining friends and their children in our house. In many ways it was the happiest of lives.

Yet there was always in me a restless quality, almost a reliving of my childhood when, secure and happy at home, I longed for a world out there. I knew I should cherish the one, but I could not dispel the allure of the other. And so, while I enjoyed my role in the household, I secretly sought the excitement of other emotional encounters, as if they would help me come to terms with the conflict in my life. Although I saw that I was living two lives, both contained features too important for me to give up, and I did not believe I would have to make a choice. I was wrong.

Finally I decided on a path which promised (quite accurately, it's now clear) to be joyful but also painful, love-filled yet lonely, but which felt like the way I instinctively wanted to travel. There was little precedent for divorce in my family, not to mention choosing desire over duty. Letter after letter from my distraught father pointed to my irresponsibility, fueling my own guilt about leaving Toni and our children. But with the passage of time and the help of psychotherapy, I was able to establish a home for myself as a single father deeply attached to his offspring.

My marriage to Toni lasted thirty years. In an earlier century, when life expectancy was considerably lower, one or both of us would likely have died in the course of three decades. Or, failing that, our understanding of the family as a workplace where we sustained ourselves and prepared our children to do likewise would have assumed greater importance than any feelings we had toward one another as husband and wife. But in the modern household, no longer workplace or school but an isolated nulcear unit in a mass society, the intensity of relationships is high, life is long, happiness is deemed an essential goal, and affluence enables its pursuit. There was a circumstantial as well as a personal dimension to our separation.

7 | Childhood

"The younger generation has more freedom." In one way or another members of the Class of 1952 made this observation about their children when I asked whether they had raised their youngsters differently from the way their parents had reared them. Some actively promoted this freedom, especially by encouraging a more open relationship between the generations. Others appeared to accept it, perhaps passively. A number noted that their improved standard of living was conducive to freedom.

We were born at the low point of the Depression, when the financial resources of most parents were severely limited. Probably emotional resources were also limited, since it was expected that parents would *tell* their children what to do, not consult with them. Empathy was not much valued, and even affection was frowned on by some professional advice-givers. Parents in search of a child-rearing manual would most likely have encountered John B. Watson's *Psychological Care of Infant and Child* (1928), which warned against "the dangers of too much mother love."

By the time we began bringing up kids conditions had improved. Unparalleled abundance in America provided better nutrition (freedom from want), washing machines and/or disposable diapers (freedom from strict toilet training), well-heated houses (freedom from hampering blankets and heavy clothes) with lots of rooms (freedom from intrusion), and higher incomes (freedom from working after school). An ideology to accompany these new freedoms, if needed, was available in Benjamin Spock's *Baby and Child Care* (1945), which advised parents to relax with and enjoy their children. Prosperity provided the leisure time to do so.

Prosperity helped produce a baby boom in the United States, but not in the Class of 1952, whose members gave birth to slightly fewer children than their parents. (True, affluent Class members had some-what more children.) If family size changed relatively little, meth-ods of child rearing were altered a lot. Only 15 percent of the mem-bers of the Class of 1952 claim to have raised their offspring as they were raised, while 28 percent saw slight differences and 55 percent noticed marked changes in child rearing. (Only two respondents re-ported radical deviation.) Those following their parents' examples generally stressed the harmonious relations that characterized their family of origin and continued into their present households.

Of those who saw slight differences, about a quarter cited "chang-ing times" as the cause, while only a tenth regarded greater prosper-ity as the reason. The rest focused not on causes but on the new quality of relationship: more love and closeness, understanding, self-expression. The emphasis on relationship was even more appar-ent for Class members who saw marked differences; furthermore, gender variations become apparent. Twice as many women as men stressed love and closeness, openness, and self-expression. Twice as many men characterized—one might say stigmatized—the new qual-ity of relationship as "permissivism," with its corollary that chil-dren were less controlled and less responsible.

The trend away from authoritarian parent-child relationships is unmistakable, but men are less friendly to it than women. Also, Class members with more recent immigrant backgrounds are apt to point to the negative aspects of permissiveness, suggesting that more conflict between generations exists in these families. Interper-sonal values are mentioned more by former students of the academic/scientific curricula than by others.

Considering the futures of their children, almost a third of the Class of 1952 saw members of the next generation following careers similar to their own. And since their attainments are a noteworthy advance over their parents' achievements (see chapter 5), this empha-sis on continuity suggests real satisfaction. Almost a sixth figured their youngsters would do even better than they had; almost none feared they would not do as well. About half the Class avoided a direct response to this question, stating either that the choice of a future must be the child's or that parents could at best express gen-eral goals for their children. (This stance seems consistent with the permissiveness discussed earlier.) Perhaps unsurprising is the fact that mothers stressed the personal happiness of their children, while fathers emphasized material success.

Probing this issue more deeply, we find Class members of more recent immigrant background are less optimistic about their children's futures—and more apt to say that children will make their own choices. The latter attitude could be interpreted to mean that parents feel they have little control, an expression of resignation rather than satisfaction. These same persons stress happiness more than achievement and, unlike longer-established Americans, express the desire that their children should become good and responsible citizens.

The following conversations, not to mention many which appeared in previous chapters, implicitly explore yet other issues of child rearing: Can parents shelter their young ones yet not be overprotective? Can they encourage the open show of affection in the face of contrary social attitudes? Can they communicate candidly yet retain authority? How can they know where control should end and liberty begin? These and other matters are considered mainly by mothers. I found that fathers seldom discussed child rearing.

———

Angie Donchez is the granddaughter of a steelworker from Hungary and a tailor from Italy. Her parents grew up on the South Side, where her father was the proprietor of a tavern near the steel plant. When she was five, the family—which now included two younger sisters—moved to the North Side. Their home, not far from Liberty High School, was a frequent gathering place for her friends. She continued to live there while attending Moravian College, not moving out until she married Bernard "Jude" Quinn, who had attended parochial schools and Villanova University, where he was then in law school.

In an autobiography written during her senior year at Moravian, she described high school as a place where she "loved every minute" and "worked my head off for the class." She was involved in a wide range of activities, as she fondly recalled: "Our crowd did everything in school. All the class officers were from our crowd; we were in plays, participated in sports, wrote for the newspaper, and did everything there was offered to us." This same enthusiasm for the past was evident when I talked to her in her home in suburban Saucon Valley, midway between Bethlehem and the posh Saucon Valley Country Club, to which she belongs.

ANGIE: High school was a very easy time for "us." There weren't any wars—well, the Korean War, but we didn't have to worry about that. You could usually get in the college of your choice—there's so much pressure on kids today, so much pressure on them to achieve, and "they" are making it hard for them to achieve.

Jude and Julie—they're the teenagers—Jude is very conscientious about school. I really don't think he knows what he wants to do. He does want to go to a good college because he thinks he'll have better opportunities there. And he's a good student. He talks about Dartmouth, Princeton, Harvard, Brown. I'd like him to go to one of those schools. Julie doesn't know as much about colleges. I think Julie should have the opportunities that Jude has. My father's friends used to say to him: "Why are you sending three girls to college when you know they're going to get married anyway?" He felt it was an insurance policy.

We moved out into the country almost ten years ago. I do a lot of chauffeuring, but I've gotten used to it. How many years of Little League, back and forth into Hellertown? But in a way chauffeuring is very good. You always know where your children are, you have more control over them. Still, I sometimes feel they run my life.

I think my children are much more sophisticated than I ever was. They talk about things that I would have been terribly embarrassed to talk about in front of my parents. I'm glad that they do. They talk about sex. One night young Jude said at the table, "If the mother has the baby, how come some people will say the baby looks like the father?" His father—I thought he would die, he was ready to leave the table—he was so embarrassed. But we explained.

I don't remember asking my parents such questions. I found a book on raising adolescents in my parents' room and read it. We never discussed *anything*. But Jude had a parochial education, and his mother was proper, almost prudish.

Sometimes I think I'm overprotective. I'm so glad I have Jude to guide young Jude. I wouldn't know when I should let him do things, when to let go. We get along fine, though he seems embarrassed when we watch him in sports.

I've been thinking about how it would be to let go of him. Last week Jude and I went to a ballgame in Philadelphia and took the subway to the park. Seeing really young boys on the subway, I realized our children know nothing about getting around in the city. It gives me a secure feeling to have them go by school bus to a place I know is safe. I don't know if I can let go of him, though I've been trying.

Jude's grandfather came over here from Ireland, by himself, when he was just sixteen. Could you picture my son going to a new country?

My sister Marie, because of Jimmy's [James Ramberger, Class of 1952] job in the Air Force, has moved around so much. Their kids are very well adjusted. I'm amazed.

I've told the children: "If you bring home people like your-selves"—and I don't mean that the father has to be a lawyer or something like that—"people who are raised like you, that's the only thing that counts to me, if the person is a good person." Maybe there were other distinctions made in high school, but I really didn't realize that there were at the time.

I guess I pretty much like things as they are. I like the way I live. I wouldn't want Jude to treat me any differently. I still want to look up to him; I really feel that the man should be the, the—if I say "master," that sounds terrible. But I really feel he should be the one you look up to in the family. I certainly would not want to have married someone less bright than I was, that I felt couldn't make decisions. Although we always discuss things, there are things he knows more about than I do. I have confidence in his decisions—about finances, for example, where he knows much more than me. Even with regard to young Jude—I came from a family of all girls—I think Jude knows better what his son can do.

I certainly want to be treated with respect. I believe women in the working world deserve equal pay for equal work, but I don't think some of them are asking for respect. I heard a story of a woman at the Steel who swears worse than the men do. I don't like that. Ladies should be ladies. And you still can be a lady doing certain types of work. Some activities go too far. I wouldn't let Julie got out for the boys' wrestling team. In fact, when she went out for the girls' basket-ball team, her brother said: "What did you do that for? I don't want you going around with that type of girl." I thought, "He really is a male chauvinist!" But they are big, husky girls, very athletic, and Julie isn't. Then I thought, what if she was the athlete and Jude wasn't?

The night we were burglarized, when I got home the only thing I could think to do was run the sweeper. Jude said, "Angie, it's two o'clock in the morning." Maybe it was a way to get rid of some anger. I'ts a funny feeling, having your home invaded. And the thing that really bothered me—it's really a dumb thing—was that they might have gotten hold of the pictures of the children, which I could never replace.

Between the time I visited Angie in 1976 and in 1983, she had moved from one very comfortable suburban house to a yet larger one, no doubt a sign of her husband's success as a lawyer. She remained unpretentious and straightforward. I arrived just a few days after the United States invaded Grenada.

I'm really patriotic, I really am. I was rally annoyed on this Grenada thing; I thought, our allies could have backed us. I was apprehensive [that we invaded another country] but I really think we should stick by our— —I don't know. I like Reagan, too, I really do. Do you think if he had more diplomatic language? . . . He just comes out and says what he says. I think he's strong. [She is pacing all over the place.] I believe the only way we protect ourselves is by being strong. I don't believe in war—I hate war. I don't think we can let our defenses down with people like the Russians.

My daughter Julie wants to join the Peace Corps. I don't want her to—isn't that terrible? She wants to go to some Spanish-speaking country. I'm afraid she'll go to Central America. When she wants something, she goes right ahead. She had us signing papers for her going to Italy before we even discussed it. Not that is wasn't a wonderful experience for her.

I was overprotective with my kids. I would never let them go to Philadelphia to rock concerts when they were in high school. We thought there were too many elements of risk. I wished we lived in a somewhat bigger city; I think they would have been a little more street wise, worldly. We can't sleep when they're out at night. I don't worry about what they're doing; I worry about what could happen to them—innocently.

At twenty-two, I think I was more ready to accept responsibility than young Jude is; I know Jude was. I don't think Jude is ready to get married. We've done so much for him; he's yet to have to do anything for himself.

I read Dr. Spock religiously, but not his philosophy of raising children. We just did what we thought was right. When I talked to you before about being overprotective, how other parents made kids find their own way to and from activities, we were always ready to take them in, pick them up—maybe we should have let them find their own way. But they've always been our life. We've always tried to do everything for them.

Angie's son Jude is following in his father's footsteps through Villanova law school. Julie is temporarily working in her father's office while searching for a more permanent career. Betsy is an undergraduate at Villanova.

———

Pat Eddy's forebears came from the British Isles, and Pat grew up on the North Side. Voted by her high school classmates the girl with the best smile—which, translated, meant she was very attractive— Pat made it clear in the yearbook that she disliked "going steady," a novel stance at that time. Perhaps it suggested some restlessness; in any case, she did not bother with college and left Bethlehem a few years after high school graduation.

When I saw her for the first time after almost twenty-five years, she was living on the rural fringe of Philadelphia's Main Line. Her husband Bill was there with us, but he spent most of the time on the phone, putting the finishing touches on the sale of his company—and looking forward, at age forty-seven, to retirement. They seemed happy, relaxed, comfortable.

PAT: We're looking for a place to go and live—and we don't know where to go. But we'd like to be close to skiing. We like water and woods and the out-of-doors.

Bill would like to go to Colorado. There's something in my mind about finishing the education of the kids. They only have a total of four or five years left, and I'm not too sure about their finishing their education in Colorado. Bill could buy a thousand acres somewhere, and there we'd be, and he'd love it. He really is just as happy in a little family. We do everything as a family. Socially, we take the kids everywhere and do everything with our kids.

I think the decision of where to live would be easier if the children were out of high school, and we didn't have to think about getting them in a good school and get the right thing and have the right opportunities for them. Although this area that we live in is so geared toward business, so geared toward everybody finishing school and going to certain colleges— everyone has to prepare himself for this big business career. He's thinking, "Well, if we go out West then they don't have the same thing."

There is a certain amount of culture, there are museums. Of course, they've probably been to most of them already, right? They've used the Franklin Institute an awful lot. They still love to go there. It probably wouldn't make any difference. But there's art and music and such things, if they want any of those things.

The two boys are totally different. Bobby is so artistic, I just can't believe it, that he has such talent. And then Brian, he handles the homework in the school like a breeze, while Bobby has a tough time.

The Waldorf School, based on the Waldorf theory of education, is basically European—Switzerland and Germany mostly. All their studies are surrounded with music and art, which is kind of a neat thing. They've got lots of languages and lots of history. Their history includes art; they do pictures with each thing they write about. My kids love to draw.

I was having a very difficult time because Bobby couldn't read. The public school here gave me the worst time in the world. First, they said it was my fault. Then they said that he was just being stubborn. And this went on. I had him tested by a psychologist who was a re-educational type and said it was my fault. I *knew* it wasn't my fault. The school said he had to go to a reading clinic, which was a bad thing because the boys were going to day camp. So he did that. Finally, I just couldn't put up with the principal and the whole thing at the school because he said, "This kid is too smart, the top 18 percent of his age group, and you're just being hyper." So I took him out of the school, and his brother with him, and

Pat Eddy with husband, Bill, and children, Bobby and Brian, on the slopes of Colorado. (Courtesy of Patricia Eddy.)

put them in this private school, which is a beautiful farm place out in the country.

They found that he did have a problem, and we took him to this place in Chestnut Hill, the Institute for the Development of Human Potential, which is for kids that have had some sort of brain damage. That is, if a kid had dyslexia or any of these types of things, a problem connected with the brain. So what they did was repattern him — or, because he was so old, he did it. Now he can read. But I had to get him out of that situation where I didn't know what to do, and they didn't know what to do either. Nobody had seen his problem; most dyslexia problems are right to left but his was up and down.

I worked a lot with him. It was really tough for him. He had to get up early in the morning and do all sorts of exercises. We had to do reading projects at night. It took a year and a half. But he went from second-grade level to an eighth-grade level in that time. It helped him in other things too. He became more confident. Brian was very understanding while

Bobby did all this. It worked out—but I know it doesn't work for everybody.

My sister-in-law has a problem, and she isn't about to do this type of thing. She's sent her kid to a tutor for about four years, and I don't think he's any better now than he was then. The place we went, the parents had to agree to do it. But it didn't occur to me to have someone else do it. I just saw this kid in trouble.

Pat described Bobby's treatment in detail and admitted she had learned a lot about the brain and human development. She had also observed and learned at a co-op nursery school. "Lots of little things you do along the way are educational," she remarked.

Pat's children remained at the center of Bill's and her lives. The family moved to Connecticut so the boys could attend the Avon School. Bob went on to Cornell and is now an architect in Santa Barbara, California. Brian graduated from St. Lawrence and is pursuing an advertising career in San Francisco. And Bill has finally lured Pat to Colorado; they live in Aspen.

As editor of *Liberty Life*, the biweekly high school newspaper, Chris Sideris was known to be both capable and creative, a doer with a flair. Her yearbook biographer observed "beautiful dark eyes and chic clothes." The activities listed under her name included the girls' hockey team and the art league. She was an American Woman in the making.

Much to the surprise of classmates who went off to Moravian College with her, she withdrew during her junior year to marry an Older Man. It probably did not seem so unusual to Chris, whose parents had been born in Greece and whose father was a dozen years senior to her mother. George Maharas was only seven years older than Chris. They settled down to raise a family but they did not become ordinary parents, as Chris informed me in 1976 in a letter attached to her questionnaire.

Nicky Nicholas Maharas, born 6/18/56, is a very special child. He was born a "Rubella Baby" (1955: German measles epidemic) with many congenital defects and is multi-handicapped with brain injury, very poor vision (he has congenital cataracts), impaired hearing, coordination problems. He is what educat-

ors call the "exceptional child," which can be misleading because the reality of that "nom" is that he is an exception to
the normal child and functions at a subnormal level. Nicky
spent the first seven years of his life on the threshold of death
and a great deal of his early life in hospitals. He was under
the care of the finest doctors possible, which in its own way
made us feel good to know we had tried our best, in spite of
cost, to give him the best. If one has to "accept" the unac-
ceptable, it's a little easier if every avenue of alternatives has
been explored.

There was no mistake. Nicky was destined to live in a
world of retardation with other physical and neurological
handicaps. He has progressed far beyond original expectations. He has far surpassed his doctor's early prognosis, although he cannot ever be self-sufficient or lead a normal life.
It was very fortunate for all of us that our two daughters
were born soon after Nicky. They were a leveling force. They
were bright, joyous, and created a "live" incentive to Nicky to
emulate them. He was gently but firmly pushed to try to
keep up with them, and this was an excellent learning experience for him when he was little.

Nicky required a tremendous amount of time, but I was
determined to have as "normal" a household as possible.
Nicky feels very much loved and very secure. He goes to
Boces Special Education and will graduate this June '77. He is
a very good, well-adjusted student and is quite a leader with
his peers. He is a very loving, altruistic youngster with much
concern for others' welfare.

He is not at all destructive, mean or selfish. We, and his
teachers, all feel that he has more ability locked up inside
him, but his sensory impairments make it difficult to develop
his full potential because of the limited communication. My
major objective has been and still is to develop his full potential. At the moment he is slated for a sheltered workshop for
the future.

His contribution to our family has been to inspire a different set of values; priorities change. Our daughters, because of
their first-hand experiences of living with Nicky, matured
much faster, and developed insights, sensitivities, and appre-
ciation of simple things which most people take for granted.

I do not mean to imply or think for a minute that one has to have something as sad as Nicky happen to them in order to gain those qualities I mentioned. Success, triumph, does not *have* to spring from tragedy. (An artist, poet, etc., does not *have* to starve to be famous someday!) I'm just trying to say that, with a positive attitude, out of a sad-tragic situation that just "happened," we've tried to see the good things that were generated. Ten, fifteen, twenty years ago I could not write this in all honesty—time, and perhaps age, does change things. Someday, I hope I'll write a book about it. Meanwhile, Nicky is our love and our problem—and society still does not make it easier to cope, but it's better.

My eventual rendezvous with Chris and George took place in Poughkeepsie, New York, at a concert of the Hudson Valley Philharmonic Orchestra. Chris was a member of its board of directors and allied associations, not to mention her service on the Dutchess County Council for the Fine Arts, the PTA, the Girl Scouts—and the county board of realtors (for she was running her own real estate business out of her house). The morning following the concert, as Chris, George, their younger daughter Karyl, sixteen, and I were having breakfast, Nicky, then twenty years old, announced himself from the hallway.

KARYL: Nicky, don't touch that. Hi.
CHRIS: Would you like to have something to eat?
NICKY: Yeah.
CHRIS: Bring me a little dish and a fork, okay?

Nicky got what was needed, making a lot of noise in the process, and when he sensed I was ignoring him—which, not being certain how to act with him, I was—he intruded himself, saying something about eating.

GEORGE: This morning Karyl and I were rather disturbed because we thought he might be ill, because he wasn't as prompt as he usually is. He loves to see people come here, and after a while he'd go and pick out their coats—he has a fantastic memory. You could have fifteen people come into the place and he identifies every garment. He'd come in with

hris Sideris with husband, George, and children, Karyl and Nicky, at home in
ıughkeepsie, New York. (Photo by JEI.)

one or two coats, which implies he wants them to leave. [Nicky
continued to talk to members of the family as this conversation
went on, asking when I'd leave, as well as other questions.]

GEORGE: Now let us talk. Would you like a glass of
orange juice?

NICKY: No.

CHRIS: You'd better find your glasses.

Nicky left, and the telephone rang. It was a work day for Chris,
who explained how she got drawn into the real estate business and
why she liked it: "Very lively, very active. And you get personally
involved with peoples' lives, but they don't get personally involved
in yours. A little like journalism."

Nine years later, sitting on the deck which I had built behind our house in San Francisco the same autumn I visited Poughkeepsie, Chris described moving to north shore Chicago, then to Fort Collins, Colorado, where the whole family is now situated.

Her daughter, Dena, after several years of working in New York as a filmmaker, has come to Fort Collins to take a rest from the pace of the city and resume work as a photographer. Karyl has married and moved from the Maharas household two miles up into the mountains. Nicky's status has changed most dramatically: he is living away from home in a new family of eight developmentally disabled men his own age. He has been employed in a workshop for some years, so his changed residence is yet another step toward independence — amazing strides considering the original prognosis for his condition. It is possible to see in his progress since his birth in 1956 an analog to the American recognition of and positive reaction to the developmentally disabled. Yet it is undeniable that the fundamental cause of Nicky's success is not due to some general change in attitude but to Chris' and George's resolution from the time of his birth. They were determined to liberate his locked up humanity, and to the extent that goal was possible, they have done so.

Nazareth was one of the rural communities founded by the Moravians and intended to supply farm products to commercial Bethlehem. It retains its village charm, and here Helen Kocher, who had been a nurse, and her husband Bob Snyder, a physician, reside in a Victorian house set up for a general practice — the first floor contains his office, the second and third, their home and three children: Leslie, Katie, and Robert, who were nineteen, sixteen, and thirteen, respectively, when I visited in 1976.

HELEN: With Bob being in the type of medicine he is, and I was a nurse, of course we pride ourselves in having a few "smarts" when it comes to psychology. And I'm sure that Bob remembers the traumas he went through. And my father died when I was eleven. I used to come home and make supper myself, and I was alone a lot. For this reason, with my mother working, I reverted the other way. I believe that I have to be home almost every day when they come home. It gives a child a big continuity to have mother at home.

I look back and remember the insecurities I felt. I knew I was missing something. I even would go down and help Angie Donchez clean someone else's house, just to be with somebody. I suppose I was looking for someone who would give me some kind of direction. My mother kind of let me on my own to make my own decisions. And growing up when I did and coming from the kind of family I did, I had no idea of doing anything wrong. I certainly wouldn't have gone out at night and walked around the streets or something. But I certainly had the freedom to do it. I didn't have to ask permission to do what I wanted.

My mother worked in the evening as a demonstrator for Stanley Home Products. She did demonstrations in the houses — brushes, mops, wax — so sometimes she had an afternoon "party" and wouldn't be home until supper, which I would make, and then she'd go out all evening.

But I actually liked being alone too. I don't know if I would have been quite as alone as I was on purpose. But even now, as an adult, I really need to be alone. It works out well. Bob has office hours in the evening. And after I would put the children to bed when they were small, I'd have a couple of hours completely by myself to sew or read or just relax. I really need this privacy.

My daughter Kate likes to be left alone. She doesn't like "hovering mothers." She has to make a speech in school on her pet peeve. I said, "Are you going to tell them that your pet peeve is when your mother pats you on the head?" And she said, "Yeah," and that's it. I'll walk out of the room after talking with her, trying to communicate with her, making a block of time, and I'll think, "Oh, we had a few nice sentences together." And I'll sort of pat her on the head. And she'll roll around and tell me she just hates that.

In our situation, we've always tried to show our children there's a wonderful, big world out there. We wouldn't want them to live here in Nazareth. We think it's very stifling for children to grow up and think they're going to stay here and give up job opportunities. We've seen that happen.

It's paradoxical, because the best place to raise a child often is a small town. We really felt good about having them go out at night to the library when they were eight years old—and things like that. We have a fine school system. I think we're fortunate that there were enough college-graduate parents around town in the last ten to fifteen years that the school system is very fine. When Leslie went to Brown she didn't have any trouble at all.

Maybe some women in our generation feel a little threatened by the women's movement. Bob and I have been very aware of the movement, and he's a great father with his girls. He always impressed upon them that he thinks women are terrific, that they have great brains, that they can do anything they want. Katie was very flattering to us the other night. She said one of the reasons she's afraid to have children is that her father and I did such a great job. She doesn't think she can raise kids as well.

We think that we have not had enough time to communicate with our daughters. They've been in sports since ninth grade, which means of course every night practice. Daddy has to be in the office again at six, they don't return until seven. This means no supper, which we think is a great communication place. So he always makes the big effort after office hours to go up and sit on the edge of the bed and ask them if there are any problems, or this or that.

We enjoy car trips with them sometimes, because we've got them right there in the car and they can't get away from us. And then we can have some discussions. Some of them have been very good. I just feel we haven't been able to discuss enough with them or communicate with them when they're pressured by school and sports and trying to pick a college. You really have to thread your way carefully about "now's the time we want to discuss your future."

With raising our son now, I try to point out the good things his sisters have accomplished. I try to wring an admission out of him that girls can do a few things, but he is quite a chauvinist and has been one since eight years old and is now thirteen. I realize that for his psychodevelopment, he's got to be chauvinistic. He's also involved in sports—basketball and tennis—and is doing well in school.

Nine years after I talked with Helen her daughter Leslie had become a local news editor (as had her husband) for a small paper in New Jersey. Katie was a nurse in Bellingham, Washington, son Robert, a business analyst in Washington, D.C. Helen had recently stepped down as president of the Medical Auxiliary of Pennsylvania. She attributed her achievements to her training:

"There's nothing better for living with a person or having children than to have a nursing background. Because not only the psychology that you learn but the interaction and the compassion for people that you display—must display— and the care for them. And I must say that Bob agrees with me; he just thinks that nurses are fantastic."

Barbara Rockstroh—Chicky, as she was popularly known—married two years out of high school and was soon stationed in the Orient with her Navy husband, Bill. When he retired from the service, they and their two daughters, Cynthia and Brenda (twenty-one and fifteen when I visited in the autumn of 1976), returned to Bethlehem, where Bill worked as a maintenance man and Chicky as a bookkeeper in an auto agency. I groped my way to their home in northeastern Bethlehem, in a suburb that did not exist when Chicky and I were in high school.

CHICKY: We've lived in the Philippines and Japan. Our youngest was born in the Philippines. The girls and I came back here in 1965. My husband also went to Nam. I miss moving around; I get bored. The longest I ever lived in one place was Japan—four years.

Brenda, her younger daughter and a sophomore at Liberty High School, entered and was introduced as "our little Filipino."

We don't have any generation gap in this house. They've had some of the teachers I had at Liberty. She's got a boyfriend, and he lives right across the street here. And the one night, he was talking on the telephone to one of his buddies from right here. And we horseplay and have conversations, and this kid [the buddy] couldn't believe it. He thought it

Chicky Rockstroh and daughter Brenda at home in Bethlehem. (Photo by JEI.).

was Brenda's sister talking. This boy had to come here and meet Brenda's mother. He couldn't believe it. We have a grand time together. The way a lot of people are having a lot of problems, it makes me feel real good.

Bill, her husband, entered, was introduced, and disappeared immediately, saying hardly a word.

They don't have a relationship with their father like they do with me. He doesn't like their music. The way they speak to me in horseplay to him is disrespectful.

I never learned too much at home. I never had any kind of a mother-daughter relationship. I was daddy's girl. And my mother never told me anything about sex. What I learned was what bits and pieces that I picked up. And you know, that's not always the right way to find it out. I could never go and ask my mother anything, because in those days that was taboo. You didn't talk about those things.

They can come and ask me anything. I'd rather they came and asked me, and I told it to them the right way than they learn it on the street corner somewhere and either learn it halfway or altogether wrong. I always said that if I had girls, I didn't want the kind of relationship with them that I had with my mother. Not that I didn't have a happy home. I did! But there were just things you didn't discuss, that's all.

We've always been very open. I don't like everything that they do. But they don't like most that I smoke cigarettes; I say, "Go on thinking that way." I've tried to teach them the same moral codes that I was raised under, but let them go along with enough of it today. I've tried to keep the rope here, not to pull it too tight that it chokes them. And I don't want to be demanding on them and say, "You can't listen to this radio and have that music on because I don't like it."

Now when we ride in that car out there, there's an FM station on, and they don't like to listen to Daddy's music. He likes the more dreamy stuff. I spent all that time in the glee club, and I like music. I like the beat. He has none of this, and he still goes along with a lot of the old ideas. One day he called here to ask whether Brenda or I knew what a marijuana plant looked like; a kid at the church where he worked was growing something. You have to learn to be flexible to survive. I've had to be flexible with them.

When her boyfriend comes over here I know the things he gets away with over here he wouldn't get away with at home because his mother wouldn't put up with it. But we all have a great time together. Like I said, some of her friends don't believe I can be her mother and behave that way. But I can go along with them.

Just like some of the terms the kids use today. We can sit, the two girls and myself, and my husband can be here, and he has to ask us what we're talking about. Because the terms don't mean anything to him. I hear them enough—she comes home from school, she tells me the things that go on in school, she's not afraid to say anything. Now the other daughter, she's a little different. This one's very open with me. The other one only tells me as much as she wants me to know, and I don't press her. Because, like I say, I tried to raise them with a set of moral standards that teach them the difference between right and wrong—and hope for the best.

I've never had any problems, so help me. I consider myself very, very lucky. My husband sometimes tells me I act too young for my age. It's the old adage that you're only as old as you feel and I'm not ancient yet. They call me their hot-rod mother, because of the way I drive.

Seven years later, I visited Chicky for the second time. She and her younger daughter, Brenda, were awaiting my arrival late on a wet November afternoon.

CHICKY: Since I saw you both daughters have married, and I've been divorced.

When I walked down the aisle in 1954—at the age of forty-nine I did not expect to be where I'm at. Three years ago I didn't think I was going to survive; your whole world falls apart. Now that's all over. I thought the divorce would be less difficult for my daughters to handle because of their ages, but it wasn't. The older one had more difficulty. I try my best to make her feel comfortable with it; she can't handle the grandfather part—she wants her two little girls to have two grandfathers. I told her: "You may find this hard to believe, but after three years it's as though those twenty-six years did not exist."

Because of the circumstances, it took three years to get over it. The biggest mistake I ever made was the day before he left here, telling him he was welcome to come here any time. For two years he behaved more like a husband and more like a father than when he lived here. He was here for holidays, gave me presents—I don't care what it means! I should have divorced him ten years ago.

He not only destroyed his own immediate family—me and his two children—but he also destroyed his whole family, because the young woman that he's living with happens to be his sister-in-law, his brother's wife! Two years younger than his older daughter. I spent my twenty-fifth wedding anniversary with all the evidence I had found in his briefcase. That's why I still have the house. I said to him: "You give me the house. I will keep quiet." Two years later he and she blew the whistle on themselves.

I visit his mother once a week. He hasn't seen her in over a year. I'm still part of the family. He is not. Ties of that many years I cannot break. At seventy-two years old she has to live with this! Brenda's father didn't walk her down the aisle: I did. Brenda insisted on that.

BRENDA: When he was here, all he did was pick on us. She was always our mother and our father.

CHICKY: And he has never called Cindy to ask about her. Or to check on her kids. He said he never got what he wanted out of life. He's got problems, and he's never done anything about them. It was the third time in our marriage he got caught. When you play a baseball game, you know—three strikes and you're out.

BRENDA: Our generation doesn't care as much. I can't see it—these girls and guys getting married, stay together two years, separate. I love to sit and listen to my mom talk about what they did in school, the bonfires, stuff like that. They couldn't do that now; kids would be lighting their joints with the fire.

CHICKY: Our lives have gotten so mixed up; nothing is the way it used to be. But you can't sit and cry about it. You have to go along with it. It's a matter of mingling families and ideas. One family does things their way; you do things your way. I always taught the girls, when you get married you have two families. Not the way my brother's wife excluded my parents. I made up my mind that when I had children of my own, it would be different. I wouldn't hide things from them, like sex. I wanted them told the *right* way.

BRENDA: It's good to be able to talk openly to my mom about things.

CHICKY: We're the Three Musketeers. When they have problems in their marriages, we talk it over.

BRENDA: And my husband appreciates that.

CHICKY: But I don't treat the boys like sons-in-law. They're sons to me. We all still stick together like glue.

When I last heard from her, Chicky had not only grandchildren but a suitor, someone who graduated from Liberty with us. She writes: "So thirty years later—two classmates from Junior and Senior high days get together—after never having seen or been in contact with each other for many, many years. We are having a ball! The tricks that life plays on you are certainly amazing, that's for sure."

———

I did not know Ed Krucli in high school but first met him and his wife Joan at their house in Buena Park, Los Angeles—turn left on Lowell, right on Frost, and there they are on Whitman, one of the arteries of the poet tract. High culture is not a rarified commodity in Southern California, a place totally unlike the South Side of Bethlehem where Ed and Joan grew up. Two of his brothers were working back there in the Bethlehem Steel Company plant, just as his Hungarian father had. Probably Ed is the most mobile member of the Class of 1952, geographically and occupationally, three thousand miles from his working-class background with a master's degree and a school principal's job under his belt. Joan works as a librarian.

When I arrived and rang, Ed answered the door in denim shorts and a Bearfoot T-shirt, introduced me to Joan who was also attired in California casual, and led me through the family room to the patio where their three children were cavorting in the blue-tiled pool. Youthful, tanned, smiling, prosperous—this was a family that had reached the Promised Land. Ed began telling me about coaching a baseball team for kids.

ED: This is based on noncompetition. The basic thing is to teach a kid the skills of the game. As a coach you are in charge of telling the parents, "No look, we're out here to teach the kids how to play baseball. Forget about winning and losing, and just enjoy it with your kids." Usually the coach asks for the participation of four or five fathers so he can break into small groups and teach these kids skills.

This year it's been most rewarding; it's my third year, and this is the year I took the step to be head coach. We came in third place out of forty teams. And it's really an honor because, like I told the coaches, it's up to us how far we bring these kids. Because they're all moldable, and you're going to teach them how to do things. You get some kids who just haven't come anywhere, and others—you wouldn't believe it!

At the very beginning I told the parents, "If you're out here to see us win every game, draw your kid out of it." Nobody did that. But we kept them alert to everything that was happening by a little newsletter every week. I kept building up the fact that "We're out there to learn skills and everything," and "Later on in life they'll have enough time for competition and everything," and "Just keep being good examples to the kids and all that." Things we learned in education.

I don't know if it's a basic feeling, though, to be noncompetitive. Sometimes when I'm coaching I almost feel like I'm role-playing. Because I know I want to win. I have to think of the kids—that I'm an example. And even in defeat, I've got to be above it all and just say, "We've played a great game, kids. You hold up your head high, you've played the best game you could." And then you go over to the other team and congratulate them and give them a cheer and everything. You role-play.

It's a gut-level feeling, that I think of. Because I know this summer I would have liked to have gone all the way with those kids. Because I thought they could do it. But . . . two outs, bottom of the last inning, and you get beat by that one run that comes across because another kid was more physical and pounded one of our little kids, and the ball flew up in the air, and the guy was safe. But I really felt that we had out-played the other team.

They were kindergarten through third grade. At the end of a game I always would say, "Go get your treat, and come back, and we'll have the after-game show." And then I would talk to them about it. You try to reinforce the positive things they've done.

When I was young, I was real hot in basketball. I remember at the high school, I really goofed. Because I guess I really never had the backing of my mother and father. They didn't understand. They were Hungarian. In fact, my father I never spoke to in English.

When I came out here I went to Compton Junior College. And I was the last man to get cut off the varsity squad up there. And if I would have had the experience, you know, I was playing ball with guys who went on to start at UCLA and Washington. These guys were tremendous! But no one gave me that extra push to keep me in there.

I loved basketball; I still do. I play baseball more than anything now. A lot of slow pitch. Three leagues. It takes up my time. Once school starts, you hardly see me because with early childhood meetings—I've got a parent advisory group I'm obligated to go to—board of education meetings, PTA—it just goes on and on. It's just that there are so many things to keep this communication thing going.

I went to Cal State, Long Beach. I did my student teaching in Bellflower. At the end of my student-teaching assignment they said, "We'd like to hire you." I picked up a second grade at that time. I was drafted for two years, came back to Bellflower, and have been there ever since: as a teacher, curriculum consultant, assistant principal, and then principal.

You know, people are mobile out here. They move within the occupation. I feel I'm kind of stagnant. Because I know many of my colleagues that are assistant superintendents and things like that. They say, "Hey Ed, five years?" And I know a lot that think this way. Educationally, people out here stay maybe four, five years, then they go to other positions.

My father worked in the plant of the steel company. One sister is out here in LaHabre; her husband's a principal also; she was the only other one who graduated from high school. But my other brothers and sisters are all back there; my two sisters are married, and my two brothers are single. One brother works in the steel plant, the other in a textile mill. Only one sister never worked; she just got married. The other sister worked before she got married.

When I was graduating from high school back there I went to the alumni meeting. And I remember this guy got up there and started talking, and he was from California. That's when I was really thinking of what am I going to do. I wanted out, and the right catalyst occurred.

My sister came back for a vacation with her husband. And they lived out here. My sister was working at Compton Junior College, and they knew I wanted out. And they said, "The service, Ed, fine. It's one way of going. But why don't you try school?" And I said, "I don't care. I'll do anything just to get out of here, because all my friendships, they've all gone in the service. What am I going to do? And I don't want to go work at the steel company." So they took me out here, and my whole life changed.

I thank the Lord that they did that kind of thing. I love it out here. I've enjoyed everything I've done out here—my schooling, my job, the mountains, the beach. As many times as I wrote people back there I said, "You wouldn't believe it, what we have out here in California." Bethlehem always reminded me of smallness. I always had to plan—you know, like if you're going to Philadelphia. It took two days of planning to go to Philadelphia to a ballgame or something like that. Where out here—I used to put a hundred miles on when I first dated a girl. It's just a different way of living.

Bigness. Openness. You've got to go through it to really live it, believe it. I know every time I've gone back there I've talked to some of my friends, like Austie Kurisco—he and I grew up together—and Freddie Jordan was another one that I met when I really started changing my thinking. And I used to write to them saying, "I can't believe that I'm sitting here in the library of Cal State, Long Beach; it's ninety degrees and I'm looking at snowcapped mountains—which I can be up there in two hours." You know, it's just an unbelievable feeling.

When I talked to Ed several years later he was program coordinator of the Bellflower Unified School District, Los Angeles. Because one of his children had to write a family history, he investigated his European background and discovered that there were educators on his mother's side of the family in Hungary. Thus, though he had come a long way from western Hungary via Bethlehem, the classroom was more home for him than he had imagined.

———

Sylvia Pearl had aged well. She obviously cared about her appearance. She was possessed of a strong social awareness as well. Sitting in her living room, looking at the rows of paperback books lining two walls, I listened to her saying that she wished we had known more, been aware of a world beyond ourselves, in high school. Her six-year-old was being better prepared. Both she and her husband—whose son by a previous marriage was a conscientious objector, a young man who left Bethlehem for California after seeing the consequences of smoking and dealing dope—are seeing to that. She spoke of her rising awareness.

SYLVIA: When the women's movement started, I admit I didn't know what it was about. And it wasn't until I read a book or two that I did really understand what it was really all about. It's not women; it's people. It has something to do with the fact that women were kept down so long, but it's better for men, too.

About four to five years ago a girl I worked with belonged to this Abortion Information Service; it's defunct now. After she dropped out they were looking for someone to take her place on the phone, so I started going to meetings, and then one night a week took the phone calls. And from that I got interested in LeVARA, which was Lehigh Valley Abortion Rights Association. Then I went to those meetings. Then I got interested in NOW, and it was all the same girls involved. But then about a year ago my dad became an invalid, and I stopped going to the meetings. I still belong to NOW, but I don't go to the meetings anymore, and LeVARA is still going.

Abortions are legal. But, it's not that well known by a lot of girls. This is why we had Abortion Information Service for a while, but now it seems that there's no problem if they want one. But still some girls don't know for sure that the Supreme Court decision is through the country; a lot of people don't realize that.

We were supposed to counsel and give information and not to tell them that they should decide on abortion, just listen to their problems and, if they wanted an abortion, give them that information, and if they didn't, refer them to the pro-life organization.

My son is six and a half, and I didn't have him till I was thirty-five. And I think what I went through when I was single is what got me so interested in Abortion Information Service because I think it was terrible, you know, what I went through. And then when I realized this was open for girls I thought it was nicer to have a choice in this way. So finally I did have a child that was well planned and thought about for years, and that's it. In fact, my husband had a vasectomy after Sean was born.

I work [on the clerical staff] at the state hospital. What always unnerved me or disturbed me and still does is that the girls I work with, their ideas are so archaic, a lot of them can't see that far, can't see through it. But it was long after I got out of high school that information was available. It was five or six years ago, before or right after Sean was born, that I heard of the AIS, and at that time it was only operating about a year.

I still belong to NOW. There aren't that many members, and at any of the meetings I've ever been, if there'd been more than twenty or twenty-five girls, that was it. And that was the Lehigh Valley organization. Most of the members are in their early and their middle twenties.

The attitude, even at work, bothers me because we're supposed to be a classless society, right? For a while I worked in administration. When I worked in administration I was a secretary, same classification as a clerk. Well it's not a classless society—it's the army. I didn't give a damn what I said, finally, so I told them, "Look at the way you do things. Do you wonder why people feel the way they do, when you put one level here, and another there? Because I work in administration, secretary is the top of the ladder." Of course it has to do with the way they think.

My boss saw what I was saying—but he didn't change his mind. He said, "Yeah, I know if I were you, I guess I'd feel the same way." It's an attitude. That's why he's in management. He started as a clerk, became an accountant, then this, then that. He could be really running the state hospital now, though he's only assistant superintendent. You must think management to be in management.

I never used to think about things like that. Up until the time I got out of high school I had my head up my back end because I didn't know or I didn't, well, I mean, it was so different. It was so very different. I think it was my middle twenties till I realized or became conscious of the world around me. But why, you know, I think it has to do with the way we were raised. High school was very nothing. I didn't remember that much. I know I went. But now I never see anyone from high school, and I'd probably never go to a reunion. I'm just not in touch with anyone.

Thinking back, because I think at the same time of my little boy, he's so young but children are so shrewd. Well, TV and everything makes—well, the way we raise them, I think makes a difference. I raised him differently because of all the damage I feel was done, not through lack of love but through ignorance years ago. The ideas are so different now. I don't know if it's good or bad. I think mostly it's good even though they certainly are different.

I used to think I was aware of the difference because of my age, but there again it isn't because my age is far above some of the kids I work with and some of the young girls I work with that are married. Their ideas are too provincial for me. And I used to think, too, that intelligence has a lot to do with it, just intelligence. Now I think it has a lot to do with perception and awareness and people's ability. You'd have to be smart to begin with, but someone's ability to think through things is very important. Some girls, even though they're very smart, they can't get past their noses.

I know for me, a big thing—and I think my husband would agree—that brought me to my senses is religion. Now, I would not take Sean to church, unless he actually wants to go. It was never that terrible in my home. I wasn't Catholic; I was raised Protestant—but all the hangups you get. Some people never ever get away from it. Not that it's bad to go to church. I don't mean that. But I think a lot of the things that happen to you—or to me—I think it was bad. You think of the moral implications of things. It's okay to sit in church and sing songs, as long as you don't take it seriously. When I was raised, I did, and I had problems with it.

And that's why I won't thrust it on my son. I'm not saying he can't or won't. So far, he doesn't want to get up Sunday morning, which is good. I work with girls my age, maybe even younger, who take their kids to church. It turns my insides a little because I think it's just the wrong way. Once in a while Sean says something about churches; in fact, he used to think they were castles. But anyway, he used to talk about church a little bit. I said I used to go, and he said, "What did you do?" I said, "Well, you sit, at your age you probably color," which he does at day school. He didn't want to go. Well. O.K. "They run around?" "No." "Go swimming?" "No. They color, they talk to each other." I said, "Anytime you want to go, Sean, I'll take you." He doesn't want to go. I think it makes a difference. Think about raising children, which is part of the myth about boys, when we were raised. I want my son to feel more open, feel he can come to me with anything and it wouldn't make any difference.

A couple of weeks ago, one of the kids said, "Why do you kiss your dad?" "Because I want to." "Big boys don't." I said, "You can kiss your dad as long as you want. It doesn't matter," I said, "big boys do." You know, he's not even seven, but that family, particularly some families, I guess, they feel after a certain age boys should not kiss their father. Now to me, I think that it is just a carry-over. There's a lot of people like that with young children. I think it's a mistake. I really do. But you get the feeling, that you don't do it after a while. Peer pressure has more, much more to do with it.

Peer pressure had its ultimate effect. Ten years after this conversation, Sylvia observed that "as a teenager, Sean raised me." It seemed ironic, given her involvement with contemporary issues that, at seventeen, Sean was uninterested in attending college. Perhaps it was more than ironic that Sylvia was working with Planned Parenthood.

––––––––––

My earliest childhood memory is of my brother Flex and me sitting on the window ledge of our first-floor apartment on Church Street in Bethlehem, talking to passers-by. Then, I think, Flex slipped off the ledge. Later in life I began to have *déja vu* experiences that always ended with a message that Flex had been hurt—or worse! It was not until I entered psychotherapy that I recognized my unconscious desire to get rid of Flex, who entered our family when I had had my parents' exclusive attention and love for only eighteen months.

The unconscious is the child in the adult. Our experiences in the nursery linger only beneath the surface of awareness to haunt us as grown-ups. Family history takes on a larger meaning when we see how the actions of our elders went into shaping our thoughts and actions, even today.

My maternal grandmother was the victim of constant anxiety, while her calm husband trusted deeply in the Lord to take care. My mother worried and prayed, often retiring early in the evening with a debilitating headache while my father washed the dishes and his sons, then plunked us four boys into bed with a hilarious story and a few math problems, after which he planned the next day's work for his construction gang. The dutiful son of industrious parents, he recognized the reassuring rewards of continual activity.

I was alternately fretful and confident, using work to ward off worry, and in choosing my future I debated between joining the ranks of the clergy or some equally ministering profession (inspired, perhaps, by the compresses I applied to my prostrate mother's head) and becoming a successful businessman, powerfully in command of events and people as my father was in command of his sons, especially me.

My parents and my maternal grandparents were not the only adult presences in my young life, however, since the rest of my mother's family lived next door. Aunt Winnie, who taught us to play cards and later introduced us to the movies and chauffeured us to baseball games, was my mother's watchful defender ("Don't upset your mother"), and I was frequently the target of her strictures on good behavior ("and don't embarrass her either").

Aunt Mary, on the other hand, encouraged me to act out feelings that might better have been repressed and seemed to take special pleasure from tales of my naughtiness in school, which inevitably got me in trouble yet made me feel special. Her husband, Uncle Shube, was the family traveler, willingly driving halfway across Pennsylvania to deliver a few cartons of canned peaches and back again that evening to engage in a lively game of hide-and-seek with his children and nephews.

I found my cousins' household so attractive that it occasionally provoked a jealous reaction in my mother, who once went so far as to pack my suitcase so I could move. I tearfully proclaimed my loyalty to home. Indeed, I can think of no stronger theme in my early years than my desire to be with my parents and brothers. But being absent from a day of school or an afternoon of swimming or, indeed, any nearby social event was not a matter I could easily tolerate either. Furthermore, I found the prospect of travel alluring, while I looked on remaining at home as a sign of weakness, even though I longed for the familiar when I was in strange surroundings. To this observation must be added the fact that travel itself—making connections from one public conveyance to another or driving a car which might fail mechanically—aroused deep anxieties in me and still does to this day.

I cite these persons, events, and consequent themes in my past not because they provide clear explanations of my thought and behavior but rather because they illustrate the hidden qualities of feeling, the subconscious nature of conflict. How else am I to say that my behavior has not always served my best interest, that my compulsivity has been self-defeating, that there has existed a gap between what I consider appropriate thought or action and what I actually have done and felt?

My childhood was long and rich. It lives on in my unconscious and frequently reappears in my dreams. No doubt the depressions I have suffered can be traced to my past or, rather, some arcane connection between the past and the present. Yet at the conscious level I retain the happiest memories of childhood. I may even have harbored the illusion that I could be born again through my own progeny.

Toni and I never doubted for a moment that we wanted children; few members of our generation thought otherwise. But after a miscarriage during our first autumn in Philadelphia, no pregnancy occurred for two years. Then came Joey, on May 20, 1959—not only *our* first child but the first grandchild on either side of the family. He responded extraordinarily, or so we all thought, by performing prodigious feats of memory and logic in infancy; by studying Chinese, the first of his many languages, at ten; by attending graduate classes in mathematics at Berkeley when he was thirteen; and by leaving home for Europe to pursue a career as a concert pianist at sixteen.

Toni, Joey, and I were a happy trio for years, whether camping across the country or playing cards on the living room carpet. When Joey was four I began telling him stories about thirteen imaginary and indistinguishable characters called FFFTs (the pronunciation of their name allowed the teller to spritz the listener), who acted out all sorts of socially frowned-upon behavior, much to the consternation of Henry, the boy who lived with them and attempted to control them. The entourage would visit Joey, who would attempt to mediate the conflicts between the FFFTs and Henry as they embarked on projects and trips. One day Toni observed that I had created through these characters the classic psychic structure of id (FFFTs), superego (Henry), and ego (Joey).

If I managed these forces in story telling (and, later, in the richly illustrated books Joey and I produced), I was less successful with them in my own life. I was dissatisfied, wanting more than I had. Since my own childhood occurred in the midst of brothers and cousins, I believed it was my assignment to create another large family. When I failed to do so I became sensitive about it, then nervous, and finally obsessive in my desire to have more children. Toni, considerably calmer, agreed that a sibling for Joey would be a joy for us all. In late February of 1969, five weeks after she was born, Katie became our adopted child. Two years later we bought a house in San Francisco, to me symbolic of the fact that I no longer lived in rural Pennsylvania.

Despite all this good fortune, when we moved into our new quarters I became depressed — and not for the first time. Issues involving home and family were deeply disturbing to me in ways I could not understand. I went into psychotherapy, a first step — but *only* a first step — toward dealing directly with these mysterious matters. Thus began the process of rediscovering my childhood. I was trying to look into myself rather than cleverly fooling with the FFFTs; Joey was beyond them by this time anyway, while Katie preferred the wonders of television to my imagination.

My research as a historian turned to questions of family and childhood, so that the emotional and cognitive sides of my character merged as never before. And scholarship gave me a perspective on my own twentieth-century predicament. Childhood, I discovered, had once been relatively short; at seven or eight years young people in early America were expected to be productive members of society. The families in which they lived were self-sustaining economic entities, as well as educational institutions and repositories of affection. But with the passage of time America was transformed, largely because of the industrial revolution, and the family lost its place as the fundamental unit of society.

Most production now was accomplished outside the home, while schools increasingly provided the tutelage that had previously been the job of parents. The family was left with its emotional duties alone, which proved to be a tremendous burden, given the strength but instability of feelings unanchored by the pragmatic concerns of

Joe Illick with children—Joey, Katie, Clara—and daughter-in-law Gina.
(Photo by Katherine Ramage.)

production of goods and instruction of youth. The wealth generated by America's mines, mills, and factories made possible longer
and longer childhoods within the emotional hothouse that was the
new family.

The household of my own childhood, whatever its idiosyncra-
cies, was very much a consequence of this dramatic social change—

and so, of course, was I. Sensitive to the needs not only of my parents but also my female relatives (one of the most distressing events of my young years was an hour-long scolding by my grandmother and my aunts, which left me so distraught that I sneaked home to bed and sobbed), my long childhood was laden with sentiment which deeply affected me as an adult.

I wanted to invest these feelings in my family, but I could not always confine them to the people closest to me. I certainly wished my own children could experience the peaks of joys without descending into the valleys of despondency. Yet when Joey, a high school graduate at sixteen, decided to make his way as a musician in Europe, I was devastated by the thought of his leaving home—which is exactly what he should have done and did so. (Toni's healthy reaction was: "He's happy, so why worry?") On the verge of his departure, Toni discovered she was pregnant; Clara, conceived when the moon was full in May, was born the following March.

Shortly afterward, I conceived the plans for this book, never considering that its gestation would be so protracted—and certainly never expecting that in the process I would become a single parent, only partially participating in the raising of my children.

Conclusion

Bethlehem. The stable and the steel mill. Is there any other name that evokes two such dramatically different images? One symbolizes traditional society, the continuity of generations within the family, the authority of religion and established wisdom, personal passivity, limited horizons, social stability. The other stands for the age of production, the ethic of ambition and success, the reality of movement upward and outward, adventure and achievement and uncertainty.

The Moravians founded a traditional society, only to see it overshadowed, then overwhelmed, by a new world whose values — the viewpoints of modern industrial managers — were realized in the railroad and the factory. Yet productive enterprise required a labor force, which was recruited from the countryside nearby — and from the farms and villages of Southern and Eastern Europe. At least until World War I the population of industrial Bethlehem was infused with immigrants from traditional societies.

These workers, old-fashioned and local in outlook, were recruited into a political machine whose center of strength lay in the South Side of town. The managers, who lived on the North and West sides of the city, were ambitious, outward-looking, and economically powerful, but politically strapped due to their smaller numbers. Hence they favored any measures — nonpartisan, city-wide elections in the early twentieth century, federal financing of urban renewal after World War II — which shifted power away from the local, popular level. Below the surface of Bethlehem's politics was a persistent tension between the old and the new. Residents clung tenaciously to time-honored practices.

Consequently, it is unsurprising that traditional values would be evident among members of the Class of 1952. The importance attached to family suggests the traditional bias. Not only did one marry for life and raise children, but one stayed close to home out of love and respect for parents. "I couldn't go my own way with any peace of mind," declared Jim Placotaris as he recalled giving up his job with a national company to enter the family bakery business. "Our ties are here," stated Don Bittenbender, explaining why he and his wife Jo did not migrate to the Southwest; then he added his mother's comment: "If you go, I'll die." Buzzy Richards, whose mother encouraged his success and whose career forced him to change residences frequently, learned the hard way: "You lose roots by moving so much. . . . it's family-wrenching." When Henrietta Diefendorfer asserted, "I'd like to get away from my parents," it was a shocking statement to hear, despite its evident truth. The idea of leaving parents behind in order to be at liberty was not and is not a popular idea in Bethlehem, Pennsylvania.

Family has always been the basic unit of traditional society—not the isolated nuclear family of modern times and mass culture but rather the porous household where the line between it and the community is easily crossed, allowing movement out of the family into a larger group of like-minded people. Bethlehem is a city that contains such communities (sometimes as neighborhoods), and its inhabitants almost instinctively know how the lines are drawn.

Race is a category which defines community in America, due to our experience with slavery and its consequences. Dorothy Lewis, one of a small minority of Afro-Americans in Bethlehem, without feeling outright discrimination, sensed a "kind of coldness" from her white classmates. Her social life existed only with other blacks. But Gus Romero (whose yearbook legend began: "Dark flashing eyes, black wavy hair . . . ") and Davy Salgado ("A dark, good-looking boy . . . ") claim that their Mexican (i.e., Indian) heritage was never held against them. And, indeed, the women they married are of German and Hungarian background.

Countries of origin appear not to have defined community. Although churches on the South Side were organized along national lines, the real religious division was Catholic/Protestant. "Marry you own kind," as Nick Begovich's father made clear, did not mean wed a fellow Croat but a fellow Catholic. Of course Jews, almost as small a minority as Afro-Americans, were beyond the pale for Gentiles. As Norma Rajeck remembered: "I grew up Jewish in the Christmas City, in a Protestant and Catholic working-class neighborhood where little boys rubbed thumb and fingers as I walked by and sneered, 'Money-money-money-money.'"

While Norma depicted her problem as partly religious, and while some of our classmates may even have considered her a member of a separate race, the reference to money is a reminder that the issue of economic class must be considered when defining community. For centuries Jews have been reviled for their economic activities, for not being *bona fide* partners in the peasant agricultural world where social class (not to be confused with social status) did not exist. Jews, as traders and money-lenders, stood in the vangard of the commercial revolution.

It was the advent of commerce that undermined traditional communities by elevating trade to a continental matter, thus breaking provincial boundaries. Then came the Industrial Revolution, with its relocation of the job from farm to factory and the pitting of manager/employer against worker/employee. In traditional society, class difference could not exist. Industrialization made the difference. Now the wealthy owner of the means of production stood in stark contrast to the mill hands who struggled along to eke out an existence.

As Gus Romero looked back at his youth, he recalled: "The South Side was poor. At that time it was the poor against the rich. I was lower class. I've never had any problems because I was Mexican. . . ." Skip John thought he saw a higher class of people when he looked across the Lehigh River as a boy; he was surprised to find working-class people in the West Side neighborhood he moved to as an adult. Margaret Crosko was less fortunate. Seeing that various sections of Bethlehem housed different classes, and quite willing to live among her own people, she found that at her church the ministers "walk right by you and put out their hand for someone that you know has position and money, and you've worked as hard if not harder doing something." It seems likely that her racism is related to her injured feelings.

Class—unlike race, national origins, and (to some extent) religion—can be changed with the acquisition of wealth and position. So goes the modern American credo. But the transition is not easy. Charlotte Cole knew how unusual it was for her to be able to attend a Russian Orthodox wedding, move on to a Lehigh University cocktail party, and have dinner at the Saucon Valley Country Club with her across-town boyfriend. In fact, it was no ordinary event to be invited to parties with the "richer kids from the North Side." Charlotte married up and moved out. For Katy Trivanovich the transformation has proved difficult. Proud of her ethnic origins but equally proud to be an American, she was at first appalled at the mean living conditions in Eastern Europe after the war, then almost equally appalled at the impact of affluence on the attitude of the upcoming generation, including her daughter. She seems ambivalent about having joined the middle class.

In the twentieth century the American high school has often been pictured as the institution that facilitates the transition from the traditional to the modern world. But at Liberty High School only one of the three curricular choices, the academic/scientific track, was designed to prepare the student for a post-secondary education and the promise of a professional or management career and membership in the modern middle class. Otherwise, the best a student could hope for was vocational training and a return to the working class.

Curricular choices were not generated by the educational enterprise itself, which might have identified the brightest students and encouraged them in their studies. Instead, choice of curriculum reflected family and neighborhood, i.e., the schooling and occupation of a student's parents, as well as his/her place of residence. The regional placement of junior high schools only reinforced this situation. The best students were known before they arrived, and their futures were assured.

Extracurricular experience did not contribute significantly to achievement in the modern world. Sports played a major role in the upward mobility of four-letter-man Billy Miller, but his many teammates did not fare as well. And athletics provided no future for females, as Pat Rose's frustrations illustrate.

School politics, which mirrored city politics, brought forward some leaders who went on to careers above and beyond their origins. But it was to their origins that they attributed their success. Savy Pasqualucci believed that in his role as Class president he could make his father proud. Buzzy Richards, the student association leader, was encouraged to succeed by his mother, while he found a supportive surrogate father at the Boys Club. Both Savy and Buzzy, their South Side backgrounds notwithstanding, enrolled in the academic/scientific curriculum.

Americans measure success by mobility, not so very different an evaluation from tracking the movement from traditional to modern values. Two of the most striking instances of mobility in the Class of 1952 are provided by the paths of Joyce Dickson and Ed Krucli, both of whom hold major administrative jobs hundreds or thousands of miles from Bethlehem. Yet both emerged from the commercial (or vocational) curriculum. The very fact that they can be regarded as exceptional helps explain the anomaly. But, in addition, the strong role played by personal initiative (and even by chance) in their respective success stories is also explanatory.

Which is not to deny the role of personal initiative in the successful careers of the academically well-prepared. Here it is interesting to note the importance of guilt as a motivating factor. Gere Bodey recalled his mother's self-sacrifice and both parents' emphasis on the work ethic, tying the latter attitude to his own "somewhat obsessive-compulsive" approach to his job. Bill Lennarz stated that because his father lacked opporunity, he (Bill) must take advantage of it. Pete Haupert connected his grade-consciousness to a desire to please his parents. Guilt itself is a modern personality trait, the other side of ambition.

But it would be misleading to attribute success to individual personality traits alone, since it is clear that a father's occupation was a major element in curriculum choice, which in turn was critical in determining a Class member's occupation. Personality and social milieu are interactive; an ambitious person is the product of a competitive culture and vice versa. If the individual is not functional in his/her environment, the consequences are usually evident. John St. Clair remained stationary in Bethlehem Steel's management hierarchy. He suggested that his father's influence may have gotten him into the executive training program at Steel (a situation not typical of modern society), but once there he, a single man, refused to "marry the company's daughter." He was not ambitious enough to get ahead in that environment.

Gus Romero and Davy Salgado could aspire to no more than blue collar jobs because their parents did not infuse them with sufficient initiative, and they have consequently tried to push their own children to achieve. In this case it is the environment that is not responsive. The postwar prosperity that lifted so many members of the Class of 1952 into good-paying jobs and a middle-class lifestyle regardless of their curriculum choices was arrested in the early 1970s. The children of the Class do not stand to fare as well as their parents.

Another postwar economic change has been the shift in activity from the secondary (mining, manufacturing) to the tertiary (services) sector, from the age of production to the age of consumption. The dramatic decline in the steel industry has been unmistakable testimony to this transformation. Nor has Bethlehem been able to recover by way of the service sector if the fate of the center city shopping mall is seen as evidence. Some Class members, however, have been able to build careers on comsumption, none more successfully than Dick Johnson.

Yet another change in the postwar economic picture has been the employment of women outside the home and its implications for the family. Davy Salgado observed: "We have girls coming into the plant. . . . When they get that money in their pocket and they know they can compete with men on an equal basis—and then you have marriage—if it isn't fifty-fifty or better you're going to have problems."

Traditional society has been patriarchal. That men should occupy a dominant position was hardly questioned. Some men, such as Sandra Styles' ex-husband Scott, still hold that viewpoint, even to the extent that their wives accepted inferiority until circumstances forced them to think otherwise—Sandra is a good example. Fran Csencsits, suffering an unhappy marriage, could state, "Yes, men are the ones in power. I think that's the way it should be, don't you?"

Yet most members of the Class of 1952 question traditional beliefs on relations between the sexes. Men will point to a "different nature between a man and a woman" (Judy Newell's husband Walt) or a "great gap" between genders (Forrest Kalmbacher), but they do not assert male superiority. Women, with the notable exceptions of Priscilla Tremper and Sylvia Pearl, gently scoff at the women's movement yet simultaneously occupy places of authority and independence, as in the case of Shirleyann Finn. Couples like Martha Marcinko and Nick Begovich quite self-consciously work for equality in relationship.

Women, formerly the oppressed gender, are more sensitive to the issue of relationship—not only with spouses but with children. In traditional society parents (especially fathers) gave orders to their young ones. Sandra Styles remarked about her father: "He put me in my place, and I accepted it. As I did in my marriage." Of course it is mothers who occupy the role of primary caretaker of children. Their continuing proximity to the young helps explain their empathy. Sally Noll pointed out the reward for listening patiently to her children, a stance her female classmates endorsed. But while mothers in the Class of 1952 welcomed love and openness with children as a healthy change from the households they grew up in, fathers complained that the young lacked responsibility and respect, attributing the change to permissiveness.

Chicky Rockstroh bluntly stated about her daughters: "They don't have the relationship with their father like they do with me." She regarded her daughters as friends with whom she could share anything. For other mothers this would be too intimate a bond. Some clearly feel their first duty is to protect and even control their youngsters. But the thought of outright ordering children to obey is outmoded.

In child rearing as in all other aspects of their lives, members of the Class of 1952 are struggling with inherited ideas and practices, sometimes successfully, moving from the traditional to the modern world, striving (not always consciously) to be at liberty by bringing the past into consonance with the present, adapting personal ideology to current material realities without sacrificing self.

Appendix A

Collecting, Coding, Computerizing, and
Analyzing Information from a Questionnaire

Five hundred fifty-four persons graduated from Bethlehem High
School in 1952. I found addresses for about 480, to whom I mailed
a questionnaire soliciting the following data about the subject's
grandparents, parents, self, spouse, and children: name; birth date;
death date; number of brothers and sisters; years of schooling; full-
time jobs (and number of years in each); religion; last church attended; dates of marriage, divorce, widowhood, remarriage; membership in clubs, fraternities, societies; language(s) spoken at home;
place(s) of residence. On the questionnaire designated "Your Children" I addressed three queries to the respondent which were not
on the other forms: What do you expect him/her (the child) to do?
What do you want him/her to do? Have you raised your children
differently than your parents raised you and, if so, how?

Several months after the first mailing I posted a second. I made
follow-up calls. I finally received completed or partially completed
questionnaires from more than two hundred people. As I scrutinized
the questionnaires I saw the need for more precise information from
some, which I usually got successfully by mail or phone. I also
found that by using the *City Directory* of Bethlehem I could get the
facts on residence and occupation for almost all my classmates and
their forebears.

This mass of data, I thought, was best handled on a computer,
an idea which interested me since I was a stranger to cybernetics.
Fortunately, I did not need a thorough understanding of the subject
to use a computer.

I proceeded pragmatically. A computer card contains eighty columns. Each column contains ten spaces (0 through 9), any one of
which can be punched to record information simply by assigning
a number to a specific piece of information; e.g., if the topic of col-

umn 5 is "Ethnicity," then 0 = English or Irish, 1 = German or Pennsylvania Dutch, etc. A *codebook* was prepared to show column topics and the specific information for which each punched column number stood.

I began by assigning each of my 554 classmates a three-digit identification number, to be recorded in columns one, two, and three. The first digit (column 1) designated curriculum (academic/scientific, general, or commercial/vocational), while the second and third digits classified each person by alphabetical sequence in his or her curriculum. Therefore, each classmate, or *case*, was assigned a computer card identifiable by the digits in its first three columns. In the remaining seventy-seven columns was recorded information about gender, ethnicity, family, religion, education, occupation, social life, residence — so-called *variables*.

The next step was to punch out control cards, which would tell the computer what to do with the information recorded on my classmates' data cards. There are three kinds of control cards: those which define and describe the data (such as listing all the variables); those that specify the statistical procedure to be used (such as measuring the absolute frequency of a phenomenon; e.g., how many persons in the academic curriculum, or correlating one phenomenon with another; e.g., how may persons in the academic curriculum were Protestant); and those which make it possible to modify the information recorded on the data cards. The control and data cards, fed into the computer, yielded the printouts. And from the printouts came the information found in the opening pages of chapters 2 through 7.

Appendix B

Gathering the Oral History of a Peer Group

Gathering oral history, unlike collecting data from documents of the past, is intrusive. Whether the subject being interviewed enjoys or detests the process, he/she cannot be indifferent to it. In such an interpersonal relationship, no interviewer should be unaware of his/her own predisposition, and no third party hearing or reading the results should fail to consider the nature of that interpersonal relationship.

My own motives and context are described earlier: I was assigning family histories to my students; I had been in psychotherapy and thus given thought to the family of my childhood; I was notified of my Class reunion and recalled the happiness of my high school years; I discovered books and conversed with friends on the subject of oral history. Of course I could not and cannot fully describe the thinking of the persons I interviewed, but I have tried to re-create the settings in which our exchanges took place.

In the beginning I had no guidelines on how to proceed. I called classmates to request visits. To the first of these meetings I took my newly purchased tape recorder and rather timidly asked whether I might put our conversation on tape. My subject confessed that she would be made nervous and asked that I dispense with the recording. I did, and I regret it. I found I could not become involved in a conversation and remember much. So, while oral history does not necessarily imply the use of a tape recorder, for me tape did seem a necessity.

But since I felt uncomfortable about introducing a machine into a conversation with a peer, I relied on a feeble joke to help me. "I'm going to immortalize you," I would say with a smile as I plugged in the recorder. Only once did a person object to being given life eternal — and then I heard a story which could not have been repeated anyway.

One of my early experiences involved a couple, with the husband doing most of the talking. He would turn to his wife to ask for her assent to his statements. Because of a later conversation with him alone, I realized that many statements he made as well as his habit of asking her for confirmation of his story were efforts to support her in a situation in which she felt very unsure. I saw what an intruder I could be.

The recognition did not come at once. I felt I could slip into the parlor with my tape recorder and my joke, affect a casual but friendly manner, and thus become a part of the furniture. It was my father, with whom I was staying during most of the time I conducted interviews, who alerted me to the possibility that I was intruding. When I remarked to him that I was struck by how clean people's houses were, he replied that I might consider that the cleaning was done for my benefit. I was an outsider, then, perhaps simply by virtue of moving away from Bethlehem but also because of going to college and graduate school, becoming a professor and—maybe most important of all—promising to write a book about the people I was talking to.

Being peers we were at the same age but not necessarily the same stage in life. We thought we shared a part of the past, but it was unclear what we presently had in common. To get that information was the reason for conducting interviews—or, rather, exchanges. For the best way to diminish my role as an outsider was to give as well as gather information. They, too, were curious.

Thus, my so-called interviewing technique was conversational, though not entirely casual. Usually we began by reminiscing. I chose as subjects some persons whom I had known well, others with whom I had a passing acquaintanceship, and yet others whom I had not ever spoken to before. Most but not all of them had answered the questionnaire. I tried to be random in my selection. It seemed no problem to recall in common some aspects of high school life.

Yet few of the discussions focused on the past. Almost always, conversation turned to our lives in the present. I had prepared no list of questions, although there were certain topics, such as the women's movement, which I might ask direct questions about. My method, if it can be called such, was to listen carefully as we talked, trying to hear what subjects they wanted to discuss. I later found very meaningful Carl Rogers' statement that "it is the *client* who knows what hurts, what directions to go, what problems are crucial, what experiences are deeply buried."

My technique failed badly only once, I think. I was waiting for a singer at a lounge he frequented and, because he was late, I overimbibed at the bar. He arrived and began our conversation with a marvelous story—which prompted *me* to tell a story, and another, and another. The tape, to my sober surprise the next day, was all me. Needless to say, this was testimony to the fact that alcohol liberated the repressed needs of the interviewer—who himself wanted to be interviewed! The exchange of information was serving more than the purpose of reducing my role as an outsider.

Indeed, the technique of listening carefully (and soberly) while encouraging the subject to pursue certain lines of thought and recollection is one which I believe I must have learned when I was in psychotherapy and the subject myself. It was and is a mode quite appropriate to therapy sessions and other private conversations. But my intent was to make these interchanges public—or, at least, to make my classmates' thoughts public. It is embarrassing to me to remember how self-satisfied I felt at the conclusion of some of these intimate discussions. Not that I was insensitive to the feelings of my peers but, rather, I took certain delight in a "good" interview, almost as if I had produced the material myself. Later I looked back and felt manipulative. In fact, this ambivalence—feeling both good and bad about a revelatory conversation—stemmed from the dual function of the interview: it was both a private and a public act, felt emotionally in the first instance but to be exploited for its content in the second. I was, after all, thinking in terms of publication.

Furthermore, I became convinced that each discussion had an integrity of its own. I wanted each to stand by itself, rather than being fragmented by my extracting parts of it for quotation in a text of my creation. Yet this decision produced an editing problem.

As I began to transcribe the tapes, I saw that the *verbatim* transcriptions did not read smoothly. Topics came up, were dropped, arose again. My side of the discussion, especially as it became repetitive in one interview after another, was unnecessary to an understanding of the subject's viewpoint. Consequently, I edited myself out of the transcript and transposed paragraphs (without changing language) so each topic was explored before the next emerged. If this editing method made my subjects seem a bit more articulate than they were in fact, I decided it was preferable to the alternative.

I do not, then, fear for the essential integrity of the transcripts. But I am rather disturbed by the matters of their candor and their meaning. My interviewing method did encourage people to speak straightforwardly about such topics as conflict in marriage, hostile feelings toward children, envy toward friends, disappointments in career. As I slowly transcribed the tapes and sent copies of the edited transcripts to the interviewees for permission to publish, I sometimes was surprised by the willingness of people to have private matters out in the open. Indeed, I worried that I had subtly coerced some of my peers into compromising positions. I began to question the complete wisdom of my technique while simultaneously seeing no better alternative except, in some instances, and usually as the consequence of a request, to falsify a name and disguise identifying places and events.

As to the meaning of the transcripts, even when they are not explicitly candid they are often laden with nuance and meaning — or so they seem to me. My acquaintanceship with the subject and my careful listening to the tape recording may make me extra-sensitive to meaning, leading me to wonder how much (beyond a paragraph or two introducing the reader to the speaker) I ought to explicate the text. My inclination has been to leave the reader on his/her own.

In the end I believe my technique has been vindicated by the transcripts. Perhaps this is best illustrated by focusing on one topic, the women's movement. Some of my subjects balked at being addressed as "Ms." — one or two even told me so by return mail. Inevitably, if I threw out the direct question "What do you think of the women's movement?" the answer would be negative — and sound as though it had been prepared for the white male media: "Oh, I like to be treated as a woman, have doors opened for me, cigarettes lit. That whole business of burning bras is silliness." However, if the same question was approached obliquely — even after such a negative answer had been given — it often emerged that the subject was in substantial agreement with the aims of the women's movement.

I think it is not an exaggeration to say that an indirect rather than a direct approach to any sensitive subject, while it still might elicit conventional wisdom, was almost always bound to lead to a personal statement of significance. It was not unusual for such a statement to stand in contradiction to other statements. This has been one of the most striking aspects of the transcripts: the person expressing an opinion is (to use terminology from David Riesman's *The Lonely Crowd*) divided between an other-directedness (which produces a conventional answer for public consumption) and an inner-directedness (which produces a more candid response). It has made me wonder about the limits of direct-question interviewing.

In any case, for the reasons already described I have gathered information through a conversational rather than an interviewing method. In the course of transcribing the tapes — a *much* longer process than I could have imagined — I became increasingly happy with the results. I learned a good deal, and not only about my peers. More than any other historical investigation I have undertaken, working in oral history has led to self-discovery. Such discovery is hard to overvalue: it allows me to separate myself from the other person and thus give a clearer picture of both of us.

Appendix C

Suggested Further Reading

Family is currently a popular subject of investigation among behavioral and social scientists. A rich sampling of their writings is available in Arlene and Jerome Skolnick, eds., *Family in Transition* (3rd ed., 1980), which treats the evolution of the family; sexuality and gender roles; love, cohabitation, marriage, and divorce; parenthood and childhood. Historical approaches to the subject can be found in Michael Gordon, ed., *The American Family in Social-Historical Perspective* (2nd ed., 1978), an anthology that includes demographic work; Edward Shorter, *The Making of the Modern Family* (1975), a lively, controversial book which depicts sentiment as a wholly modern phenomenon generated by the self-interest endemic to capitalism; and Carl Degler, *At Odds: Women and the Family from the Revolution to the Present* (1980), a provocative account focusing on the conflict between female autonomy and family responsibility. Economic, psychological, and gender themes are also the concern of Eli Zaretsky's *Capitalism, the Family, and Personal Life* (rev. ed., 1986).

Few commentators doubt that the modern family faces problems. A way of coping is explored in Lynn Hoffman's *Foundations of Family Therapy: A Conceptual Framework for Systems Change* (1981), while the intrusion of professionals (such as family therapists) into the household is deplored by Christopher Lasch in *Haven in a Heartless World: The Family Besieged* (1978).

The issue of *Marriage*, as well as family, is examined in Lillian Rubin's psychologically oriented *Intimate Strangers: Men and Women Together* (1983), her feminist perspective being that the divergence between the way boys and girls develop in today's mother-dominated home produces men and women who are mutually incompatible. Studies of the two genders include Carol Gilligan, *In a Different*

Voice: Psychological Theory and Women's Development (1982); Daniel J. Levinson, *The Seasons of a Man's Life* (1978); Rayna B. Reiter, ed., *Toward an Anthropology of Women* (1975); and Eleanor B. Leacock, *Myths of Male Dominance* (1981). For an interpretation of the consequences of recent legal changes in gender relations, see Mary Ann Mason, *The Equality Trap: Why Women Are in Trouble at Home and at Work* (1988).

If marital conflict poses one problem for the family, the changing nature of *Childhood* poses another. Daniel Elkind's *The Hurried Child: Growing Up Too Fast Too Soon* (1981) and Neil Postman's *The Disappearance of Childhood* (1982) are thought-provoking but present-minded, largely because there is no easily accessible history of the young in America. Joseph F. Kett's *Rites of Passage: Adolescence in America, 1790 to the Present* (1977) covers one phase of immaturity. Joseph M. Hawes and N. Ray Hiner have edited two useful volumes: *Growing Up in America: Children in Historical Perspective* (1985), an anthology; and *American Childhood: A Research Guide and Historical Handbook* (1985).

A third problem faced by today's family concerns the social context within which it exists: the *Community*. Two sociological treatments of the subject which demand attention are David Riesman's *The Lonely Crowd: A Study of the Changing American Character* (1950), a theoretical work which traverses centuries in linking personality to society, and Robert S. and Helen Merrell Lynd's *Middletown* (1929), the classic study of life experience in Muncie, Indiana, during the 1920s.

Political scientists Robert Dahl (*Who Governs?*, 1961) and Nelson Polsby (*Community Power and Political Theory*, 1963) take issue with the Lynds' class-oriented approach, arguing for the vitality of democracy and equality. In "Problems in the Historical Study of Power in the Cities and Towns of the United States, 1800–1960," *American Historical Review* 83 (1978), David C. Hammack examines different perspectives taken on community. John G. Clarke et al., *Three Generations in Twentieth Century America: Family, Community, Nation* (1977) is a fact-filled but fascinating account of rural and urban communities as well as of a variety of American families.

This variety could be experienced by straying outside the guarded circle of the household into a *Neighborhood* composed of many families besides one's own. Testimony to the heterogeneity of the

American urban community is the international assortment of its citizens, thoroughly described in Stephan Thernstrom et al., *Harvard Encyclopedia of American Ethnic Groups (1980)*. In *The Uprooted* (1951), Oscar Handlin argues that immigrants to America left their culture in the Old World, while in *The Transplanted: A History of Immigrants in Urban America (1985)* John Bodnar thinks otherwise. See also Bodnar's book on Steelton, Pennsylvania, entitled *Immigration and Industrialization. Ethnicity in an American Mill Town, 1870–1940* (1977), as well as Milton Gordon's *Assimilation in American Life* (1964) and Will Herberg's *Protestant-Catholic-Jew* (1964).

In early America the English immigrant household combined the functions of *Work* and a *School*; it was the place where the young were instructed, mainly, for their adult jobs. Economic change, especially the Industrial Revolution, robbed the family of both these functions. The accomplishments of American education are highlighted in books by Lawrence Cremin, while the defects are pointed out by Michael B. Katz, among others. Basically the conflict in interpretation hinges on whether schools offer the same opportunities to all students, thus promoting equality of opportunity, or whether they reflect the inequities of economic class in American society. See also James S. Coleman, *Equality of Educational Opportunity* (1966) and Christopher Jencks et al., *Inequality: A Reassessment of the Effect of Family and Schooling in America* (1972).

The creation of industrial America—what David Riesman calls "the age of production"—is explained well in Samuel P. Hays, *The Response to Industrialism, 1885–1914* (1957). In 1972 the U.S. Department of Health, Education and Welfare published an interesting survey, *Work in America*, which should be supplemented with Studs Terkel's oral history *Working* (1972).

Focusing on the industry which dominated Bethlehem, if not the age of production itself, see David Brody, *Steelworkers in America: The Non-union Era* (1960); Robert Hessen, *Steel Titan: The Life of Charles M. Schwab* (1975); Donald F. Barnett and Louis Schorsch, *Steel: Upheaval in a Basic Industry* (1983); and John Strohmeier, *Crisis in Bethlehem: Big Steel's Struggle to Survive* (1986).

Appendix D

Members of the Class of '52

Edwin W. Ahlum
Geraldine Anna Albert
Barbara Jean Alexy
Bernard Stephen Joseph Anderko
Rosemarie Grace Andre
Carol S. Andrews
Gloria Ruth Anthony
Shirley Ann Anthony
Allen R. Arnold
Leonard J. Arnold
Franklin T. Athis
Joseph Ralph Atkinson
Marie Dorothy Auer
John Christiano August
Ruth Diana Aykroyd
Ellen Davies Baber
Earl Marcus Bachman
John Balaz
Franklin Richard Balliet
Robert George Barber
Richard Arlen Barndt
Nancy Christina Barnett
Betty Jane Bartholomew
Anna Mae Beatrice Batley
Anna Jane Beahm
Gloria Margaret Beahm
Peter Beckage
John R. Bedics
Irene Agnes Bednar
Nicholas Joseph Begovich
Roger Leroy Behler

Madeline Mary Belgrasch
Barbara Ann Beltzner
Loretta Kay Bender
John Dwight Bentley
Willard Berger
Evelyn Irene Berkenstock
Kenneth A. Bernd
Jeanne Ann Bernstein
John Hamilton Berry
Matilda Berry
Erma Catherine Bigley
Mildred Marie Bitler
Donald Bittenbender
Dolores Olga Blatnik
Bernice Blinderman
Gerald Paul Bodey
Robert Paul Bohning
Edward Boksan
Elwood Borger
Richard Charles Borghi
Paul Stephen Bosak
Joan Barbara Boyer
Pearl Gladys Brader
John Edward Bragg
Ruth Arlene Brauchle
Esther Mae Breyfogle
Elizabeth Jane Bright
Paul William Britt
Eleanor Webster Brown
Ernest Leroy Brown
Carol Mae Bruch

William Richard Buckfeller
Eileen Marie Bunsa
Barbara Louise Buss
Thomas William Callahan
Elaine Kathryn Carter
George William Carvis
Anthony Louis Casciano
John Francis Casey
Marilyn Florence Castles
Eleanor Mae Chasar
Wasyl Chase
Geraldine Louise Chiz
Virginia Frances Chrisman
William Carl Christenson
Louis Chuck
Shirley Mae Clark
Gloria Elaine Clause
Froso Collins
Joanne Mary Eva Comoglio
Robert William Conover
Charles Trexler Cook
Betty Jean Cooke
Lois Christine Cowden
Richard Bruce Crabb
Lois Arlene Crandell
Annamae Cressman
Curtis Richard Cressman
Barbara Ruth Crosland
Frances Irene Csencsits
Julia Mary Csuk
Josephine Frances Dalint
Corinne Lucille D'Ambrosio
Mario Orazio D'Angelo
George Edward Darazsdi
Lucille Edna Darrohn
Maryjane Loretta Davis
Shirley Ann Davis
Donald Deasey
William Deasey
Robert Norman Debuigne
Robert Julius Delre
Elaine Catherine Demkovitz
John Demyan

Joyce Edythe Dickson
Geraldine Anna Diconcetti
Robert Charles Diehl
Donald Aaron Dilliard
Marilyn Louise Dimmick
Agnes Sibbald Doan
Frank Dollak, Jr.
Ethel Ann Dominko
Angeline Marie Donchez
Francis Joseph Donchez
Francis Robert Donchez
Jeanette Cleo Doster
Jack William Dougherty
Marlene Ann Dougherty
Carolyn Dorothea Dunton
Henry Walter Durkop
Marilyn Ann Durn
Melvin Francis Eberly
Royce Arlington Ebner
Patricia Edna Eddy
Helena Florence Edelman
Jane Ellen Edinger
Thomas Edwards
Sally Ewing
Thomas Dominic Falcone
Joanne Irene Farrell
Marlene Louis Farrington
Anna Mickaline Fattore
Mickaline Lucy Fattore
Donald Richard Faulstick
Lina Frances Fehnel
Maryjane Lorraine Fehr
Shirley Irene Feltault
Shirley Louise Fenner
Jane Caroline Ferenczy
John Francis Ferry
Juliette Ann Filo
Shirleyann Marie Finn
Nancy Ruth Fleming
Franklin Steven Fliszar
Shirley Mae Flores
Althea Mae Florey
Marvin Floyd Fluck

Robert John Fluck
Nancy Ann Fox
Stephen William Fox
Leonard Martin Fraivillig
Ellsworth Frankenfield
Patricia Ann Frankenfield
Martha Henrietta Frederick
Nancy Lou Frey
Richard G. Frisoli
Richard A. Fryer
Joanne Nancy Gall
Maryann Barbara Gallagher
Carmen M. Gallo
Kenneth Richard Gangewere
Rosemary Ann Garcia
Richard Anthony Garin
Clayton Earl Garland
Robert Gasdaska
Lloyd M. Gehret
Janet Elois Gemberling
Shirley Ann George
Frank John Gerencser
Richard Arthur Girard
Edward David Glass
Jeanette Catherine Glass
Joan Larue Glose
Pelagia Dorothy Golab
Rosalie Wilma Gombosi
Manuel Anthony Gonzalez
Carl Gottshall
Florence Marion Grabias
Norma Irene Green
Richard Ellis Green
Norman Edward Greth
Dorothy Frances Ann Grobelski
James Thomas Groeger
Lucille Ellen Gross
Edward Gubish
William Ernest Gubish
George Michael Guignet
Robert Charles Gundrum
David Paul Gunkle
Richard Joseph Gutierrez

Joy Myrene Haas
Joseph Charles Habakus
Regina Elizabeth Hader
James George Hageter
Louise Elizabeth Hahn
Shirley Ann Hahn
Elsie Lillian Halleman
Rosemarie Teresa Halleman
Ruth Elaine Handwerk
Patricia Ann Harpel
Robert James Harte
Georgine Marie Hartzell
Robert Lockhart Hartzell
Frances Hassick
Suzanne Martha Hassick
Albert Peter Haupert
Betty Norine Henn
Robert John Henry
Roy R. Henry
Donald Francis Heptner
Elizabeth Herczeg
Laverne Ruth Hess
John Joseph Higgins
Judith Ann Hill
Donald Melvin Hinkle
John Andrew Hochella
Eunice Elizabeth Housenick
James Mekeel Howell
Charles John Hoydu
Veronica Ann Hrin
Joseph Steeven Hrivnak
Francis Leonard Hyatt
Joseph John Iampietro
Marie Ann Iampietro
Marlene Ann Ihle
Joseph Edward Illick
William Joseph Jablonski
Charles Dean Jackson
Frances Mae Jacoby
Catherine Cecilia Janek
Thomas Edward Jankowski
Lennart Gustav Johansson
George John

Richard George Johnson
Charles Howard Jones
Ferdinand Joseph Jordan
Mary Kalafatides
Edward John Kametz
John William Kardos
Joann Henrietta Kashner
Bruce Allen Kelchner
Ruthanne Kelchner
Arlene Magdalene Kelemen
Gwendolyn Irene Keller
Nancy Ann Keller
Richard Charles Kiefer
Mary Louise Kilpatrick
Muriel Carmen Kimminour
Edward Kirk
Miriam Marjorie Klausen
Theodore Siegfried Klein
Marian Georgine Klinkhoff
Irene Dorothy Kloo
Laureen Ann Knauss
Lowell Austin Knauss
Nancy Louise Knecht
Elaine Marie Knerr
Henry Earl Knies
Victor Edward Kobordo
Dawn Lucille Koch
Frank M. Koch
Helen Louise Kocher
Phyllis Jean Koehler
Delbert Martin Kohn
Lois Jeanne Kollarik
Francis George Komenas
Elizabeth Ann Konuch
Frank Stephen Konya
Frank Joseph Korpics
John Charles Korpics
James Theodore Kostenbader
Elsie Christine Kovacs
John Herman Kovacs
Bernadine Ann Kozak
Edward Eugene Kozo
Elsie Roseann Krause

Nancy Lee Kresge
Leroy David Kressly
Edward Francis Krucli
Kathleen Ann Kuchera
Walter Stanley Kucsan
Austin Kurisco
William Robert Kvochak
Neal Anthony Lamana
Charles Albert Lambert
Paul Alfred Larson
Kalman Michael Lasko
Gloria Patricia Laskowski
Earl Ralph Laub
Wilbur John Laub
Pauline Annie Laubach
Stephen Joseph Lawrence
Ann Marie Leh
Robert Franklin Lehman
Priscilla Lucille Leiser
William Joseph Lennarz
Gladys Mae Lerch
Dorothy Lee Lewis
Lillian Marie Lewis
Jean Marie Linsenbigler
Betty Jane Lobach
Frances Barbara Long
Roberta Susan Lozensky
Gertrude Lutz
Thomas Macarro
William Joseph Maioriello
Joseph M. Majewski
Lorraine Mary Major
Charles David Malloy
Anna Marie Mandic
Joseph Tido Marcantognini
Martha Helen Ann Marcinko
Joseph Mari
Josephine Marie Marino
Nancy Carol Marsh
Evelyn Marie Martin
Frances Marie Martin
Erma Arlene Martz
Edward J. Marx

Helen Eva Mavis
Lucy A. McCall
Richard Lee McClarin
Robert T. McClarin
James William McGovern
Nancy Jean McKelvie
Barbara Mae Meckler
Maureen Doris Medgie
Arthur Nelson Meixell
Ralph Henry Meixell
John J. Mellon
Stephen Thomas Michael
Katherine Marcella Mihalakis
George Winfield Miller
Leroy Robert Miller
Marian Mae Miller
Nancy Ada Miller
William H. Miller
Wilbur James Miltenberger
Joseph Steven Minarik
Lamar Mindler
Dolores Louise Mingora
Walter Paul Lewis Minnich
Rudolph Stephen Mitman
Jeanne Elizabeth Mohr
Kenneth J. Moore
Lois Nancy Moore
Clarke Morgan
Patricia Ann Morrill
Lorraine Mae Moser
Stephen Andrew Moss
Edward Harold Moyer
Jane Joan Moyer
Ruth Jane Moyer
Frances Joan Mriglot
Larry Donald Muhlberger
Shirley Mae Mundy
Mary Ann Muntian
Helen Mae Muschlitz
Nancy Jane Muschlitz
Josephine Musike
Charles C. Navle
Adolfo Ralph Negrete

Joseph John Nemesch
Judith Alida Newell
Irene Nicholas
Sarah Ann Noll
Laverne Nonnemacher
Joseph Lewis Novak
Anna Marie Dolores Olay
JoAnne Olay
Louis Oravec
Richard Stephen Oravec
Nemesio Anthony Padua
Argiro Pappas
Saverio Anthony Pasqualucci
Paul Peter Patelis
Helen Marie Pavkovic
Mary Ann Pavkovic
Sylvia Pearl
Dolores Rita Perschy
Alex Petkavich, Jr.
Eleanor Elaine Pipok
James John Placotaris
Joseph Michael Polefka
Cyril Charles Polenchar
Elda Marie Polentes
Marion Elaine Ponoski
Marquerite Ann Ponticelli
Nellie Press
Bernard Matthew Prime
Floyd Clinton Rader
Norma Rajeck
James Harvey Ramberger
Gloria Angeline Ramos
Walter Rasich
Joseph Raykos
Wilson William Reed
Marie Louise Reslie
Jean Arline Reynolds
Donald Leroy Rice
Thomas Ramsay Richards
Warren David Richards
Audrey Jean Rieger
Geraldine Ann Ringhoffer
Susanne Rose Rios

Rauline Ruth Ritter
Barbara Ann Rockstroh
Robert Richard Roebuck
Augustine Romero
Betty Jane Ronca
Rocco John Rosamilia
Patricia Ann Carol Rose
Shirley Ann Rothrock
Susan Roumfort
Patricia June Russo
Donald Leroy Ruth
Shirley Ann Ruth
Donald Rutt
David Salgado
Juyne Esther Sanders
Charles Rudolf Santly
Catherine Geraldine Sauer
Shirley Ann Sayer
Carolyn Ann Schaffer
Shirley Ann Schaller
Ronald Pearson Schantz
Ruth Janice Scheirer
Samuel Scheltzer
John Francis Schimmel
Lucille Irma Schneider
Mary Ellen Schneider
Mark Leo Schoch
Carol Marie Schrader
Ralph La Verne Schreffler
Gloria Elsie Schultz
James Stephen Schumacher
Mary Lee Schussler
James Charles Segesdy
Alan Philip Seifert
Margaret Ada Seifert
John Ralph Selvaggio
Victor Michael Francis Shimko
Bruce Mallard Shortell
Frederick Harold Shunk
Alma Margaret Shurts
Mary Chris Sideris
Ernest Wayne William Siegfried
Paul Ernest Siegfried

Mildred Ann Siftar
Robert David Sigley
Nancy Lou Silfies
Thomas Joseph Silvester
Dennis Howard Singer
Charles Howard Skinner
Andrew Joseph Slabikosky
Jean Marie Slapinsky
Earl Abraham Smith
Frank John Smith
Jack Lawrence Smith
Marie Louise Smith
Walter Barry Smith
Calvin Edward Snyder
La Rue Diane Snyder
William Andrew Snyder
Elsie Betty Spishak
Ralph Springer
James Francis Stankus
Mary Evangeline Starner
John Beidler St. Clair
Richard L. Stefanik
Lee Steffen
Mildred Stein
Lawrence Joseph Steirer
Nancy Marcia Stocker
Robert Franklin Stocker
John Matthew Stofanak
Joseph Matthia Stofanak
William Charles Strobl
James Supeck
Richard David Sutch
Lynwood Vernon Sweigard
Eleanor Jane Szakmeister
Joan Karilyn Talijan
Henry Robert Tarola
Loetta Irene Thomas
Vivian Jeanette Thomas
Henry Belin Tinges
Robert Edgar Tinsman
Edward Daniel Tkacik
David Tomko
Harry Tomolovski

Jacqueline Anne Torpey
Doris Mae Toth
Edward Peter Townsend
Melvin Eugene Townsend
Jean Elizabeth Toy
Shirley Mae Transue
Priscilla Marie Tremper
Patricia Ann Tressler
Katherine Trivanovich
Rosemary Louise Tronovich
Charles Robert Troutman
Paul Emil Ulicny
Margaret Alice Unangst
Stanley Vincent Urban
Donald Richard Urello
Nancy June Vaitekunes
Eleanor Marian Valentine
Michael Francis Vidumsky
Bruce Evans Villard
Audrey Jo Vollman
Lucille Ruth Voytko
Jane Leonarda Vrabel
Francis William Vresics
Marian Ann Wagner
Mary Jane Walker
Paul Franklin Walters
Patricia Ann Ward
Damaris Helen Weaver
Gilbert Earl Weaver
Joseph Charles Weaver
Nancy Ellen Weaver

Russell C. Weber
John H. Webster
Elizabeth Ann Weiss
John Weiss
John Robert Welsh
Patricia Jane Wenner
Geraldine Grace Werner
Jean Ann Werst
Paul Erdman Wetzel
Paul Ephraim Wieand, Jr.
Charles Ernest Wiggin
Betty Jane Wimmer
Gerda Martha Wolden
Miriam Ruth Wolfe
Nancy Estelle Woodring
Marvin Samuel Wuest
Joseph Michael Yankovich
Roseanne Yanosik
Mary Ann Yasenchok
Frederick Lester Yeakel
William Yost
Rodger Edward Young
Ronald Lee Young
Elizabeth C. Yovakimaglou
Andrew Michael Yurasek
Joseph Bartholomew Zaun
Millie Rose Zeiner
Louise Irene Ziegenfuss
Nancy Jane Ziegenfuss
Donald Zoltack
Teresa Marie Zulli

Epilogue

Bethlehem

There they gathered, where the Monocacy flowed into the Lehigh:

First, the Delawares in their longhouses, families together;

Then the Moravians in their German dormitories,
  segregated by age and sex,
  determined to save the Indians

Then the Austrians and the
  Irish and the Pennsylvania Dutch farmers,
  looking for work on the south side of the river;

And the English entrepreneurs,
  establishing railroads and iron mills and an Episcopalian church,
  providing work for the needy;

Finally the gates opened wide, and in rushed the peasants
  of Eastern and Southern Europe, leaving behind their plowshares
  in the hurry to make steel.

The furnaces burned twenty-four hours a day, the ingots glowed in the night,
  odes to the open hearth were recited in the Roosevelt Grill;

Wars were fought, and after the second big one everybody got a car,
  even the Hunkies got a piece of the action.

And then it was over.

The mills closed, and the children slipped away, and there was peace.
  Just as the Moravians promised the Indians there would be.

Joseph E. Illick

Index

At Liberty: The Story of a Community and a Generation was designed by Dariel Mayer, composed by Lithocraft, Inc., printed by Cushing-Malloy, Inc., and bound by John H. Dekker & Sons, Inc. The book is set in Sabon and printed on 50–lb Glatfelter Antique.